Eco-Concerns in Indian Religious Traditions

Interfaith Treasures Uncovered

Under this Series, the Publishers endeavor to focus on Comparative Studies pertaining to Christian Faith & Living in the central matrix and Hinduism, Buddhism, Sikhism, Islam, Judaism, etc., on the peripheral. The Studies shall cover topics like Literature & Poetry, Indigenous Philosophizing, Ethical response towards Agriculture, Health & Healing, Science & Technology, Ecofeminist Theology, Sociological approach towards Human Rights, Law & Politics, Arts, History of Ideas, Ancient Civilizations, Cultural Contiguity, Religious Cosmologies & Mysticism, Footsteps of famous Theologians, World Peace & Harmony, Global Capitalism, Network Marketing, Cybertheology, Population & Demographics, Epigraphic Studies, Contextualized Education, and many others. We welcome a Mss. on any topic/s mentioned, whether they are original works, scholarly monographs, collections of conference papers, revised dissertations, or translations of historical documents. Through the Series, we are striving to put forward published works that may help Institutions, Academic Bodies, Researchers, Scholars and the World at large in furthering their respective knowledge and understanding on the concerned subject. We welcome your comments on our efforts and further suggestions on how we can foster the upcoming books on parallel interfaces between and among Christianity and other religions.

Interfaith Treasures Uncovered - 16

Eco-Concerns in Indian Religious Traditions

Inter-Religious Cooperation Towards Healthy Environment

T. Swami Raju

CWI

Christian World Imprints™

First Published in 2018 by

Christian World Imprints™
Christian Publishing & Books from India
H-12 Bali Nagar, **New Delhi-110015**
info@christianworldimprints.com
www.ChristianWorldImprints.com
Phone: +91 11 25465925

ISBN: 978-93-5148-302-1 (HB) ISBN: 978-93-5148-303-8 (PB)

Cataloging in Publication Data--DK
Courtesy: D.K. Agencies (P) Ltd. <docinfo@dkagencies.com>

Swami Raju, T., 1959- **author.**
Eco-concerns in Indian religious traditions : inter-religious cooperation towards healthy environment / T. Swami Raju.
pages cm. -- (Interfaith treasures uncovered ; 16)
Includes bibliographical references.
ISBN 9789351483021 (HB)
ISBN 9789351483038 (PB)

1. Ecology--Religious aspects. 2. Ecology--India. 3. Environmental protection--Religious aspects. 4. Environmental protection--India. 5. Religions--Relations. I. Title. II. Series: Interfaith treasures uncovered ; 16.

LCC BL65.E36S93 2018 | DDC 201.77 23

Printed in India.

DEDICATED TO

My Guruji

Professor

Dr. Eric J. Lott

In honour of
his literary and scholarly
contributions to the
field of Religious Studies
especially in the area of
Ecology and
Indian Religious Traditions

Contents

Foreword

Swami Raju has once again enriched the resources on Religious Studies and Social Concerns in India. He deserves an appreciating applause for producing this resourceful book which reflects hard work, engaging research with detailed documentation. It introduces the ongoing debates and reflections on environmental health with special reference to a comprehensive spirituality of environment as practiced by some iconic activists. It is my delight to write this foreword and am grateful to the author for asking.

Human beings do not exist by eating, clothing, breathing and sleeping alone. Many more needs are there than these basics, i.e., atmosphere, air, water, vegetation and soil which can be either purified or polluted, maintained or maimed, loved or raped. Modern technology may have the capacity to help in acting for the positive effect or equally if not more to be instrument of ruthless exploitation and destruction. The visions, traditions and practices of religious communities can inform and inspire or warn.

The primal (tribal) traditions have maintained an eco-spirituality supported by a sacred kinship involving persons, nature and unseen powers (or mysterious spirits) resulting in an integrated life. Hinduism is poly-paradigmatic and its master narrative is in Sanskrit language describing the Brahmanic tradition starting from the Vedas. The Vedic vision is 'cosmotheandric' as R. Panikkar called and it implies the nexus of gods, humans and the cosmos sustained by ritual order and social order. Though the social order disintegrated by the prophetic challenges of renouncers such as Buddha and Mahavir, the proliferation and ramification of castes pushed to the cruel end of untouchability. While there is greater awareness of this process, in all the Hindu traditions including popular cults sun, planets, trees, rivers, mountains, certain animals and birds, etc., are regarded as sacred.

The Buddhist and Jaina traditions extend the compassion and kindness to all the creatures. Toleration of many views and the celebration of the ideal of un-harming (ahimsa) and controlling craving and greed, the instincts for overindulgences are taken as the cardinal ethical principles. The Judeo-Christian tradition has passages in the Bible about God limiting (signified by the tree in the middle of the garden Eden) the human knowledge, power and enjoyment, commanding to till and guard the garden, and living a crucified life. Islam holds that humans were created to be the trustworthy vicegerents of the earth. The Sikhs by praising the holy Name attributes ultimate ownership to God, who is also the Truth expecting truthfulness and equality from his devotees. Parsees and Bahais also might have visions and insights to complement the above.

This book does not limit to a study of eco concerns in religious traditions. The idea of *ecosophy* (wise perception and introspection of the intricacies and integrity of the life world) is fascinating. An introduction to the prominent ecological movements are not only informative but also instructive. The author adequately acknowledges the contributions of the ecologically enlightened, scientists and thinkers, thus stimulating to redefine the meaning of enlightenment.

Interreligious cooperation for maintaining the ecological balance for the welfare of all life through partnerships, forums and networks is rightly emphasised. Earlier, there have been voices for interreligious cooperation for social transformation and nation-building. However, concrete initiatives and experiments have been not encouraging. Ecological concerns need not be separated from social transformation and national integration. Therefore, a follow up study could be on case studies of interreligious engagement.

By undertaking research into an important theme, Swami Raju has proved not only a teacher as he has been for decades but also a prophet. Readers may be stimulated to question existing norms and practices in India as well as around the world. For example, we have diet-related obesity on the one hand and malnutrition on the other; flood on the one side and drought on the other; calls for peace on the one side and escalation of weapons of war and instigating conflicts on the other. In such a world of obscene contradictions religions may be rightly discredited if they still turn a blind eye. There are those highly religious having their eyes fixed on sky, but in possessions and enjoyment are selfish. Do we bless the unrepentant prodigal sons while pitying on the poor? However, those who are pleasing the promises of false teachers for a luxurious heavenly life, their actual position is like the following picture: a man sitting on the top branches of a fruit tree enjoying fruits and looking to heaven without realising a slow and noiseless sawing going on at the bottom of the tree!

Israel Selvanayagam
Methodist Church, Evesham, England

Acknowledgement

It is, indeed, a time for me to acknowledge my heart-felt gratitude to our dear God, who is genuine source of my strength, knowledge and wisdom, which certainly enabled and empowered me and perhaps used me as His instrument to produce this 16th book for His glory on *Eco-Concerns in Indian Religious Traditions*. I experienced His presence and support in all stages – collecting information, writing and publishing in book form.

I am personally thankful to two of my gurus (teachers) – Dr. Eric J. Lott and Dr. Israel Selvanayagam for their timely support and suggestions to bring out this book in a proper order. Eric J. Lott as an authoritative and eminent resource person on Indian Religious Traditions and Ecological concerns of India, author of many scholarly publications, indeed, helped me much by sharing his views, correcting my thoughts and allowing me to refer his scholarly articles on eco-concerns particularly. I am also much thankful to him for his kind acceptance to dedicate this book in honour of his scholarship to my subject "Religions". I indebted much to Israel Selvanayagam, a well known scholar of Religions and author of many scholarly books, addressing Hinduism and inter-faith relations, for reading my draft, suggesting corrections and providing well thoughtful and much encouraging "foreword" to this book. I salute, from the bottom of my heart, to my gurus for their encouragement while celebrating "Teachers Day" on September 5th 2018.

Major source and inspiration of this book is my teaching/lectures on "Ecology and Indian Religious Traditions" to M.Th students of Hinduism and Islam in Advanced Institute for Research on Religion and Culture (ARRC), a joint program of ACTC, HMI and CIT, affiliated to Senate of Serampore University. I need to appreciate my students for their research works, paper presents and interactions which helped to make this text book publication possible. I appreciate Rev. K. Jason, M.Th-I, for his skill in designing cover page to this book.

I drafted this book in May, June and July 2017, while I was in Edmonton, Canada with my children – my son Mr. T. Samuel Karun Kumar, his wife and my spiritual daughter Mrs. Vani Bhatt and my last daughter Ms. Susheela Grace, who indeed loved me and provide me peaceful time to work on, therefore, I utilize my leisure time to focus on thinking and working on this book. I am grateful to the publishers Christian World Imprints for publishing this book with an attractive design. I am thankful to Mr. Sudhanshu Kanda, who helped me much in publication process. Finally, I appreciate the love and cooperation of my wife and all children.

Teachers Day (September 5th, 2018) **T. Swami Raju**

Introduction

"Eco-concern" is one of the major contemporary issues today in world hot debates, conferences, seminars, workshops and environmental movements; perhaps, it became an important academic issue of educational curriculums of world universities. Scientists and scholars; theologians and philosophers; sociologists and environmentalists; preachers and poets are talking and thinking about "eco-crisis" and "environmental changes" that took place in today's world.

The world today suffers irregularity and abnormality due to changes in nature against to the order designed by the Creator of this universe. The air has been polluted out of some from our kitchens, traffic fumes, chimney smokes to big industries, therefore, the *Oikos*[1] experience drastic change in nature's equilibrium in the form of thinning of the "Ozone layer", "Global warming", and changes in climatic conditions effecting the seasons. Along with this is the dumping of toxic waste, usage of pesticides which pose a threat to the aquatic animals which in turn affect the whole eco-system; the world is not a safe place to be in. We live in the age of 'wants' thereby over spending natural resources. This is a self suicidal attempt and the complete annihilation of the whole *Oikos* has been continued by human's limitless desires.

Keeping these issues in serious consideration, Senate of Serampore College (University) gave considerable place by including "Eco-Concerns" in it's recent revised curriculum offering courses on "Ecology and Environment" from almost all disciplines. This book attempts to study the terms "Ecology" and "Environment;" the underlying factors responsible for the Ecological Crisis, the Cosmos face today and paying major attention to investigate reliable resources from Indian Religious Traditions in order to reconstruct an "Inter-Religious Cooperation" to promote respect among people towards healthy environment and bring awareness that

---

[1] *Oikos* (Greek) in English translation renders it as 'house; 'it also mean the whole world or the whole inhabited earth. The rendering of the word house is a metaphorical usage reflecting upon the live of a family in a household inclusive of every house members and where there is love and acceptance. When used with the world, we can say that the world is a place where every beings and things of God's creation co-exists sand live harmoniously together (*Oikoumene*).

every human being has responsibility to protect the creation of God as stewards of this creation. This book is designed as per the objectives and syllabus of M.Th course on "REL-B-I-4 (a) Ecology and Indian Religious Traditions". The major objectives of this course, as it is mentioned in course, are as follows:

- To assess the ongoing discussions on ecological issues and their relevance in the multi-religious context of India.
- To consult select key texts of the different religious traditions concerning nature and its integral role in human life.
- To explore the theological foundations such as the vision of creation, its goal and the way it affects human life individually and socially.
- To study the thinking and involvement of prominent figures of different religious traditions.
- To explore the possibility of interfaith cooperation in saving and maintaining the environmental health and integrity.

Many ecological discussions seem to be guided by common observation and focused on certain ideologies, justice concerns, and human right of communities who are in vulnerable conditions and international voices and experiments. There are many writings on ecology from scientific, environmental and social aspects, but there is no much enough discussion from the perspective of religious resources. Interfaith cooperation for social transformation has been a concern in discussions on interfaith dialogue initiated by the ecumenical agencies. The Indian pluralistic situation presents a unique reality of living together "inter-religiously" in such a multi-faith context. By joining with people of other faiths, Christians in India create a great opportunity to witness to the gospel insights, particularly to work together and promote healthy environment with the cooperation of people of different faiths in India. This book provides basic insights to the candidates on "eco-concerns" and helps to search for the resources from major Indian Religious Traditions. Let me explain briefly here some important concepts that directly related to main chapters of this book

1) Conceptual Clarifications:

1.1) "Ecology": The term 'Ecology' was coined by German Zoologist Ernst Haeckel in 1866 in his book *Generelle Morphologie der Organismen*. It is derived from the Greek "οικοσ" (oikos; house, household, also dwelling place, family) and "λογοσ" (logos; word, language, language of reason).[2] It is the study of the interrelationship of organisms with their environment; a relationship of organism

[2] Felix M. Podimattam, *The Ten Commandments in the Law of Christ –Ecological Ethics,* vol. ix (New Delhi: Media House, 2013), 10; also see Astrid Schwarz, "Etymology and Original Sources of the Term 'Ecology,'" http://link.springer.com/chapter/10.1007%2F978-90-481-9744-6_9 (31-07-2016).

to one another and to their physical surroundings.[3] It attempts to study the causes and effects of all ecological problems by delving deep into nature's secrets.

Types of Ecology: Ecology may be classified into three kinds as follows:

a) **Plant Ecology:** This studies ecological patterns and process in plant kingdom. It is the study of plant performance, structure and dynamics of plant communities and how plant contributes to the function of ecosystem. It includes study of evolution of plant life and their interaction with animals.[4]
b) **Animal Ecology:** This study deals with the relationship of animals their environment by studying the pollution dynamics, distribution, behaviour and their interrelationship with their environment.[5]
c) **Human Ecology:** This is the study of the relation and interaction of human social system with the ecological system on which they depend. It studies the influence of Human on environment, the influence of environment on human behaviour. It is also regarded as the wholistic approach to address and enhance human potential within their near environment.[6]

1.2) "Environment": The term environment refers to the collective material factors and conditions surrounding the living organism and their components. Therefore, it includes both the external and internal factors.[7] It is the sum total of all surroundings of a living organism, including natural forces and other living things, which provide conditions for development and growth as well as of danger and damage.

The environment is the combination of all those present on the planet. It is a space of interaction, relationship and communication between and among the constituent of the environment which may be with or without life. This interaction develops constant changes brought about by external agents that disrupt and modify the internal environment and vice versa. The environment is constituted by abiotic elements and biotic. The main abiotic elements are: atmosphere, water and soil. The biotic elements constitute all living organisms that inhabit the environment such as plants, animals, and humans. Each of

---

[3] T. Swami Raju, *Christian Theological Responses: Contemporary Contextual Concerns* (New Delhi: Christian World Imprints, 2014), 92; also see Podimattam, *Ecological Ethics*..., 10.

[4] Podimattam, *Ecological Ethics* ..., 11.

[5] Podimattam, *Ecological Ethics* ..., 11.

[6] Podimattam, *Ecological Ethics* ..., 12.

[7] J.E.M. Arputhamurthy, "Ecology, Economics and Ecumenics," in *TBT Journal,* edited by Ken Gnanakan and Paul Mohan Raj (Bangalore: The Theological Book Trust, 2000), 40.

these, are complementary and interrelated. For instance, while plants perform photosynthesis and the entire process to develop, the animal feeds on their properties to exist and the man with his capacity of reasoning manages first two organisms to survive and keep their environment sustainable.[8]

2) Indian Religious Traditions and Environmental Issues:

Living in harmony with Nature has been an integral part of Indian culture. This has been abundantly reflected in a variety of traditional practices, religious beliefs, rituals, folklore, arts and crafts, and in the daily lives of the Indian people from time immemorial. The present day global concerns for sustainable development and conservation of natural resources spanning the two decades between the Stockholm Conference of Environment in 1992 and the United Nations Conference on Human Environment and Development (Earth Summit) at Rio de Janeiro in Brazil on 20-22, June 2012[9] are of recent origin in comparison to the long tradition and cultural ethos of nature conservation in India.

Virtually all the countries of the world have rich traditions embedded in the ethics of protecting nature. Many ancient cultures tell us how communities lived in harmony with nature, with a tradition of reverence for the elements that constitute ecosystems, drawing their sustenance from natural resources and at the same time protecting the environment that sustains them. Modern man tends to look down upon indigenous people as primitive, backward and superstitious. They may be poor, illiterate, and disadvantaged in many other ways, but they have a tremendous understanding of eco-spirituality and the factors that sustain them. They still look upon life as a gift to be celebrated; and this ancient Earth as one to be praised, worshipped and also celebrated. They are the one to whom the earth is not something to be used, not a possession or an object for exploitation but a living entity, an object of reverence, and the relationship is one of sacred trust and loving intimacy. For, they believe as much in celebrating one's life in this world as in remembering, adoring and celebrating the world in one's life. The sacred soil of ancestors into which one is born is thus a part of one's fundamental psychic experience of life and is a part of its spiritual dimension. The earth, the land, the village enter into and are secure in racial memory and it is only an ethical imperative to worship the Earth goddess, the Mother Earth.[10]

The worship of Mother Earth is a universal phenomenon in many indigenous cultures. There are innumerable examples of festivals, rituals, songs, and myths

---

[8] "What is the Meaning of Environment? Concept, Definition of Environment," https://edukalife.blogspot. in/2013/01/definition-of-environment.html (31-07-2016).

[9] United Nations' Conference on Sustainable Development, Rio+20, https://sustainabledevelopment.un.org/rio20, Rio+20 Conference website ☐ (accessed on June 29th 2017).

[10] S.M. Nair, "Cultural Traditions of Nature Conservation in India", refer his article in http://ccrtindia.gov.in/readingroom/nscd/ch/ch11.php (accessed on June 28th 2017).

that celebrate the gifts of Mother Earth all over the world, revealing the intimate sense of togetherness and harmony that exists between man and nature in tribal societies. Indigenous people in many countries attribute supernatural powers to plants, animals, rivers, oceans, mountains, the wind, sun and moon. Respect for nature is inherent in many religious faiths. Many Hindu gods and goddesses are shown to use animals as mounts. Sacred groves or sacred forests preserved with reverence have been part of Hindu and Buddhist culture. In Christianity as well as in Islam, conservation of the environment is based on the principle that nature and its components are created by God, and humans are entrusted with the responsibility of protecting it. Many religions and moral philosophies have professed the unity of all life on earth and the obligation of human beings to care for them.

Today, when people throughout the world are perturbed by the degradation of the environment and the disastrous consequences of this, traditional ethics of nature conservation could be looked upon as a source of inspiration and guidance for the future. Perhaps, no other culture can provide such a profound variety of cultural practices and ecologically sound relationship with nature as the Indian. This book is an attempt to bring together some of the information available on this aspect of Indian Religious Traditions from various sources. For the people of India, environmental conservation is not a new concept. Historically, the protection of nature and wildlife was an ardent article of faith, reflected in the daily lives of people, enshrined in myths, folklore, religion, arts, and culture. Some of the fundamental principles of ecology-the interrelationship and interdependence of all life-were conceptualized in the Indian ethos and reflected in the ancient scriptural text, the *Isopanishad,* over 2000 years ago. It says, 'This universe is the creation of the Supreme Power meant for the benefit of all his creation. Each individual life-form must, therefore, learn to enjoy its benefits by forming a part of the system in close relation with other species. Let not anyone species encroach upon the other's rights.

The oldest visual image of the human fascination, love, and reverence for nature in India can be found in the 10,000 year-old cave paintings at Bhimbetka in Central India depicting birds, animals, and human beings living in harmony. The Indus Valley civilization provides evidence of human interest in wildlife, as seen in seals depicting images of rhino, elephant, bull, etc. Historically, conservation of nature and natural resources was an innate aspect of the Indian psyche and faith, reflected in religious practices, folklore, art and culture permeating every aspect of the daily lives of people. Scriptures and preachings that exhort reverence for nature and relate to conservation can be found in most of the religions that have flourished in the Indian subcontinent. Primal Religions, Hinduism, Buddhism, Jainism, Sikhism, Christianity, Islam; and others place great emphasis on the values, beliefs, and attitudes that relate to the cross-cultural universality of respect for nature and the elements that constitute the universe. The concept of sinning against nature existed in various religious systems. Classical Indian myth is replete with similes of man in unison with the environment. Many of the rituals which to modern society may seem meaningless and superstitious were traditional strategies to preserve the intrinsic relationship between man and nature. The worship of trees, animals, forests, rivers, and the sun, and considering the earth itself as Mother Goddess, were part of the Indian tradition.

One of the finest examples of traditional practices in India based on religious faith which has made a profound contribution to nature conservation has been the maintenance of certain patches of land or forests as "sacred groves" dedicated to a deity or a village God, protected, and worshipped. These are found all over India, and abundantly along the Western Ghats, the west coast, and in several parts of Kerala, Karnataka, Tamil Nadu, Telangana, Andhra and Maharashtra. In Kerala there are hundreds of small jungles dedicated to snakes *(Sarpakavu, Sarpa* meaning snake, *kavu* meaning jungle). There are also Ayyappan *kavus* dedicated to Lord Ayyappa, the most famous of which, visited by millions of devotees every year, being the sacred hill of Sabarimala with an Ayyappan temple. In spite of the depletion of forests in many parts of India, some sacred groves still remain intact as oases in deserts, conserving rich biological diversity. The maintenance of sacred groves can thus he considered to be an outstanding example of a traditional practice that has contributed to forest conservation, albeit in a small measure. There are also examples of sacred ponds attached to temples in many parts of India. Some of these have been responsible for the protection of certain endangered species of turtles, crocodiles, and the rare fresh water sponge.

Many plants and animals have from historical times been considered sacred in India by various communities. The most outstanding examples are the Papal tree *(Ficus religiosa).* The banyan tree *(Ficus 'bengelensiss,* and Khejdi tree *(Prosopis cineraria),* Margosa tree and so on have been traditionally revered and therefore never cut. There are a number of other trees and plants considered sacred and grown in temple premises and are protected in other localities. More than a hundred such species of trees/plants in India are considered sacred by various communities and religious faiths. These include the sandalwood, beetle-nut, neem, coconut, palm, juniper, champa, lotus, tulsi, pepper and so on. Such traditional cultural attitudes, though based on religious faith, have made significant contribution in the protection and propagation of various species of trees and plants in India.

Many animals are considered sacred and worshipped by several Hindu and other communities, and have thus received protection for centuries. The peafowl, sacred to lord Karttikeya is never hunted, the blue rock pigeon is considered sacred to Saint Hazrat Shah lalal and is protected in the Bengal region. Even rodents are considered sacred and are allowed to breed in the famous temple of goddess Karnimata in Rajasthan. The tiger and the cobra, though greatly feared, are afforded protection on religious grounds. In the pre-Aryan society of India tiger worship was in vogue from the remotest past. The seal engraved with the image of Siva, lord of beasts, that has been discovered at Mohenjodaro has also, among other four principal beasts, the figure of a tiger engraved beside Siva. Siva, the god of the ancient non-Aryan race of India, is clad in a tigerskin and it is a tigerskin which is his seat. Probably the tiger was the most primitive vehicle of Siva. Later, when cow-worship started in society, Siva was made to ride on a bullock, but a tigerskin was preserved for his wearing cloth and seat. The legitimate conclusion form the association of this particular beast with the god Siva is that the tiger-worship of primitive society has subsequently got mixed with the Saiva cult. Another proof of the special vogue of tiger-worship in regions lying outside the pale of Aryan society in Northern India is that there is a community named Baghel Rajputs in Rajputana. Perhaps, they are the descendants of some primitive community of tiger-worshippers. They worship tigers and never hunt them.

Snake worship has been an established cult among the Telugu speaking people in Andhra and Telangana and Nairs of Kerala. Snake groves - *puttalu* or *kavus* abounding in wild trees and creepers housing a cobra's head carved in granite were found near the homes of many Kerala Hindus. The celebrated Padmanabaswami temple in Thiruvananthapuram has Lord Vishnu reclining on a mighty serpent. Many other animals are also worshipped as they are considered vehicles of gods and goddesses. Cow has been a sacred animal to Hindus from centuries, which now became a current debate in India.

In Buddhist mythology, the *Jatakas* or the stories of the Buddha's previous life are replete with several incarnations of the Bodhisattvaas an animal. Among the Jains, eighteen of the twenty-four Tirthankaras have an animal as their cognizance. It is interesting to observe that the first, second and the eleventh Tirthankaras have a bull, an elephant and a rhinoceros as their cognizances. Their antiquity could be traced to the Indus valley period (c. 2500-1750 BC). The famous Pasupati seal, for instance, shows a deity seated with a horned crown and surrounded by an elephant, a tiger, a rhino and a bull/buffalo. On the other hand, those of the first, second, third, and twenty-fourth, viz., the bull, elephant, horse and lion make their appearance on the Ashokan pillar capital at Sarnath in the third century BC. All these accounts vividly show how the ancient culture and traditions of Indian society contributed to the conservation of natural ecosystems, and the plants and animals that inhabited these.

Indian painting, sculpture, architectural ornamentation, and the decorative arts is replete with themes from nature and wildlife reflecting love and reverence, and therefore the ethics of environmental conservation. A wide range of images of forests, plants, and animals are to be found in Indian miniature paintings and sculpture. The theme of the Hindu god Krishna's life depicted in miniature paintings underlines an appreciation of ecological balance. He is shown persuading people to worship the mountain in order to ensure rainfall. Krishna swallowing the forest fire also signifies a concern for the protection of forests and wildlife. Numerous examples of the status given to plants and animals can also be seen in the traditional sculptural art of India. The concept of *vana devatas* (tree goddesses), vehicles of gods and goddesses, sacred trees, tree and animal worship,' etc., are depicted in stone and metal sculptures independently, or as part of temples, palaces, and historical buildings.

In literature and scriptures too there has been considerable depiction of the appreciation and love for nature. Mahakavi Kalidasa, a prominent poet of the ancient period visualized, a cloud as a messenger in his *Meghaduta* and went into raptures when describing various seasons in his *Ritusamhara.* Such an involvement with nature is reflected even in the visual arts which excel in their minute depiction of nature. Indian literature effectively mirrors the ethos of its deep and sympathetic understanding of animals through innumerable stories. Even amongst these one could pertinently mention are the *Hitopadesha,* the *Panchatantra* or the *Shuka-saptati, Mitralabam* and *Mitrabedam* and so on which abound in allegorical references to the animal and bird world.

Emperor Ashoka decreed, twenty-two centuries ago, that it was a king's duty to protect wildlife and the trees of the forests. He got edicts inscribed on rocks and iron pillars throughout his kingdom, prohibiting the destruction of forests and the killing of various species of animals. This historical evidence, surviving to this day, perhaps, is the first recorded measure on conservation anywhere in the world. In more recent historical times, Mughal Emperor Babur's memoirs *(Baburnama),* Guru Nanak's hymns on *'Baramasa'* (the seasons) depicting each month with a dominant bird image, and Emperor Jehangir's memoirs showing his keen interest in and study of wildlife provide fine illustrations of this Indian tradition.

The love for nature has been handed down the ages, becoming an integral part of the Indian psyche. Nowhere is this better exemplified than in the martyrdom of the Bishnois in Khejarli village in Rajasthan. In 1730 AD the then ruler of a native state had ordered the khejri *(Prosopis cineraria)* trees to be cut in order to bake lime for the construction of a fort. This sparked off a strong collective protest from the local Bishnoi community. Nearly 363 men and women, young and old, one after the other, placed their heads against the trees to prevent them being cut and were axed along with the trees. The ruler of the state was so moved by this sacrifice that he sought pardon from the people and issued an order that no green trees should in future be cut in the Bishnoi village. This happened over two centuries ago when the world had scarcely become conscious of ecological consequences of the reckless felling of trees. This legend is now celebrated by singers on stage and in the streets during the Tree Festival.

This long tradition and belief in the conservation of nature is also vividly alive in contemporary times. One of the most successful conservation movements in India today is the Chipko movement spearheaded by the womenfolk of Gopeswar village in Garhwal in the Himalaya. Commercial felling of trees was effectively stopped by them by hugging the trees when lumbermen arrived to cut them. This simple yet effective action eventually saved 12,000 sq.km., of a sensitive water catchment area. There was a similar Apiko movement in the southern state of Karnataka.

India is no exception to the global phenomenon of environmental degradation brought about by developmental activities. Rapid industrialization, growing urbanization, intensive cultivation, extensive construction of irrigation/ hydro-electrical projects and other developmental activities, coupled with increasing biotic pressure has had a very adverse impact on India›s environment. The major areas of environmental concern today include, (i) deforestation, (ii) degradation of land resources, (iii) pollution of air and water, (iv) threat to natural living resources - wildlife, fisheries, etc., and (v) problems associated with urbanization such as - slums, sanitation, pollution, water shortage and widespread diseases.

Human and animal pressures have led to considerable deforestation. Deforestation leads to soil erosion and sedimentation that shortens the economic life of reservoirs, hydroelectric facilities, and irrigation systems. The problem of water and air pollution is assuming serious proportions in various parts of the country. With eighty per cent of industrial production confined to ten cities, atmospheric pollution is concentrated principally in the major cities and industrial towns. Apart from industries, the density of traffic is also contributing substantially to air pollution.

Habitat destruction has endangered the survival of a number of plants and animals.Two species of mammals - the Indian cheetah and the Lesser Indian rhinoceros, and two species of birds-the Pink headed duck and the Mountain quail-have become extinct during twentieth century alone. Eighty-one species of mammals, 38 species of birds, and 18 species of amphibians and reptiles are now listed as ‹rare› and ‹threatened›. Among these are the tiger, leopard, Asiatic elephant, and all-the three species of the Indian crocodile. About 1500 species of plants are on the endangered list.

While the annual per capita income in India has been rising over the years, about 40 per cent of the people are still below the poverty line. Environmental degradation has adversely affected the poor who depend upon the resources of their immediate surroundings. Thus, the challenge of poverty and the challenge of environmental degradation are not two different challenges, but two facets of a single challenge. In a developing country attempting to achieve rapid economic growth, there are often tensions between the claims of environmental protection and those of development. That environmental conservation cannot be isolated from the general issues of development and must be viewed as an integral part of it, and an essential prerequisite for sustainable development, is being increasingly understood today. Conscious efforts are now being made to integrate environmental concerns into policies and programmes relating to economic development. It is at this juncture that we should look back upon our rich tradition of living in harmony with nature, which over the years has been overshadowed by the Western utilitarian approach to scientific and technological developments.

India obviously needs a new strategy of resource use and a new common belief system to hold the society together and put this strategy into operation. The present strategy of resource-use intensification, leading to increasing levels of outflows from the countryside to the urban-industrial sector, which is heavily subsidized by the state, and from the country as a whole to the developed world, and the belief system centred on development and national prestige, which has replaced the unifying theme of a national struggle against the British, have proved inadequate. The new strategy has to be grounded in efficient, sustainable use of resources and supported by a belief system based on respect for the natural endowments of the country. There are welcome signs that such a strategy and such a belief system are beginning to emerge, although not enough has happened in terms of concrete action. What does ultimately happen will depend critically on how far society recognizes the real power of those whose well-being is organically linked to the health of the resource base of the country the peasants, the tribal peoples and the nomads[11]

The main focus of this work is to search and re-examine major Indian Religious Traditions in order to identify resources to reflect from eco-perspective and re-construct eco-spirituality to promote ecological enlightenment among people, particularly in India, generally all people. Two kinds of religions are examined, they are, religions originated in India, such as Primal Religions, Hinduism, Buddhism, Jainism and Sikhism; as well as religions originated outside and came to India, such as Christianity and Islam. Though Christianity and Islam, treated as "semitic religions" by some critics in the sense of that these religions originated outside India and still getting support from outside, but these two religions have been played vital role in India since many centuries, hence they are treated as major religions in India along with Indian Primal Religions, Hinduism, Buddhism, Jainism and Sikhism. These major religious traditions contained excellent resources to reflect from ecological perspective and bring awareness on today's ecological concerns of the world.

[11] Refer for information, S.M. Nair, "Cultural Traditions of Nature Conservation in India".

3) Eco-Concerns:

One of the major and urgent concerns before the world is "eco-concern". Scientists, Theologians and Environmentalists have been highlighting the great danger of ecological disaster to the living beings on this globe – the earth. The Bible scholars and religionists identified that the creation is not as it is created by God the creator. There are signs leading to ecological disaster, such as, rapid increase in temperatures, changes in seasons, acid rains, floods, tsunamis, declension of ozone layer and diminishing of species, air and water pollution and so on made "ecology and environment" as an important concern of present world academics, so also it became the primary concern of our theological education and endeavours. Therefore this work is, indeed, an attempt of theological reflection on Indian Religious Traditions from an eco-perspective.[12]

4) Brief Chapterization:

First chapter on "Eco-crisis and Eco-spirituality: Contemporary Contextual Concerns" deals with basic conceptual questions such as "what is eco-spirituality?", "why eco-crisis?" and various dimensions of eco-crisis, exploitations of ecological resources, threats from modern technologies to environment, and finally why eco-spirituality is needed. Second chapter on "Environmental Issues in India: A Critical Review" is indeed an analytical attempt to study various environmental problems Indians are facing. Brief history on Environmental policy of India is, perhaps, an historical attempt of Indian policies on environmental issues. It is also an attempt to identify and discussed on various causes that lead to ecological crisis in India.

Third chapter on "Eco-sophy and Eco-spirituality" is a philosophical and theological attempt to understand ecology/environment, which highlights the importance of eco-sophy and dire need to develop eco-spirituality in our Indian pluralistic context. Fourth chapter deals with "Primal Religious Traditions and Ecology", which indeed is an attempt to study Primal/Tribal Religious Traditions from eco-perspective highlighting primal religious ecological resources to reflect on our contemporary environmental concerns. In a similar way a special research has been done on different religious traditions from eco-perspective. Fourth chapter is on "Hinduism and Eco-spirituality"; sixth chapter is on "Buddhism/Jainism and Ecology"; seventh chapter is on "Eco-concerns in Sikhism"; eighth chapter is on "Christian Attitude on Environment" and ninth chapter is on "Islam and Eco-concerns". All these are research findings of major religious

[12] The course I taught for M.Th students on "Ecology and Indian Religious Traditions" and research papers I presented at various seminars are provided basic information to the publication of this present work. I am also acknowledging and appreciating the research findings of my M.Th students who joined Advanced Institute for Research on Religion and Culture (ARRC) Hyderabad for their M.Th studies in Islam and Hinduism since 2016.

traditions which, indeed, reveal the fact that they contain rich resources to reflect on contemporary environmental concerns and reconstruct eco-spirituality and eco-theology in India.

Tenth chapter deals with "Prominent Eco Movements in India" which developed in recent past to fight against the policies and projects of government that affects environmental balance in India. It provides information on "Eco Movements in India: Issues and Concerns", "Prominent Ecological Movements developed in India" such as *Chipko* Movement, *Appiko* Movement and *Narmada Bachao Andolan* in protest of environmental concerns of India. Eleventh chapter on "Contributions of Ecologically Enlightened" is a search for the contributions of prominent ecologists and environmentalists those who worked and lived for the cause of ecology and environment. This chapter is an attempt to record the major contributions of prominent persons who have both from worldwide and Indian nation wide recognition as prominent ecologists.

Final chapter on "Inter-Religious Cooperation for a Healthy Environment" is, indeed, an attempt to highlight the present dire need and crucial importance of "Inter-Faith/Religious Cooperation to safeguard healthy environment in multi-faith/religious context of India. The ways and means are discussed to achieve such a healthy cooperation by bringing ecological awareness among various religious communities about present ecological crisis and environmental degradation, so that they may protect at least locally their surroundings and work for the improvement of healthy environment nationally and globally. It is essential responsibility of every human being, that's what every Religious Tradition of India highlighted.

Chapter 1

Eco-Crisis and Eco-Spirituality Contemporary Contextual Concerns[1]

One of the important/imperative dangers/challenges of the world, facing our contemporary society, is from "ecological crisis" and "environmental degradation", hence, it becomes not only a Christian concern, but also worldwide contemporary concern to heal the nature/environment and world in order to restore its' purity. Nowadays it seems, the whole world is heading towards "ecological bereavement". The environmental and biological balance of the earth's biosphere which is home to multi-millions variety of plants and animals, both aquatic and terrestrial, is endangered. All ecosystems around the world and their life supporting structures – atmosphere, water, air and soil are under damage; hence, we are threatening from air and water pollution, ozone depletion, global warming, acid rains, climatic changes and unseasonable happenings. As human beings, particularly as Christians, we will have a special concern to protect the environment of our inhabitant planet – the earth. We need to strive for and development of a sustainable "eco-spirituality" that brings ecological awareness among masses making "an ecological movement" to protect the environment around every one of us and save it from degradation and destruction.

[1] This chapter is first published in T. Swami Raju, *Christian Theological Responses: Contemporary Contextual Concerns* (Christian World Imprints, New Delhi, 2014), 91-110; which is revised/updated and published here.

What is Eco-spirituality?

"Ecology" and "spirituality" are key terms used in this chapter; let me give some conceptual clarifications of these terms related to this topic in order to have comprehensive understanding about what is "ecology" and "eco-spirituality". Ecology is the branch of biology dealing with the relations of organisms to one another and to their physical surroundings. Ecology is a relatively new science; the word is said to have been coined by E.H. Haeckel in 1869. It may be concerned with the study of single species in its environment, or of a complete ecosystem.[2] Within the biosphere - the total expanse of water, land, and atmosphere able to sustain life - the basic ecological unit is the ecosystem. An ecosystem may be as small as a tidal pool or a rotting log or as large as an ocean or a continent-spanning forest. Each ecosystem consists of a community of plants and animals in an environment that supplies them with raw materials for life, i.e., chemical elements and water. The ecosystem is delimited by the climate, altitude, water and soil characteristics, and other physical conditions of the environment.[3] "Ecological crisis" occurs when the environment of a species or a population change in a way that destabilizes its continued survival. "Eco-spirituality" is another term used in terms of "well being" of whole eco-system. Eco-spirituality is also known as "Evolution Spirituality". Eco-spirituality is a non-violent spirituality and spiritual activism informed by the principles of progressive evolution, the sustainability movement and the New Universe Worldview.[4] The main aim of "eco-spirituality" is to enlighten people to give due respect to the environment as it is created by God for the well being of all "living organisms" by taking preventive steps against the activities leading to "eco-crisis" and adopting inclusive positive activities that ensure restoration of "ecological balance" in this universe.

Why Eco-crisis?

There are many possible causes of eco-crisis:

- It may be that the environment quality degrades compared to the species' needs, after a change of abiotic ecological factor (for example, an increase of temperature, less significant rainfalls).

[2] Cf. Judy Pearsall and Bill Trumble (eds.), *The Oxford English Reference Dictionary* (Oxford University Press, Oxford New York, 1995), 446.

[3] http://encyclopedia2.thefreedictionary.com/biosphere; en.wikipedia.org/wiki/ ecology. For information See E. P. Odum, *Fundamentals of Ecology* (3d ed. 1971); R. L. Smith, ed., *The Ecology of Man: An Ecosystem Approach* (1971); P. A. Colinvaux, *Introduction to Ecology* (1973); R. M. Darnell, *Ecology and Man* (1973); T. C. Emmel, *An Introduction to Ecology and Population Biology* (1973); D. B. Sutton and N. P. Harman, *Ecology: Selected Concepts* (1973); K. E. F. Watt, *Principles of Environmental Science* (1973); D. Worster, *Nature's Economy* (1977); R. Brewer, *The Science of Ecology* (1988).

[4] http://www.universespirit.org/eco-spirituality-definition-principles-history http://www.universespirit.org/node/286/backlinks

- It may be that the environment becomes unfavourable for the survival of a species (or a population) due to an increased pressure of predation.
- Lastly, it may be that the situation becomes unfavourable to the quality of life of the species (or the population) due to raise in the number of individuals (overpopulation).[5]

From the early days of "industrial revolution", there have been voices against the destructive development methods, but they are considered as reactionary. It was assumed that technological development and economic progress would take care of the environmental problems, but in fact, the problems are multiplied and are merging into global threats. The progressively increasing amount of toxic emissions contributes to global warning, which causes rising sea levels and climatic changes with potentially disastrous effects. Climate change,[6] global warming, species extinction, the destruction of forests, pollution of water and air resources, are some of the dangers to ecological balance which are threatening the very basis of living existence of not only human beings, but also animals and plants on this globe. Vandana Shiva, the world renowned environmentalist, is of the opinion:

> Even as we attempt to grapple with the pollution and externalities of the first two industrial revolutions based on fossil fuels and chemicals, in the form of climate change and toxic pollution, new threats of genetic pollution are being unleashed by the third industrial revolution in the form of biotechnology and genetic engineering.[7]

It illustrates how technological progress and industrial development affect the environment leading to climate changes, which escort to "eco-crisis". We need to review various dimensions of "eco-crisis" in order to understand the problem comprehensively.

Various Dimensions of Eco-crisis:

Ecological Crisis is a "multi-dimensional" issue, hence, it is needed multi-dimensional approach to understand the problem and estimate its effect on this planet.

---

[5] Visit - en.wikipedia.org/wki/Ecological-crisis. Also refer Takis Fotopoulos, "The Ecological Crisis as Part of the Present Multidimensional Crisis and Inclusive Democracy", in *International Journal of Inclusive Democracy,* (Vol. 3, No. 3, June 2007).

[6] Cf. Bas Wielenga, *Towards an Eco-Just Society*, Center for Social Action, Bangalore, 1999, p. 9 and Ch. Vasantha Rao, *Let the Mother Bird Go*, National Christian Writers Forum, Hyderabad, 1996.

[7] Cf. Vandana Shiva, *Earth Democracy, Living Democracy: Rebuilding Security in an Age of Insecurity*, (Ecumenical Christian Centre, Whitefield-Bangalore, n.d.), 1-2.

I) Pollution

Once we didn't have distrust to breath air and drink water, but now we fear to breath 'air' and drink 'water' due to "pollution". We find age-old and new forms of air pollution today. The age-old practice of cooking on wood, dung and crop residues continues in rural areas among poor families affecting their lives to some extent. More recent surveys are exhorting how pollution affecting the lives of people who are living in metropolitan cities like Delhi, Kolkatha, Bangalore, Chennai, Hyderabad and other towns in India. High alert is declared in Hyderabad city about the danger of increasing ground level "ozone" limits in atmosphere due to vehicular and industrial pollution as per the recent survey and report of Pollution Control Mandali. Generally it is not harmful, if ozone is below 100 micro grams in one cubic meter, but it is now 138 micro grams in Hyderabad city. Many people are suffering from breathing problems due to oxides of nitrogen and hydro carbines released by vehicles.[8] Polluted particles released by industries and vehicles are polluting air. If this polluted particles density will be 10 micrometers, that will be calculated as "particulate mater 10 (pm 10)". People will suffer more, if the density is increased. Death rate due to pollution increased 300% during last 13 years. Every year 6,20,000 people died due to pollution in India.[9] The Centre for Science and Environment (CSE) has highlighted the threats to health especially in urban areas due to the rapid increase of "motorized traffic". It's report of 1984-85 foresaw the danger of air pollution has come true.[10]

The cities are choked by four, three and two wheelers emitting toxic substances which cause a wide range of health troubles, especially respiratory diseases and cancer. One of the damaging factors of air pollution is that 90% of the vehicles on India's roads are using "lead" in the fuel they use, which can cause brain damage in children, leading to lowering of IQ, hyperactivity and lack of concentration. The increasing use of "diesel", which pollutes air effectively, contributes to the sickening result of thousands of premature deaths.[11] Another major contribution to air pollution is from industries. As per survey reports, the rapid increase can be illustrated with figures from Mumbai, "Transport in 1978 contributed 399 metric tonnes per day to air pollution, and industries 438 tonnes. This is the toxic price for motorization and industrialization, causing bronchitis, asthma and other ailments.[12]

---

[8] "Denger Zonelo City", in *Sakshi*, (Tabloid, Saturday, April 13, 2013) 1-2. Also refer for the problem of vehicular emissions, "The way out of the mess on road", in *The Hindu*, (Daily News Paper in English, Hyderabad, Sunday, April 14, 2013), 12.

[9] Patangi Rambabu, "Mana Nagaralu "Bhopal"ku Nakallu!" in *Sakshi*, (Daily News Paper in Telugu, Thursday, Hyderabad, April 04, 2013), 4.

[10] Cf. *The State of India's Environment, 1984-1985,* The Second Citizens' Report, (Centre for Science and Environment, New Delhi, 1985), 131.

[11] Bas Wielenga, *Op.Cit.*, 13.

[12] "Survey of the Environment 1997", *The Hindu*, p. 54ff quoted by Bas Wielenga,Loc..Cit.

Vehicles, industries and coal-based thermal power plants release tonnes of nitrogen oxides, carbon dioxides, sulphur dioxides, which cause further damage in the form of "acid rain" that destroys forests and lakes.[13] Another important damage from air pollution is "declining ozone layer". Ozone layer protects human and non-human living beings from deadly ultraviolet –B radiation. Chlorofluorocarbons (CFCs) used in refrigeration and in aerosols are eroding and destroying the ozone layer in the stratosphere – 15 to 50 km above the earth that causes direct effect of ultraviolet radiation on living beings.[14] Global warming is another dimension of "eco-crisis" now affecting living planet - the earth. Generally we feel summer in the months of April and May, but this year we are experiencing summer temperatures, more than 41⁰C, in Andhra Pradesh from the middle of March due to the effect of global warming.[15] While criticizing America for it's responsibility to global warming, ABK Prasad writes, "The reason for burning sensation of many World Nations like in ravaging fire is due to releasing poisonous gases (greenhouse gases) from industries in view of development. Though it is the responsibility of developed countries, it blamed other developing nations like India. Poisonous wastes from their industries are dumping at the sea boarders of other nations."[16] Industries have been releasing uncontrolled and unlimited dangerous gases into air that affects our earth planet pushing into a global "eco-crisis". This increases "greenhouse" effects leading to raise sea-levels and climatic changes which will affect environmental conditions for agricultural production and the livelihood and health of millions of living beings. Due to global warming many species have been disappearing affecting biodiversity.

The air and water have become "poisonous" due to pollutants particularly from pesticides, toxic wastes and plastics. One of the most striking and incisive factors in the evolving eco-crisis is the accumulating impact of the great strides which chemical science and, in its wake, chemical industry has made. Invention and production of chemicals may not be wrong, but it becomes problem when chemical industry produces/releases eco-destructive products that affects environmental healthiness. Industries or scientists need to give much importance to "eco-friendly" substances/products. Chemical industry has been releasing dangerous pollutants into air and water, which affects not only urban population but also people involved in agriculture sector. Toxic waste is another pollutant releasing from industries, which poison the water of both flowing streams and

---

[13] Cf. "Acid Rain", *Down to Earth*, May 15, 1999.

[14] Arjun Makhijani et at;, "Ozone Depletion: Cause and Effects" in *Economic and Political Weekly*, March 10th 1990.

[15] Recorded temperature on March 28, 2013, as per TV channel and News Papers, is above 41⁰C in some parts of Andhra Pradesh, which was never before in the month of March. It indicates "global warming" affect. Refer, www.sakshi.com, Sajjala Ramakrishana Reddy (Editorial Director), *Sakshi,* Daily News Paper in Telugu, (Jagathi Publications Limited, Hyderabad, March 29, 2013), 1.

[16] ABK Prasad, "'Agni' ki Ajyam America!", in *Sakshi*, Daily News Paper in Telugu, (Hyderabad, Thursday, April 11, 2011), 4.

rivers as well as stagnate/storage water from wells, tank bunds and ponds, and thus affecting safe drinking water supply. Chemical wastes dumped in rivers, streams and on grounds are drastically affecting both air and water resources. The toxins eventually enter into the food-chain and damage human health. Tanneries, dyeing processes, paper factories and many other chemical factories multiply health problems.[17]

Another rapidly increasing and uncontrollable hazardous pollutant of our contemporary environment is "plastics". Plastic products have been occupied human life, perhaps, it may not be an exaggeration, if we say that plastic industry dominates life of the world today. Plastic products entered all areas of human life, because they are very convenient, light in weight, water proof, cheaper in cost and easily available. We are hearing now that plastic eggs, plastic cabbage, plastic rice and plastic sugar entered into daily essential commodities of human life. Plastic wastes dumped in rivers and oceans cause death of many water species and plastic wastes dumped on grounds kill many animals and birds. They get swallowed up by animals, birds and fishes and eventually they cause their death. The World Watch Institute in Washington estimated that up to 1 million seabirds and 1 lakh whales and dolphins died because of plastic pollution of the seas in 1987.[18] It is reported in newspapers that 55 kg plastic waste was removed from the belly of a cow.[19] Toxic and plastic wastes caused to raise sea water levels flooding many areas. Plastic contain dangerous substances such as *polyvinylchloride* that can cause cancer. When plastic products burnt, *polyvinylchloride* releases *vinyl chloride* gas which causes liver cancer, and eventually contributes to acid rain though the release of hydrogen fluoride that can cause to the death of trees. Plastics are "non-biodegradable", unlike paper and jute; they don't decompose when we throw them away. They remain in the environment for thousands of years affecting climate.

Using pesticides in agriculture sector is another dimension of eco-crisis, which polluting air, water, soil and food. Modern agriculture with its chemical inputs is posing a threat to health and environment. Genetic engineering introduced number of hybrid crops in order to yield high quantity of food grains, but these crops introduced numerous pestilences into agriculture sector, therefore, pesticides are increased its use to attack them. Cultivation has become commercialization and chemical industry developed rapidly expanding pesticides production. Chlorine plays an important role in the production of pesticides. Through the massive use of pesticides chemical poisons have entered into the surface-waters of rivers, ponds, lakes and seas and have even penetrated into aquifers, poisoning the sources of water for drinking and irrigation. Pesticides are particularly dangerous because they may wreck the human immune system and

---

[17] Cf. Desrochers et. al., *Social Movements, (*Centre for Social Action, Bangalore, 1991), 89-90.

[18] Bas Wielenga, *Op.Cit.* p. 21.

[19] The Indian Express, (December 9th, 1997).

thus make us vulnerable to a wide range of diseases.[20] Anil Agarwal rightly pointed out that "elite of our nation have failed to internalize the ecological principle that every poison we put out into environment comes right back to us in our air, water and food. These poisons slowly seep into our bodies and take years to show up as cancer."[21] When farmers spray pesticides and different chemicals on crops, they deposited in food grains and threaten consumers when they eat. Washing and boiling don't remove all poisons. Using the pesticides produce dangerous gases into air affecting environment and people living surrounding.

II) Exploitation of Ecological Resources

Resources we are discussing here are non renewable resources of energy such as coal, gas, oil, and various other raw materials which are in limited reserve. However, large these stocks may still be, the rapid spread of exploitation shall eats them away and leaves the coming generation with the prospect of dwindling resources.[22] We are facing "energy crisis" due to increasing industrialization and rapid exploitation of natural resources – such as coal, gas and oil as well as petrol, diesel and so on. Now many countries are facing "power problem" due to "energy crisis", especially we are experiencing in Andhra Pradesh "power cuts" in electricity supply from six to twelve hours in a day. Eighteenth century industrial revolution brought a radical shift away from renewable and almost inexhaustible solar energy to the use of non-renewable fossil fuels as basic sources of energy. These resources have been exhausting very speedily due to increasing use and need of industries and transportation. In such way petrol, diesel and gas reserves are being emptied rapidly leading to "energy crisis" and wars for these resources.

"Deforestation" is another important area of exploitation of ecological resources leading to "eco-crisis" of our time. Forests, with thick trees, are the divine plan of God to protect human beings from destructive natural calamities like cyclones, tsunamis and floods. These thick forests have been cut down in many areas due to either "industrialization" or "urbanization", hence, sea waves have been touching/reaching and flooding even towns and cities far away to sea. For example, in one of the recent cyclones, Bhubaneswar was badly affected due to deforestation of popularly known "*mada forestes*" on the border of the Bay of Bengal. The National Forest Policy of 1952 has set a national target of bringing at least one third of India's land area under forest cover, but unfortunately this target has not yet been realized, perhaps, deforestation is still continued. The statistics of Forest Department claim about 23% of India's total area as forest lands, but

[20] Cf. Anil Agarwal's article in *Down to Earth,* (December 15th 1996), 27ff.

[21] Anil Agarwal, "Facing a Silent Spring, Pesticides and Ecological Devastation and Cancer: The Story of an Environmental Victim" in *Down to Earch,* (November 30, 1996).

[22] For details refer, *World Resources, 1994-1995,* A Report by the World Resources Institute in collaboration with the United Nations Environmental Program (UNEP) and the United Nations Development Program (UNDP), Delhi, 1995 particularly chapter 11 on "Atmosphere and Climate".

it doesn't mean that all forest area covered by trees. As per National Committee on Environmental Planning, not more than about 12% of the total land surface is under adequate tree cover. The main pressure on forests is cutting trees for industrialization, agriculturalization and urbanization. Deforestation takes place for commercial purposes, providing material for industries (paper industry), therefore, the wealth of forests has been commercialized.

Millions hectors of forests have been disappearing through "deforestation" either converting to "agricultural, industrial, urban projects" or leaving as "deserts". Forests became rich sources of production of woody biomass for commercial purpose, as raw material for industries, particularly for timber merchants. The interests of the timber merchants and their customers clash with the interest of the *Adivasis* who live in the forests and with the forests, and depend on the sources that are available in forests, economically as well as spiritually. Deforestation affects to a larger extent the life of *Adivasis* – Tribes and wild life of many forest living creatures. The trees, either in the forests or in villages and towns, have been playing crucial role in keeping ecological balance. Human beings at large need the trees/forests for the sake of fresh air, stabilization of climate, supply of living sources - oxygen and water; prevention of soil erosion, droughts and floods; and the preservation of biodiversity. Through the "living mechanism" designed by the Creator God, trees absorb CO_2 – harmful gas from climate and release Oxygen – living gas, through the process of "photosynthesis". CO_2 is the harmful gas which has been evicted by human beings and other living creatures that pollutes the atmosphere, but trees have been playing a positive role while absorbing "carbon" from CO_2 and release oxygen - O_2.

This is the chemical process of "photosynthesis" that can be possible only by trees; and trees are sustainable resources of both living elements "oxygen and food". When trees are cut down irregularly, CO_2 content rapidly increased in atmosphere, which inevitably caused to negative effects like global warming, acid rains and other ailments. Trees regulate the supply of water through the seasons by preventing excessive run-off of rain water and allowing it to percolate. Trees reduce temperature and provide shelter to living creatures. I experienced this as a fact in Andhra Christian Theological College (ACTC), Hyderabad, where we have been working and living in the campus. In ACTC we have very big trees and we observed ecological principles on the campus, so I experienced difference in temperature, for example, if it is 41^{0}C outside campus, it is only 38^{0}C inside campus. It is only because of trees and plants we have inside the campus. Therefore, if we want to live, let the trees be alive. Trees have prominence and significance in almost all religious communities. Tribes (Adivasis) believe forests, trees and jungles are abode of their life existence; Hindus even believe trees are divine abode and worship them; Buddhists and Jains due to their belief in "non-violence" they respect trees as living beings; Christians and Muslims do respect trees as the creation of God. There are many resources and possibility to develop "eco-spirituality" from religious point of view, if we search religious scriptures from "eco-perspective".

"Diminishing Biodiversity" is another area of ecological concern to which we need to give considerable importance.[23] Biodiversity is also divine plan of God for the survival of life on the earth. God created different kinds of living creatures before He created human beings (Genesis 1-2 Chapters). God instructed Noah to take care of all kinds of living beings – animals, birds, creepers and so on before He sent destructive floods to punish the wickedness of human beings on the earth. It is mentioned how the wickedness of human beings corrupted the whole earth "The LORD saw that the wickedness of humankind was great in the earth, and that every inclination of the thoughts of their hearts was only evil continually" (Genesis 6:5); "Now the earth was corrupt in God's sight, and the earth was filled with violence" (Genesis 6:11). Therefore, God determined to destroy the wickedness on earth and said to Noah, "I have determined to make an end of all flesh, for the earth is filled with violence because of them; now I am going to destroy them along with the earth" (Genesis 6:13). But God has taken special concern to continue "biodiversity". While instructing Noah, God suggested:

> But I shall establish my covenant with you, and you shall come into the ark, you, your sons, your wife, and your sons' wives with you. And of every living thing, of all flesh, you shall bring two of every kind into the ark, to keep them alive with you; they shall be male and female. Of the birds according to their kinds, and of the animals according to their kinds, and of every creeping thing of the ground according to its kind, two of every kind shall come into you, to keep them alive" (Genesis 18-20).

It indicates clearly the intention of the creator God on protection of "biodiversity" giving importance to both male and female; and of all kinds of living creatures.

The loss of species which is increasing day by day is one of the greatest dangers facing humankind. Scientists distinguish "genetic diversity", "species diversity" and "eco-system diversity."[24] "Genetic diversity" is the variation within a particular species, for example, the estimated 1,20,000 types of rice plants in the world of which Indian farmers might have cultivated 30,000 in the past, whereas at present due to the "green revolution" only 50 varieties are being cultivated.[25] This diversity is the basis for countering pest attacks and adjusting to climatic conditions. "Species diversity" indicates the variety of plants, animals and other

---

[23] The lovers and scientists of biodiversity exhorted the danger from diminishing biodiversity in recent "International Biodiversity Conference" held in Hyderabad from October 1st to 9th 2012 at Hyderabad International Convention Centre.

[24] *World Resources, 1994-1995*, Op.Cit., Chapter 8.

[25] *Second Citizens' Report, (*Centre for Science and Environment), 229 ff.

living creatures within a particular region. It provides the basis for a variety of uses, for food, medicines, construction and so on. "Eco-system diversity" is the variety of habitat within an area, i.e., grass land, marshland and woodland.[26] The endangering fact is "extinction of variety of species" effecting "biodiversity", which in turn lead to "eco-crisis". Every living creature is created and designed for a particular purpose, if one creature exits permanently from life that affects unity, integrity and continuity of "biodiversity".

Frogs, for example, appeared in large quantity everywhere in the fields three decades ago during my school days, but now they are in scarcity and sometimes zoology practicals are postponed due to lack of frogs availability.[27] Frogs were hunted during 1980s and 1990s; and exported to other nations on profit basis. So, frogs also became a delicious diet for human beings. Today nothing is taboo for human beings food. No limitations of food today to vegetarian, chicken, birds, goats, rams, buffalos, cows and so on. It appears today that there are no restrictions to eat such animals, or prohibit such animals, but everything becomes eatable, so human beings are eating dogs, horses, donkeys, elephants, frogs, snakes, scorpions, lizards, cockroaches, locusts, lukewarm, insects and so on. As per the survey of one of the Australian ecologist, human beings are eating nearly 20,00,00,000 frogs every year in the world. This is only as per government calculations, but in fact this number should be four times higher.[28] Recently in UK airport one passenger was caught by airport authorities for transporting dried worms in four bags. That passenger replied, "These worms are transporting to somebody on high price for their food."[29] This indicates how human beings are interesting to eat everything they want.

Frogs helped, indeed, to the "life-cycle" of ecological process. Frogs eat insects, snakes eat frogs, eagles eat snakes – this life cycle is continued as a natural process of food security for the sustenance of life. It is the divine plan of God to continue living beings in biodiversity. There are many life cycles in living beings. If in any life cycle the partner living being – animal or bird or insect, either decrease in quantity or extinct permanently, then the problem of food security arise to other living beings depending on that particular creature, which lead to diminishing of biodiversity. For example, dependant snakes, eagles also suffer, if frogs disappeared. Frogs, lizards eat insects – mosquitoes and other worms, if frogs and lizards disappear, the insects and warms increase rapidly and destroy crops and vegetation. Farmers are using highly powerful destructive chemicals and pesticides to kill these insects, which in turn effect the environment and leading to

---

[26] Cf. Bas Wielenga, *Op.Cit.*. 29.

[27] "kappa(frog) bathikipoyindi (escaped alive), in *Sakshi*, (Daily Newspaper in Telugu, February 3, 2010), 5.

[28] "Kids Special – Mother Earth" in *Sakshi*, (Daily Newspaper in Telugu, February 15, 2009), 8.

[29] *Funday, Sakshi Sunday Magazine*, (Sunday, April 14, 2013), 5.

food poisoning that affects consumers' health. Human beings irrespective misuse of living beings lead to diminishing of several species, thus "eco-biodiversity" has become a big problem today to food security of living beings.[30]

Ecologists estimated that eleven percent of world species may become extinct between 1975 and 2015. Special attention has been given already to endangered species such as tigers and whales. Nearly eighty percent of the flowering plant species depend on insects and birds for producing seeds and bearing fruit. Many pollinator species are rapidly declining in recent years.[31] Pollution, loss of fragmentation of habitats, over-exploitation and introduction of exotic and alien species into other habitats are some of the reasons for increasing extinction of species. Deforestation, mining, industrialization, urbanization, construction of roads, railway lines, harbours and economic globalization, commercialization of agriculture products are often has unexpected consequences for extinction of species. Agriculture sector has been economically globalized in view of promotion of big mono-crops for export is, indeed, destroying the peasant culture of local communities which is based on the utilization of nature in its diversity. Traditional agriculture has lost its vitality and peasants have come under debt traps of "commercialized mono-crops", which eventually end their lives by "suicides". Mono-cultures are not, perhaps always, ecologically sustainable and expose agriculture to the danger of devastating pests, which then require more harmful pesticides. Artificial homogenization is also found in industrialized livestock farming. Traditional varieties (local animals like cows, buffaloes etc.) are giving way to cross breeds which are more vulnerable to diseases and to extinction of local varieties.

The recent threat to ecology is from "genetically manipulated organisms" through genetic engineering revolution, which is also termed as "counter-evolution". It goes against the ways in which nature organically evolves, and against the ways in which the peasant cultures based their work on knowledgeable respect for the interconnected patterns and processes of nature. This counter-evolution is basically driven by the economic calculations of the big multinational seed, food and oil companies and the genetic-technological researchers. They push for the patenting of seeds and life-forms. In such a way they try to establish globalized control over the production process in order to maximize profit. It is indeed, "enclosure of commons", i.e., preventing local peasants from their control on traditional agriculture.[32]

---

[30] "Kids Special – Mother Earth" in *Sakshi*, (Daily Newspaper in Telugu, February 14, 2009), 6; www.sakshi.com.

[31] "Where are all the Pollinators going", in *Down to Earth,* (cover story), (August 15, 1998).

[32] Cf. Vandana Shiva, "The Enclosure of the Commons", in *The Third World Resurgence*, No. 84, August 1997. Refer for more details, her *Earth Democracy, Living Democracy: Rebuilding Security in an Age of Insecurity*, Op.Cit.

"Land and water" resources have been exploited both locally and globally. Land and water resources are limited and declining. Competition over the use of these resources is increasing, perhaps, the poor and dalits have been losing their lands becoming workers on daily wages; sometimes pushed their lives into debt traps ultimately becoming bonded labourers. Both land and water are living resources, but now they are converting as commercial commodities. Agricultural and food productive lands are converted for industrialization, urbanization and other non-food productive purposes. Lands once used for food production– rice, wheat, etc., have been converted to grow commercial crops like tobacco, cotton, etc. Even fisheries are turning from the sea to the land. Fertile paddy lands are turned into aqua-culture farms, which leave the land unusable within a few years time.[33] Many fertile agricultural lands in coastal areas have been converting into fish and prawn ponds, which perhaps created ecological problems polluting not only air, water, atmosphere, but also fertile lands become useless – unfertile for growing food crops like rice and wheat. Surrounding environment has been polluted due to bad smell out of prawn ponds and use of dangerous chemicals. Once sea was far away from living areas, but now human beings, with their lust and greediness, brought sea water nearer to their houses, hence, the lands frequently floods with sea water thereby losing its fertile quality. This aquaculture has been polluting soil, air and water rapidly, fertile land is losing its fertility, fresh air is being polluted and sweat drinking water is becoming salt water losing its savour.

III) Threats from Modern Technologies

New technologies have been developed and are being developed, perhaps, it is only later that we discover side effects and problems which were not anticipated earlier. We are now seeing the deadly dangers of discoveries which earlier had been welcomed as solutions to our problems. Dichlorodiphenyltrichloroethane (DDT), for example, would put to an end to malaria, but now is being banned in most places and malaria is on increase. Scientists thought that "nuclear energy" would solve the energy problem, but now we learn that nobody has a "safe-solution" for the disposal of nuclear waste. The splitting of uranium or plutonium atoms produces radioactive fragments and activation products which cause the ionization of normal atoms. This radiation leads to deformations and cancer.[34] In nuclear reactors, most fission fragments are trapped in the fuel rods in which the fissioning takes place, but activation products can be formed in the surrounding air, water, pipes and building, thus posing a threat to workers and life in the vicinity. One of the unsolved problems is the disposal of radioactive waste,

[33] Cf. "The Aquaculture Disaster", in *The Ecologist Asia*, (September-October, 1995).

[34] For detailed information refer, for example, Rosalie Bertell, *No Immediate Danger, Prognosis for a Radioactive Earth*, (The Women's Press, London, 1985); T. Shivaji Rao, *Nuclear Plants – The Silent Killers*, (Navya Bharathi Publications, Hyderabad, 1989).

which poses a massive threat to forthcoming generations. Nuclear reactors pose immense risks on environment, health and life. A nuclear reactor in Chernobyl melted down and released radiation far beyond the borders of the Ukraine, where has been a massive increase in thyroid cancers in Ukraine, Belarus and Russia. The soil and its food products are contaminated and this causes leukemia and other blood ailments leading to breakdown of immune systems.[35] The risks of radioactive contamination have spread far and wide.

Genetic engineering, perhaps, is the latest hope as a solution to the food production. New products are coming in the market, the results of what is "genetic engineering" or "biotechnology". Eco-scientists and activists protested for a moratorium on the release of such products outside the research labs until it has been made sure that they don't carry any hazardous risks for environment and health.[36] This appeal has not been heeded by companies in a hurry for profits and by governments under the pressure of industrial lobbies. Scientists argued that "biotech" is the method followed similar to humans over the centuries that have been crossing plants and cross-breeding animals; and the very terminology of "biotechnology" and "genetic engineering" suggesting that the processes are fully determined and under control – as in mechanical engineering. But this is a reductionist approach, as Vandana Shiva argued, which ignores that life-forms are much more complex and characterized by inter-determinacy and uncertainty.[37] We need to note that "genes" are not like iron nuts and steel bolts, but they are part of a complex organism. The researcher or scientist may isolate and transfer a particular gene for its colour or drought resistance or herbicide quality, but it may bring about other modifications as well. Scientific researches in laboratories cannot predict all the possible mutations and effects of the transfer of genes; therefore, we don't know forthcoming ecological problems. Environmentalists are principally worried about the danger of reducing natural biodiversity through the introduction of powerful transgenic organisms, the spread of new resistant weeds, and possible emergence of new viral strains.

People are threatening economically along with ecological hazards. Organic farmers and substance peasants who have so far survived the green revolution are now threatened in the context of globalization. The debate on the "terminator" seeds shows what is in store. These have been jointly developed by the US Department of Agriculture and a cotton-seed company which is a subsidiary of Monsanto. They acquired the patent for the "Control of Plant Gene

---

[35] Cf. Vladimir Chernousenko, "We Shall be Killed in Silent Ways", in *Third World Resurgence, (*No. 69, May 1996).

[36] International Conference on "Redefining the Life Sciences", held in July 1994 in Malaysia. See for more information, *Third World Resurgence*, (No. 53-54, January – February, 1995), 16-24.

[37] Vandana Shiva, "Why the Engineering Paradigm in Life-Forms is Flawed", in *Third World Resurgence*, (No. 53-54), pp. 25ff.

Expression", extending to plants and seeds of all species. This technology sterilizes Deoxyribonucleic Acid (DNA) to kill its own embryos. This forces farmers to buy seeds each year afresh. Farmers are struggled for acquiring these seeds and many have been going into debt traps leading many of them to adopt "suicide" as means of only solution to their life problem. It was not happened previously when farmers followed traditional crops, they stored seeds and use them for next crop. Biogenetic seeds would create total dependency on the big companies and would be a mortal blow to the peasantry. A further threat is "High-Tech Piracy", which takes genetic material from southern countries and then patents it. The "bio-pirates" are not only interested in microbes and plants but also in the bodies of indigenous peoples.[38]

Why Eco-spirituality?

How do we see our relationship to life in its rich diversity as it is given to us and on which we depend? Is it something which we can manipulate and terminate at will, in the pursuit of profits? Or are we meant to live with it in a more supportive and co-operative way? Basically, perhaps, it is not only an ecological, economic and political question, but a philosophical, cultural and religious one. Ecological problem is not the problem of only scientists; it is also problem to people of all faiths. Ecological endurance is the responsibility of the people professing different religious traditions and confessing various faiths. A multi-religious coalition representing eighty religious faiths and denominations in the US, including Christian leaders of both Protestant and Catholic, Jewish, Muslim, Hindu and Buddhist faiths, has come out against the patenting of life, which World Trade Organization (WTO) and business are pursuing. They affirmed, "We ...oppose the patenting of human and animal life-forms... We believe that humans and animals are creations of God, not humans, and as such should not be patented as human inventions."[39]

Life is the gift of God and whole universe is the creation of God, therefore, as part of God's creation, we – human beings respect our environment, not for the benefit of the creator, but for the survival and continuation of human beings and other living forms on this globe – the earth. We need to reorient our approaches to environment and rededicate to the nature.[40] I am not suggesting to worship the nature, but I beg to respect "the universe" as the creation of God being the abode of all living creatures. God created everything in this universe in a proper order for the origin, sustenance and continuation of life. After every day creation, God

[38] "High-Tech Piracy" in *Third World Resurgence,* (No. 71, July 1996).

[39] "Broadest Religious Coalition in US History opposes Life Patenting" in *Third World Resurgence,* (No. 63, Nov. 1995), 28.

[40] "Prkruthiki Punarankitam" in *Sakshi – Fun-day,* (Sunday Magazine, March, 17th 2013), 10-12.

examined and affirmed that His creation is good, "And God saw that it was good" (Genesis 1:4, 12, 18, 21, 25), and finally He confirmed, "God saw everything that he had made and indeed, it was very good" (Genesis 1:31). Why this very good creation (environment, climate) corrupted and polluted? What happened to God's good creation? Who were responsible? Why living beings are pushed into life-surviving crisis? The Bible states clearly that it is the responsibility of human beings for the development of unwanted happenings in universe leading to "eco-crisis".

The Bible says, "The LORD saw that the wickedness of humankind was great in the earth, and that every inclination of the thoughts of their hearts was only evil continually. And the LORD was sorry that he had made humankind on the earth. And it grieved him to his heart" (Genesis 6:5-6). Human beings need to develop "eco-spirituality" – a spirituality of respect and honour towards God's creation. Human beings are only "stewards of creation", but God is the author and owner of this universe. As stewards we are here to protect God's creation, not to destruct in any way, since we are accountable to God for everything we do. Christians do play an active and a positive role in ecological movements and organize programs to bring ecological and environmental awareness among congregations. We need to reorient our attitude towards environment and promote "eco-friendly" activities. Our lectionaries, pulpit sermons, order of worships, other religious programs need to include our contemporary "eco-concern". When we respect "life" in universe, it protects our "life" from destruction. Let us respect the creation of God and be the channels of its continuation with its original beauty in diversity.

Chapter 2

Environmental Issues in India
A Critical Review

"Environment is not good today as it was before" is one of the repeated statements we have been hearing every often. "The present environment is not very good as it was designed/intended by the creator God at the time whole creation", is perhaps the words we are hearing from the people who have faith in the Bible and other religious scriptures. Theologians, sociologists, vedantins and philosophers are searching for the reasons to present "ecological crisis" and identified that human irresponsible involvement and greediness are some of the important reasons for the present state of environmental emergency. Scientists have been done researches on environmental changes that took place in the universe and have been exhorting the world community about the forth coming ecological catastrophe. I think that the present environmental state in India may not be different to other parts of the world, but this book focussing much on Indian context, therefore this chapter is a brief attempt exclusively to identify the present environment issues in India, though it was addressed in first chapter to some extent.

There are many environmental issues in India to consider, for example, air pollution, water pollution, garbage waste, and pollution of the natural environment are all challenges for India today. The situation was worse between 1947 through 1995. According to data collection and environment assessment studies of World Bank experts, between 1995 through 2010, India has made one of the fastest progresses in the world, in addressing its environmental issues and improving its environmental quality[1]. However still, India has a long way to go

---

[1] *The Little Green Data Book,* The **World** Bank, 2010; *Environment Assessment, Country Data: India*, **The World Bank, 2011;** also refer http:/web.worldbank.org; http:/data.worldbank.org/country/India, accessed on June 10th 2017.

to reach environmental quality similar to those enjoyed in developed economies. Pollution and climate changes remain major challenges in India threatening healthy environment. Environmental issues are one of the primary causes of disease, health issues and long term livelihood impact for India.

1) Brief History of Environmental Policy of India

British Government in India saw several laws related to environment. "Shore Nuisance (Bombay and Kolaba) Act" of 1853 and "the Oriental Gas Company Act" of 1857 were some of the earliest acts related to Indian Environmental Policies. The Indian Penal Code of 1860 imposed a fine on anyone who voluntarily pollutes the water of any public spring or reservoir, in addition, the Code Penalised Negligent Acts. British Government in India also enacted laws/acts intended at controlling "air pollution". "The Bengal Smoke Nuisance Act" of 1905 and "the Bombay Smoke Nuisance Act" of 1912 were some of the prominent acts of the time related to control air pollution. While these laws/acts failed in controlling air pollution, British Government enacted legislations pioneered the growth of environmental regulations in India.

Independent India adopted a constitution and numerous British-enacted laws, without any specific constitutional provision on protecting the environment. India amended its constitution in 1976. Article 48(A) of Part IV of the amended constitution, read: "The State shall endeavour to protect and improve the environment and to safeguard the forests and wildlife of the country". Article 51 A(g) imposed additional environmental mandates on the Indian state. Other Indian laws from recent history include "the Water (Prevention and Control of Pollution) Act" of 1974, "the Forest (Conservation) Act" of 1980, and "the Air (Prevention and Control of Pollution) Act" of 1981. The Air Act was inspired by the decisions made at Stockholm Conference. The Bhopal gas tragedy triggered the Government of India to enact the "Environment (Protection) Act" of 1986. India has also enacted a set of Noise Pollution (Regulation & Control) Rules in 2000.

The Indian government formed the "Ministry of Environment and Forests" in 1985. This ministry is the central administrative organisation in India for regulating and ensuring environmental protection. Despite active passage of laws by the Central Government of India, the reality of environmental quality mostly worsened between 1947 and 1990. Rural poor had no choice, but to sustain life in whatever way possible. Air emissions increased, water pollution worsened, forest cover decreased. Environmental reforms were introduced from the beginning of 1990s. Since then, there is some improvement in controlling the pollutants,[2] but still there are many issues to be dealt seriously.

---

[2] *"Global Forest Resources Assessment 2010"* (PDF). FAO. 2011.

2) Possible Causes for Ecological/Environmental Crisis

There are many causes/reasons for ecological degradation and environmental problems. Some scholars are of opinion that economic development as the cause regarding the environmental issues. It is suggested that India's growing population is the primary cause of India's environmental degradation. Systematic studies challenge this theory. Empirical evidence from countries such as Japan, England and Singapore, each with population density similar or higher than India, yet each enjoying environmental quality vastly superior to India, therefore suggests population density may not be the only factor affecting India's issues.[3] Floods are a significant environmental issue for India. It causes soil erosion, destruction of wetlands and wide migration of solid wastes. Major environmental problems are forest and agricultural degradation of land, resource depletion (such as water, mineral, forest, sand, and rocks), environmental degradation, public health, loss of biodiversity, loss of resilience in ecosystems, livelihood security for the poor.[4] Let us discus important factors to present eco-crisis and environmental degradation keeping our attention to Indian environment.

A) Deforestation

Deforestation in India is one of the widespread destructions of major forests in India. It is mainly caused by environmental degradation by stakeholders such as farmers, ranches, loggers and plantation corporations. In 2009, India ranked 10th worldwide in the amount of forest loss, where world annual deforestation is estimated as 13.7 million hectares a year.[5] Deforestation started with the growth of agriculture, but was exacerbated in the nineteenth century when British commercial forestry operations destroyed Indian forests mainly in western and southern areas.[2] Several causes supported deforestation, including colonization, agricultural expansion, firewood collection, timber harvesting and extension of cultivation on slopes. Due to the colonization from all over the country trees are cut down as a primary source of fuel. These trees are used for cooking food and other daily needs which require fuel. Deforestation has affected the lives of wild animals and birds including bats. Birds like sparrow, pigeon and crow are becoming rarer due to deforestation. India is facing water problems in urban cities and villages due to deforestation.

The slash and burn method of Jhum-cultivation as one method of shifting cultivation that requires slashing and burning the forest is one that is directly or

---

[3] Henrik Urdal, "People vs. Malthus: Population Pressure, Environmental Degradation, and Armed Conflict Revisited". *Journal of Peace Research*, (42 (4), July 2005), 417–434.

[4] Cf. Ramesha Chandrappa and Ravi. D.R, *Environmental Issues, Law and Technology – An Indian Perspective.*, (Research India Publication, Delhi, 2009).

[5] Gore, Al . *Our Choice: A Plan to Solve the Climate Crisis,* (Rodale Books, 3 November 2009). pp. 174, 192, 184, 186, 192, 172.

indirectly responsible for the cause of climate change, increase in temperature and drought. The climatic changes due to deforestation, global warming brings about extreme heat, flood and draughts.[6] The felling of trees is also responsible for the decrease in rainfall, pollution of air, floods and increase in disease and epidemics. It is also responsible for species extinction. It is found that in Ecuador with increased felling of tress since 1960 for cash crops, the original rainforest has been almost eliminated while a small remnant at Rio Palenque of less than one kilometre is the only remaining site for 43 plants species.[7] This was deforestation ugly side to the environment. Moreover excessive rain, floods, drought and all these uneven climatic changes is the result of deforestation.

B) Emissions

The excesses and emission of green house gases, like carbon dioxide, methane, nitrous oxide, carbon monoxide and others creates imbalance in temperature, pollution, global warming, etc.[8] Smoke, pollutants, waste from the factory, causes air pollution, water pollution, soil pollution. For instance, the water is rendered unfit for drinking, so is the polluted air harmful for the health and the soil that is unfit for cultivation. The exhaust fumes from factories and cars caused severe health problems. Due to the decrease in ozone, higher amount of ultra violet radiation enter into the earth and that caused leukaemia, breast cancer and other skin disorder.[9]

Greenhouse gas emissions

India was the third largest emitter of carbon dioxide, a major greenhouse gas, in 2009 at 1.65 Gt per year, after China and the United States. With 17 percent of world population, India contributed some 5 percent of human-sourced carbon dioxide emission; compared to China's 24 percent share. On per capita basis, India emitted about 1.4 tons of carbon dioxide per person, in comparison to the United States' 17 tons per person, and a world average of 5.3 tons per person.

C) Pollutants

The major sources of pollution in India include the rapid burning of fuel wood/ fire wood and biomass such as dried waste from livestock as the primary source of energy, lack of organised garbage and waste removal services, lack of sewage treatment operations, lack of flood control and monsoon water drainage system,

---

[6] George Zachariah, *Gospel Groaning World: Climate Injustice and Public Witness* (Thiruvalla: CSS & NCCI, 2012), 23.

[7] Jaison Thomas, "Cosmic Groaning for Creation Stewardship: Excavating Green Theology" in *Olive Theological Institute* 4/ I (February 2014), 45.

[8] Zulunungsang Lemtur, "Climate Change and Climate Refugees," in *Green Theology*, edited by Wati Longchar (Kolkata: SCEPTRE, 2014), 40.

[9] Thomas, "Cosmic Groaning for Stewardship: Excavating Green Theology...," 43.

diversion of consumer waste into rivers, cremation practices near major rivers, government mandated protection of highly polluting old public transport, and continued operation by Indian government of government owned, high emission plants built between 1950 and 1980.[10] Air pollution, poor management of waste, growing water scarcity, falling groundwater tables, water pollution, preservation and quality of forests, biodiversity loss, and land/soil degradation are some of the major environmental issues India faces today.[11] India's population growth adds pressure to environmental issues and its resources. Rapid urbanization has caused a build-up of heavy metals in the soil of cities and these metals are being ingested through contaminated vegetables. Heavy metals are hazardous to people›s health and are known carcinogens.[12]

i) Air Pollution

Generally in rural area stoves are using biomass cakes, firewood and trash as cooking fuel. Surveys suggest over 100 million households in India use such stoves 2–3 times every day. It is one of the major causes of air pollution in India, and produces smoke and numerous indoor air pollutants at concentrations 5 times higher than coal. Clean burning fuels and electricity are unavailable in rural parts and small towns of India because of poor rural highways and limited energy generation infrastructure.

Air pollution in India is a serious issue with the major sources being firewood and biomass burning, fuel adulteration, vehicle emission and traffic congestion. Air pollution is also the main cause of the Asian brown cloud, which is causing the monsoon to be delayed. India is the world›s largest consumer of firewood, agricultural waste and biomass for energy purposes. Traditional fuel (firewood, crop residue and dung cake) dominates domestic energy use in rural India and accounts for about 90% of the total. In urban areas, this traditional fuel constitutes about 24% of the total. Fuel wood, agri waste and biomass cake burning releases over 165 million tonnes of combustion products into India's indoor and outdoor

---

[10] For details refer, Milind Kandlikar, Gurumurthy Ramachandran (2000). "2000 India: The Causes and Consequences of Particulate Air Pollution in Urban India: A Synthesis of the Science", *Annual Review of Energy and the Environment,* (25, 2000), 629–684; "Drowning in a Sea of Garbage", *The New York Time,* 22 April 2010; Tripathi, Anshuman; Mishra, Rajesh Kumar; Bouskill, Nik; Broadaway, Susan C.; Pyle, Barry H.; Ford, Timothy E.; et al,. "The role of water use patterns and sewage pollution in incidence of water-borne/enteric diseases along the Ganges River in Varanasi, India", Steve karthik kjournal, *International Journal of Environmental Health Research;* (16 (2) (2006), 113–132.

[11] "India: Country Strategy Paper, 2007–2013", *European External Action Service,* (European Union, 2007).

[12] *Human and Ecological Risk Assessment: An International Journal.* ***22*** *(3):* 736–752.

air every year.[13] These biomass-based household stoves in India are also a leading source of greenhouse emissions contributing to climate change.[14]

The annual crop burning practice in northwest India, north India and eastern Pakistan, after monsoons, from October to December, are a major seasonal source of air pollution. Approximately 500 million tons of crop residue is burnt in open, releasing smoke, soot, NOx, SOx, PAHs and particulate matter into the air. This burning has been found to be a leading cause of smog and haze problems through the winter over Punjab, cities such as Delhi, and major population centers along the rivers through West Bengal.[15] In other states of India, rice straw and other crop residue burning in open is a major source of air pollution.[16]

Vehicle emissions from metropolitan cities are another major source of air pollution. Vehicle emissions are worsened by fuel adulteration and poor fuel combustion efficiencies from traffic congestion and low density of quality, high speed road network per 1000 people.[17] On per capita basis, India is a small emitter of carbon dioxide greenhouse. In 2009, IEA estimates that it emitted about 1.4 tons of gas per person, in comparison to the United States' 17 tons per person, and a world average of 5.3 tons per person. However, India was the third largest emitter of total carbon dioxide in 2009 at 1.65 Gt per year, after China (6.9 Gt per year) and the United States (5.2 Gt per year). With 17 percent of world population, India contributed some 5 percent of human-sourced carbon dioxide emission; compared to China's 24 percent share.[18] The Air (Prevention and Control of Pollution) Act was passed in 1981 to regulate air pollution and there have been some measurable improvements.[19] However, the 2012 Environmental

---

[13] Ganguly; et al., "Indoor Air Pollution in India – A Major Environmental and Public Health Concern", *Indian Council of Medical Research*, (New Delhi, 2001); David Pennise and Kirk Smith. "Biomass Pollution Basics", The World Health Organisation.

[14] Kirk Smith et al., "Greenhouse Implications of Household Stoves: An Analysis for India", *Annual Review of Energy and the Environment*, (Vol. 25), 741-763.

[15] Streets et al., "Biomass burning in Asia: Annual and seasonal estimates and atmospheric emissions", *Global Biogeochemical Cycles*, (17(4), 2003).

[16] Gadde et al., "Air pollutant emissions from rice straw open field burning in India, Thailand and the Philippines", *Environmental Pollution*, (Volume 157, Issue 5, May 2009), 1554–1558

[17] "The Asian Brown Cloud: Climate and Other Environmental Impacts", *United Nations Environmental Programme. 2002*, Archived from the original on 26 May 2012; "Gridlocked Delhi: Six years of career lost in traffic jams", *India Today*. 5 September, 2010.

[18] "CO_2 Emissions from Fuel Combustion Highlights - 2011 Edition", International Energy Agency, France. 2011; "Country Analysis Brief: India", U.S. Energy Information Administration-2011.

[19] "Emissions and Pollution in South Asia", The World Bank – 2010, Archived from the original on 12 April 2011.

Performance Index ranked India as having the poorest relative air quality out of 132 countries.[20]

ii) Water Pollution

Water pollution is the major problem in Indian environmental issues. Discharge of untreated sewage is the single most important cause for pollution of surface and ground water in India. There is a large gap between generation and treatment of domestic waste water in India. The problem is not only that India lacks sufficient treatment capacity but also that the sewage treatment plants that exist do not operate and are not maintained properly. The majority of the government-owned sewage treatment plants remain closed most of the time due to improper design or poor maintenance or lack of reliable electricity supply to operate the plants, together with absentee employees and poor management. The waste water generated in these areas normally percolates in the soil or evaporates. The uncollected wastes accumulate in the urban areas cause unhygienic conditions and release pollutants that leach to surface and groundwater. [21]

According to a World Health Organization study,[22] out of India's 3,119 towns and cities, just 209 have partial sewage treatment facilities, and only 8 have full wastewater treatment facilities. Over 100 Indian cities dump untreated sewage directly into the River Ganges.[23] Investment is needed to bridge the gap between 29000 million litre per day of sewage India generates, and a treatment capacity of mere 6000 million litre per day.[24] Other sources of water pollution include agriculture run off and small scale factories along the rivers and lakes of India. Fertilizers and pesticides used in agriculture in northwest have been found in rivers, lakes and ground water. Flooding during monsoons worsens India's water pollution problem, as it washes and moves all sorts of solid garbage and contaminated soils into its rivers and wetlands. According to NASA, groundwater declines are highest on Earth between 2002 and 2008 in northern India. Agricultural productivity is dependent on irrigation. A collapse of agricultural output and severe shortages of potable water may influence 114 million residents in India. In July 2012, about 670 million people or 10% of the

---

[20] "Data Explorer: Indicator Profiles – Environmental Performance Index", Yale University. 2012, Retrieved 5 September 2012.

[21] "Evaluation of Operation and Maintenance of Sewage Treatment Plants in India-2007", Central Pollution Control Board, Ministry of Environment & Forests, 2008.

[22] "Our Planet, our Health: Report of the WHO Commission on Health and Environment", (World Health Organization, Geneva, 1992).

[23] "Water: A Story of Hope", (Washington (DC), National Geographic Society, 1995).

[24] "Status of Sewage Treatment in India", Central Pollution Control Board, Ministry of Environment & Forests, Govt of India. 2005.

world's population lost power blame on the severe drought restricting the power delivered by hydroelectric dams.[25]

iii) Solid Waste Pollution

Solid waste like trash and garbage is accumulated in India. Trash and garbage disposal services, responsibility of local government workers in India, are ineffective. Solid waste is routinely seen along India's streets and shopping plazas. Trash and garbage scattered everywhere is a common sight in urban and rural areas of India. It is a major factor of pollution. Indian cities alone generate more than 100 million tons of solid waste a year. Street corners are piled with trash. Public places and sidewalks are despoiled with filth and litter, rivers and canals act as garbage dumps. In part, India's garbage crisis is from rising consumption. India's waste problem also points to a stunning failure of governance.[26] The tourism regions in the country mainly hill stations are also facing this issue in the recent years.[27]

Supreme Court of India directed, in 2000, all Indian cities to implement a comprehensive waste-management programme that would include household collection of segregated waste, recycling and composting. These directions have simply been ignored. No major city runs a comprehensive programme of the kind envisioned by the Supreme Court. Indeed, forget waste segregation and recycling directive of the India's Supreme Court, the Organisation for Economic Cooperation and Development estimates that up to 40 percent of municipal waste in India remains simply uncollected. Even medical waste, theoretically controlled by stringent rules that require hospitals to operate incinerators, is routinely dumped with regular municipal garbage. Half of India's medical waste has been disposed improperly that pollutes the environment. Municipalities in Indian cities and towns have waste collection employees. However, these are unionised government workers and their work performance is neither measured nor monitored. India has few solid waste landfills near its major cities, but some of them are overflowing and poorly managed. They have become significant sources of greenhouse emissions and breeding sites for disease vectors such as flies, mosquitoes, cockroaches, rats, and other pests.[28]

Some metropolitan cities of India embarked, in 2011, on waste-to-energy projects of the type in use in Germany, Switzerland and Japan. For example, New Delhi is implementing two incinerator projects aimed at turning the city's trash

---

[25] "Decade of drought: A global tour of seven recent water crises", *Guardian*, 12.6.2015.

[26] "Drowning in a Sea of Garbage", *The New York Times*, 22 April, 2010.

[27] Kumar, S., Dhar, H, Nair, V. V., Bhattacharya, J. K., Vaidya, A. N. and Akolkar, A. B., (2016). "Characterization of Municipal Solid Waste in high altitude sub-tropical regions", *Environmental Technology*, (37 (20), 2016), 2627-2637.

[28] "India: Urbanisation, Sustainable Development and Poverty Alleviation", University of Oregon, USA. Spring, 2010.

problem into electricity resource. These plants are being welcomed for addressing the city's chronic problems of excess untreated waste and a shortage of electric power. They are also being welcomed by those who seek to prevent water pollution, hygiene problems, and eliminate rotting trash that produces potent greenhouse gas methane. The projects are being opposed by waste collection workers and local unions who fear changing technology may deprive them of their livelihood and way of life.[29]

iv) Land and Soil Pollution

The issue of "uranium poisoning" in Punjab attracted press coverage in March 2009. It was alleged to be caused by "fly-ash ponds" of thermal power stations, which reportedly lead to severe birth defects in children in the Faridkot and Bhatinda districts of Punjab. The news reports claimed the uranium levels were more than 60 times the maximum safe limit.[30] In 2012, the Government of India confirmed[31] that the ground water in Malwa belt of Punjab has uranium metal that is 50% above the trace limits set by the United Nations' World Health Organization. Scientific studies, based on over 1000 samples from various sampling points, could not trace the source to fly ash and any sources from thermal power plants or industry as originally alleged. The study also revealed that the uranium concentration in ground water of Malwa district is not 60 times the WHO limits, but only 50% above the WHO limit in 3 locations. This highest concentration found in samples was less than those found naturally in groundwaters currently used for human purposes elsewhere, such as Finland.[32] Research is underway to identify natural or other sources for the problem of uranium.

v) Noise Pollution

It is another major problem the people of India has been faced. Freedom from noise pollution is true freedom indeed. Noise pollution or noise disturbance is the disturbing or excessive noise that may harm the activity or balance of human or animal life. Noise-wise India can be termed as the most polluted country in the world. The source of most outdoor noise worldwide is mainly caused by machines and transportation systems, motor vehicles, aircraft, and trains. In India, the outdoor noise is also caused by loud music during festival seasons. Outdoor noise is summarized by the word environmental noise. Poor urban planning may give

[29] "Indian waste workers fear loss of income from trash-to-electricity projects", *The Washington Post,* 20 November, 2011.

[30] Yadav, Priya, "Uranium deforms kids in Faridkot", *The Times of India,* (2 April 2009); Jolly, Asit, "Punjab disability 'uranium link", *BBC News,* (2 April, 2009).

[31] "Uranium in Ground Water", Ministry of Drinking Water and Sanitation, Government of India (2012).

[32] "Atomic Energy Report - Malwa Punjab Uranium", Question & Answer in Lok Sabha, Government of India (2012).

rise to noise pollution, since side-by-side industrial and residential buildings can result in noise pollution in the residential areas.

Indoor noise can be caused by machines, building activities, and music performances, especially in some workplaces. Noise-induced hearing loss can be caused by outside (e.g. trains) or inside (e.g. music) noise. High noise levels can contribute to cardiovascular effects in humans and an increased incidence of coronary artery disease. Noise can increase the risk of death by altering predator or prey detection and avoidance in animals, interfere with reproduction and navigation, and contribute to permanent hearing loss. The Supreme Court of India which is in New Delhi gave a significant verdict on noise pollution in 2005.[33] Unnecessary honking of vehicles makes for a high decibel level of noise in cities. The use of loudspeakers for political purposes and for sermons by temples, churches and mosques make noise pollution in residential areas worst day by day. Government of India published norms of permissible noise levels in urban and rural areas in January 2010.[34]

D) Urbanization and Industrialisation

Urbanization and industrialization add problems to environment. Few of the characteristics of urbanization and industrialisation are, increase in transportation, fuel combustion, disposition of solid waste which aggravate air pollution and water pollution. In the name of urbanisation rich agricultural lands are misused while there is also increased misuse of raw materials in urbanised area. For instance, it may be recorded that in urbanised area most of the water source is exhausted due to deep filtration of water. With the increase in urban population, industrialisation has badly exploited natural resource to meet the wants of the consumerist society. The waste and toxic materials outlet from the industry, the smoke emitted from the chimney is one of the most dangerous pollutants of air, water and land.

E) Nuclear and other Modern Technology

Nuclear and Modern Technology pose a great threat to well being and continuation of healthy environment in the world. For instance, the Fukushima Nuclear meltdowns and the subsequent danger it poses on environment and health is presented by Dr. Med. Alex Rosen, University Clinic Düsseldorf, and Department of General Paediatrics on March 9th, 2012. Aalex Rosen reported that The *Tōhoku* earthquake on March 11th, 2011 led to multiple nuclear meltdowns in the reactors of the Fukushima Daiichi nuclear power plant in Northern

---

[33] "Noise Pollution: Restricting use of loudspeakers", Court: Supreme Court of India, Justices: Lahoti and Bhan,. *Ecolex*,. 18 July, 2005.

[34] "Amendment to Noise Pollution Regulation and Control Rules-2000 and setting up of a National Noise Monitoring Network", Ministry of Environment & Forests, Govt of India. 4 January, 2010.

Japan. Radioactive emissions from the plant (nuclear reactor) caused widespread radioactive contamination of the entire region. Soil and water samples, as well as marine animals have been found to be highly contaminated. The people exposed to harmful radioisotopes have an increased risk to develop cancer or other radiation-induced diseases. Food, milk and drinking water have been contaminated as well, leading to internal radiation exposure. Most severely affected are children, as their bodies are more susceptible to radiation damage. It was also reported that massive amounts of water which were used in a desperate attempt to cool the reactors and led to equally large amounts of radioactive wastewater, which was continually discharged into the sea, seeped into soil and ground-water deposits or evaporated into the atmosphere.[35]

F) Dams, Hydro-Electric Thermal Projects and Others

The accumulation of agricultural land at the expanses of human habitat, human livelihood and animal and the danger such big dams pose to the environment is worth pondering. Let us take a look at the Koodankulam Nuclear Energy Project of India in partnership with Russia which has been vehemently opposed by **Peoples' Movement against Nuclear Energy (PMANE)** with the support of the local, national and international pacifist in Tamil Nadu. The main reasons for the opposition to such nuclear power project were the issues that relates with the subsistence economy of the local people and the threat to the environment post Fukushima Nuclear crisis. The cry of the fisher folks, farmers, shopkeepers, dalits, workers, beedi-rolling women and others near the southernmost tip of India, who have been fighting against the Koodankulam Nuclear power Project (KKNPP) since the late 1980s appealed,

> They promise FDI, nuclear power, development, atom bombs, security and superpower status. We demand risk-free electricity, disease-free life, unpolluted natural resources, sustainable development and harmless future. They say the Russian nuclear power plants are safe and can withstand earthquakes and tsunamis. But we worry about their side-effects and after-effects. They speak for their scientist friends and business partners and have their eyes on commissions and kickbacks. But we fight for our children and grandchildren, our progeny, our animals and birds, our land, water, sea, air and the skies....[36]

---

[35] Dr. Med. Alex Rosen, "Effects of the Fukushima nuclear meltdowns on environment and health," (March 9th, 2012) http://www.ippnw.de/commonFiles/pdfs/Atomenergie/FukushimaBackgroundPaper.pdf (02/08/2016).

[36] http://www.dianuke.org/letter-from-koodakulam-to-citizens-of-india (02/08/2016).

G) Globalization and Capitalism

Globalisation and Capitalism that emphasise the global linkage based on European capitalist feeds on accumulation of profit through the exploitation of the third world, extracting resources from the domestic economy, interacting and accumulating resources.[37] The threat to creation and the injustice against the poor of the third world, most deplorable being children and women are not two but one issue.[38] For instance, the globalisation threat to the third world poor and ecology is the report that in the year 1983, about 1.8 million metric tons of hazardous waste was dumped in the developing countries. In 1987 and 1988, it was estimated that millions of tonnes of waste, including nuclear waste from the industrialised countries were exported to the poor developing countries of Latin America and West Africa, to be dumped in their Oceans.[39] No doubt, the *Oikos* and the poor inhabitants are the victims of the capitalist trend of globalisation.

Today with the onset of globalisation infected capitalism of companies, lands that once serves us to provide food crops has been used to export crops for the global market.[40] The capitalist agenda of pseudo development that serves the influential out of the very resources of the third world is a thread both to human poverty and the exploitation of the ecology.

H) Consumerist Life Style

Milton-Friedman asserts, "The social responsibility for business is to increase its profits;" so is Brain Griffiths who says, "The business of business is business in which a moral standard has no relevance."[41] To reflect upon these two statements reveal a horrible state of the poor and the equilibrium of the ecosystem. In the earlier subsistence economy natural resources were meant to sustain people to a fulfilling life. But today natural resources are meant to be exploited for extravagant life of few. The environment has enough for the needs of human being but not wants. It may be mentioned here that consumerist lifestyle has in fact exhausted the natural resource. The problem with this lifestyle is those human beings are consuming without giving back anything to the *Oikos*.

---

[37] James Petras and Chronis Polychronism, "Critical Reflections On," in *Economic and Political Weekly* September 6, 1997, 2249 cited by Indukuri John Mohan Razu, *Global Capitalism as Hydra- A New Look at Market, Money and MNCs* (New Delhi: ISPCK, 2006), 23.

[38] Wati Longchar, "Ecumenical Responses to Ecological Crisis: A Critique from the Indigenous Peoples' Perspective," in *Green Theology - Asian Ecumenical Response to Eco-Justice*, edited by A. Wati Longchar (Kolkata: JTCA, 2012), 153.

[39] P.J. Sanjeeva Raj, "Ecology and Development: A Theological Perspective," in *Ecology and Development*, edited by Daniel D. Chetti (Chennai: United Evangelical Lutheran Churches in India, Gurukul Lutheran Theological College & Research Institute, BTESSC, 1991), 58.

[40] Bas Wielenga, *Towards an Eco-Just Society* (Bangalore: Thomas K.C., 1999), 33.

[41] Razu, *Global Capitalism* ..., 220.

I) Use of Plastics, Fertilisers, Pesticides and Other Chemicals

Artificial fertilizers, pesticides and other chemicals used for the preservation, productivity of the crops is also one responsible factor for ecological crisis. It may be mentioned that these are harmful for the health of human beings and the environment. For instance, chemicals used in the paddy field resulted to water pollution, which in turn results to death of aquatic beings which in turn directly affect the environment. One may recount the pollution of land and the danger it poses to the terrestrial animal. By nature plastics are mostly incombustible

To all these direct factors and many other indirect factors added fuel in India to degrade it's environment, for example, government policies such as against to eco-friendly; lack of sincerity and commitment in implementing laws of nature; negligence of government employees; destruction of natural environment in the name of so-called development; selfishness and greediness of industrialists, contractors and government officials and so on are played major role in India to corrupt environment causing eco-crisis. Therefore, India has been faced great challenges from environmental changes, such as global warming; rapid increase in day temperatures; natural calamities such as floods, tsunamis; unseasonal rains and drought; and highly polluted atmosphere caused hazardous diseases to the citizens such as bronchitis, asthma, heart and lung diseases. Government should adopt constructive eco-friendly policies and implement them sincerely. As well as it is the problem to solve by the government alone, but peoples active participation is highly needed. Inter-faith and inter-religious co-operation is more essential in India due to its pluralistic context. For that environmental awareness programs to be arranged to educate people and universities incorporate and integrate courses in their academic curriculums to educate students and make them aware of the present eco-crisis. Researchers and writers should be encouraged to focus their talents and efforts on promoting healthy environment in India. Religious scholars and devotees strive for developing respective eco-friendly religious spiritualities.

Chapter 3

Eco-Sophy and Eco-Spirituality[1]

The contemporary transnational capitalist-technocratic society, with its profit interests which claims to have mastered the techniques of controlling and conquering Nature, is, unfortunately, faced with the problems of environmental degradation, a basic threat to global living. The egoistic human potency to corrupt and pollute has eroded the phase of nature, while Nature has all along been nourishing, protecting, sheltering, life-giving, creative and maternal. Nature, earth, its biosphere and atmosphere have been mortally wounded, due to the immortality of man. The life giving mother earth (terra mater) is turned to be life destroying, to the extent of self-annihilation. The scientific community, partially describe this crisis-situation as deforestation, depletion of ozone layer, global warming, impoverishment, pollution and so on. However, this factual description is only one side of the coin, i.e., the technological. The reasons for this crisis are many. They include factors such as racial discrimination, economic exploitation, casteism, world-wars, socio-political colonization, cultural invasions, religious fundamentalism and so on. Hence, the reasons for the crisis, is not merely scientific and technological, but also non-scientific. In other words, ecological problem is multi-faced.[2]

Deep down, the radicality (root cause) of the crisis is, philosophical (ideological). It is philosophical in the sense that the worldviews (perspectives

[1] This chapter is revised article which is first published in K.L. Richardson (ed.), *Samaikya*, (Andhra Christian Theological College, Hyderabad, April 2015), 29-32.

[2] For details, S. Lourdunathan, "Ecosophical Concerns in the Sikh Tradition" a Faculty member of Arul Anandar College, India, presented as a paper at a conference Sikhism and Global Living, organized by Guru Nanak Devji Chair, School of Religions, Philosophy and Humanistic Thought, Madurai Kamaraj University, Madurai, April 1996. http://www.ecosikh.org/wp-content/uploads/2011/09/Ecosophical-Concerns-in-the-Sikh-Tradition.pdf accessed on 13-07-17.

or the ways of looking at) of those who are responsible for destruction of Nature often tend to be partial (monolithic) dualistic, and non-earthly (other worldly); for instance, the idealism of Plato denying the reality of the World, affirms only the Archetype, and hence it is partial, not ecological. Naive realism and materialism assert that Cosmos is what ranks first, and consciousness is only secondary (one sided); Existentialists, like Sartre, affirm the world and consciousness as primary, and confuse the real cosmos with the human-world alone. In the Indian philosophical tradition, *Vedanta,* for example, affirms the primacy of the ideal of the 'identity of *atman* or *Brahman*', to the extent of giving only a relative or no importance to the existence of the world *(maya* – theory of illusion).

The frontier-mentality of human-centricism (humanism) of the 18th century, proved to be not sufficiently human, as it implied the development of the dominant class and the Western scientific man's interests. These are some of the instances to point out the fact, that, our worldviews that shape human attitude to life and Nature, were predominantly partial and other-worldly, implying an inbuilt-insensitivity to ecology. Given this context of metaphysical exclusion of Nature, it is high time that we search for philosophical foundations that are eco-relational. It is the moral responsibility of man to establish a new humanism without 'human-centricism' of the West. In other words, the practical relationship of man with Nature must be redefined or deconstructed, outside the 'wrong kinds of philosophizing'. Perhaps, one of the ways of responding to the situation, is to investigate the philosophical foundations of the South Asian ethos, and that too, of those, who are neither monolithic nor other-worldly. In contrast to the European individualism, the remarkable characteristic of West Asian Religious ethos, (that of Buddhism, Taoism, Confucianism and so on.) is holistic - these religions are in general anti-individualistic, not consumerist and indiscriminative. The spirit of peace, justice, global living, harmony with Nature, is foundational to these religions.

Therefore, it is a philosophical/theological attempt to understand the relation between philosophy and ecology. "Ecosophy" and "Eco-spirituality" are very recent concepts used frequently in our contemporary times by philosophers and theologians in their philosophical and theological attempts in relation to ecology and environment. Our contemporary society has been facing several crucial problems, eco-crisis is one of many, which perhaps compelling human beings to search for it's healing. In search of healing and restoration of "fallen-creation", scientists, ecologists, environmentalists, philosophers and theologians are attempting for resources from their respective fields and undertake several ecological & environmental researches and awareness programs to prevent eco-destruction/environmental degradation and protect the very life on this globe – mother earth. A theme like "Eco-Justice and Spirituality" is an appropriate one, which is very necessary for our contemporary socio-religious, theological and philosophical reflections on this contextual issue. By improving "eco-spirituality", I believe, we will bring "eco-justice", keeping in view of this "quest for contextual eco-spirituality" of our times, this chapter, perhaps, is a brief attempt to search for relevant resources contributing to the development of "eco-spirituality" both from philosophical and theological stand point of views.

"Eco-sophy and eco-philosophy" are neologism formed by contracting the phrase "ecological philosophy". Ecosophy is used to designate different and often contradictory, though conceptually related, concepts by the Norwegian father of "deep ecology" Arne Naess and French post-Marxist philosopher and psychoanalyst Felix Guattari. Arne Naess introduced the concepts "deep ecology movement" and "ecosophy" into environmental literature in 1972 while he was working as a professor at University of Oslo. Naess based his article on a lecture he gave in Bucharest in 1972 at the Third World Future Research Conference "Eco-philosophy, Ecosophy and the Deep Ecology Movement: An Overview". Naess, in his talk, discussed the longer-range background of the ecology movement and its connection with respect for "Nature" and the inherent worth of other living beings. Naess's view of human beings as an integral part of a "total-field image"[3] of Nature contrasts with the alternative and more anthropocentric construction of Ecosophy outlined by Guattari. The term ecological wisdom, synonymous with ecosophy, was introduced by Naess in 1973. The concept has become one of the foundations of the "deep ecology movement". All expressions of values by "Green Parties" list "ecological wisdom" as a key value – it was one of the original "Four Pillars of the Green Party" and is often considered the most basic value of these parties. It is also often associated with indigenous religion and cultural practices. Naess stand point is:

> By an ecosophy I mean a philosophy of ecological harmony or equilibrium. A philosophy as a kind of sofia (or) wisdom, is openly normative, it contains both norms, rules, postulates, value priority announcements and hypotheses concerning the state of affairs in our universe. Wisdom is policy wisdom, prescription, not only scientific description and prediction. The details of an ecosophy will show many variations due to significant differences concerning not only the 'facts' of pollution, resources, population, etc., but also value priorities.[4]

Felix Guattari is a psychoanalyst, poststructuralist philosopher and political activist who refer "ecosophy" to a field of practice. Guattari's use of the term

---

[3] Drengson, A. and Y. Inoue (eds.), *The Deep Ecology Movement: An Introductory Anthology*, Berkeley: North Atlantic Publishers, 1995, also refer for details - http://en.wikipedia.org/wiki/Ecosophy

[4] *Ibid.* For information refer, for example, Naess, Arne, "The Shallow and the Deep Long-Range Ecology Movement: A Summary" in *Inquiry*, 1973, 16:95-100; Drengson A. & B. Devall (eds.), *The Ecology of Wisdom Writings by Arne Naess,* Berkeley, Counterpoint, 2008.

demarcates what he observes as the necessity for the proponents of social liberation whose struggles in the 20th century were dominated by the paradigm of social revolution and Marxism to implant their arguments within an ecological framework which understands the interconnections of social and environmental spheres. Guattari holds that traditional environmentalist perspectives obscure the complexity of the relationship between humans and their natural environment through its maintenance of the dualistic separation of human (cultural) and nonhuman (natural) systems; he envisions ecosophy as a new field with a monistic and pluralistic approach to such study. Ecology in the Guattarian sense then, is a study of complex phenomena, including human subjectivity, the environment, and social relations, all of which are intimately interconnected.[5]

The term eco-sophia, literally means the wisdom of the Universe that is required for the promotion of sustainable and peaceful ecology. The combination of the two Greek words, Oikos + Sophos gives rise to Eco-sophia; (Oikos means the Cosmos, the household of being). Eco-sophia is a philosophy of ecological harmony and equilibrium. It is the kind of wisdom (sophia) that is suggestive of norms, ways of perceiving Nature, as against dominant world-views. It is an attempt to go beyond anthropocentrism; towards holistic consciousness of the universe. It is a new mediation of humanity and society with Nature. It involves developing a certain religious attitude towards nature-eco-spirituality. It views that social and environmental problems are the consequence of specific social relations of dominations.

Within this frame, ecology (mere environmentalism) is elevated from a scientific description to philosophy, in this sense, it is called deep ecology. It is to view that the problems of human society are not to be treated in isolation with other social systems and norms, for "systems are integrated wholes, whose properties cannot be reduced to those of its parts." Eco-sophia is the articulation of religious and philosophical world-views that provide a "face to face relation with Nature." The eco-sophical paradigm, aims at the liberation of life - that necessarily includes the liberation of Nature, women and the underprivileged. It is an attempt to contact with intrinsic dignity/worth of Nature, women and the downtrodden. It aims to establish relation in justice. Cosmic unity and bio-centric equality are the two ultimate norms of eco-sophia. Eco-sophism essentially recognises that both human and non-human life on earth has intrinsic values. It abnegates any form of domination and subjugation. People and Nature is the core of eco-sophia(ism).[6]

Another important concept is "eco-spirituality", which indeed is a spiritual view of, and context for, our relationship with the universe and the earth. It

[5] Guattari, Félix, "Remaking Social Practices", in Genosko, Gary (Hg.), (1996): *The Guattari Reader,* Oxford, Blackwell, 1996, pp. 262-273.

[6] S. Lourdunathan, "Ecosophical Concerns in the Sikh Tradition."

has the potential to transcend boundaries between spiritual traditions and also between science and spirituality. On a personal level, it can foster a deep sense of belonging to the universe and the earth and a deep sense of participation in the unfolding mystery of this universe. It is now self-evident to anyone who looks out and observes the environmental conditions at our doorstep that this earth is in trouble. It is important that we know our cosmology as well as possible in order to better savor God's grandeur and glory. We need to create the conditions so that spirituality can emerge as something so deeply inside us that we need not even think about it, but we simply live the presence of God in everything and of everything in God.[7]

Eco-spirituality is the humble way of caring for the earth. It is the area where modern ecology and the resources of the spirit overlap and cry out for all of us to abandon destructive behavior of the natural world and to transform our attitudes towards the earth. The New Testament says that "God is spirit" (Jn 4:2) and that "the spirit of life" (Rom 8:10). Spirit means everything that breathes that inhales and exhales; everything living is spirit or bearer of spirit. That means God above all, then human beings and animals, then vegetarian, and finally earth itself everything that it holds. The earth is seen as full of spirit, for the wind surrounding it is earth's breath. If life is the spirit of God, then we must respect such life in this universe, therefore, "eco-spirituality" aims at developing such respect towards living organisms believing as divine sparks.

The human spirit is most open and universal in what exists, a node of relationships and connections in all directions and dimensions. If spirit is life, then the opposite of spirit is not matter but death, and the realm of death includes all the processes that lead to breakdown and prepare the way for death, such as oppression, injustice, and neglect of living conditions, which cause illness and dehumanized human relations, as well as the destruction of the landscape and the loss of the physical and chemical balance of the soil and atmosphere. Spirituality accordingly entails a true basic life-direction that confronts the logic of death as it exists in the current process of accumulation and total market, which are maximum organized expressions of the assault against nature and community around the planet. Eco-spirituality is an attempt to discover the ecological dimensions of our responsibility for peace, justice, and the integrity of everything created.

---

[7] For detailed discussion on "eco-spirituality" refer this author's other writings, for example, T. Swami Raju, *Christian Theological Responses: Contemporary Contextual Concerns,* (particularly chapter VI on "Eco-spirituality, a Contemporary Concern", Christian World Imprints, New Delhi, 2014, pp. 91ff; T. Swami Raju, "Eco-Justice: Contemporary Global Concern" in *Social Justice and Eco-Concern,* Published in connection to ACTC Golden Jubilee One Day State Level Women Meet held on Thursday, February 27th 2014, pp. 14-26; for Telugu see Acharya Tadivaka Swami Raju, "Paryavarana Aadhyathmikata – Aavasyakatha: Samakaleena Samaja Badhyata" in *Samaikya,* Golden Jubilee issue, ed. Praveen Prabhu Sudheer, ACTC, Hyderabad, pp. 39-44.

"Eco-spirituality" is a contemporary form of nature spirituality, present-day part of every religion and philosophy, a very precious form of spirituality, part of the Franciscan vision and the insight expressed in the metaphor of "creation as a great book that human beings must learn to read". Every religion has a dimension of nature as a whole. It projects a cosmology or world view, as Durkheim explained very well, not in the sense of doing science but of showing the connectedness of everything with the Divine reality, therefore, perhaps there is always a religious ecology. It is not necessarily aimed at conservation or integration, however, but may foster an aggressive stance that destabilizes ecosystems, as, for example, in one particular understanding of the Jewish and Christian doctrine of the human being as lord and king over creation. But it may also, as in the case of natural mystics, internalize the Christian truth that we are all children of the same eternal Creator-Parent and on that basis emotionally experience the bond of radical kinship that unites all beings from the ant on the roadside to the most distant star, from the tiniest elementary particle to the largest galaxy or quasar in the universe. The result is an attitude of deep reverence for each being in creation, an attitude that is absolutely necessary today if we to ensure the preservation and integrity of whole creation.

Eco-spirituality is linked to the spirit of this age. Human beings of the world, inspired by the same Spirit, are increasingly, feel the same way about environment. As we awaken spiritually to understand the connection between man and nature, we ourselves are healed of the former attitude of dominance toward earth. We begin to see the natural world as a source of the divine. We begin to discover at the heart of the universe a source of love, goodness, and affection for the entire earth community. We experience earth as the source and basis of our life and we celebrate oneness with the earth, a spirituality with the land. As we reflect on our origins, we start to understand ourselves in communion with the universe. The universe discovers itself in us and we celebrate our journey with earth as our spiritual journey. Eco-spirituality teaches that divine life extends to all reality, and the cosmos is an integral part of God's self-revelation. It studies our relationship to God as it develops in the context of our relationships with the cosmos in its totality. Ecology studies our total environment and all the living or non-living creatures that dwell with us in this cosmic house *(oikos)*.

The present religious and non-religious understanding of our relationship with nature can be categorized as follows: First type is "**dominion-spirituality**" where people feel that they can rightfully exploit natural environment. The emphasis here is that humans are not at all at home in nature. It stresses differences between humans and the rest of nature, while we are not above the nature but with the nature. The danger is the arrogant disdain for material world; subjugating and empowering nature and environment, which leads to exploitation. Second type is "**stewardship-spirituality**" in which people take care of creation, which is intended to serve our needs. The emphasis is that there is a wide gap between humans and the remainder of creation; anthropocentrism, in which the human person is the center of creation. There is the danger of overemphasis on mastery, with focus on conquering and controlling nature; speciesism; no sense of solidarity with other species.

Third type is, "**Creation-centric-spirituality**" where people are not so much caretakers as fully part of creation the emphasis is on intrinsic value and sacredness of nature, so all species deserve protection; recognizes interdependence within the web of life. The danger is in the call for sustainable development leaves many unresolved issues! It is unclear how to balance human needs with solidarity with other species. Fourth type is "**deep eco-spirituality**" which is the radical re-visioning of the relationships and boundaries between human beings and the rest of creation. The emphasis is on the call for revival of asceticism, human renunciation, and mysticism; eco-theology views nature as a medium for the mystery of the sacred, which humans must not presume to know fully. The danger is overly romanticized view may make creation into an idol; danger of totally neglecting legitimate human needs. Finally, "**eco-friendly spirituality**" which, indeed, is a recent development in environmental concerns that promotes friendly relations of human beings with whole creation particularly surrounding environment. Such kind of spirituality doesn't limited to "theological thoughts" or "philosophical speculations", but needs to develop and promote as a "**practical spirituality**" that involves in practicing eco-friendly life and "**participatory spirituality**" which aims at peoples active participation in ecologically sustainable activities.

Chapter 4

Primal Religious Traditions and Eco-concerns

Primal Religious Traditions have been dominated the life of Indians even today. A number of corrective measures, resources and future course of action have been initiated in both at the level of international and national conferences, summits, workshops and dialogues since the latter half of the twentieth century pertaining to the matter of environmental issue we are being faced with. Many scholarly researches have been focussed on classical religious traditions but not many sadly have look back and to rediscover the enormous wealth of knowledge and wisdom that primal religious traditions has to offer humanity to save the mother earth. This chapter is a brief attempt in search of wholistic vision of the mother earth long forgotten; therefore, it gives an overview of the Primal Religion and re-visioning the values inherent to the people as we search for resources to protect the environment.

1) The Concept "Primal Religion"

There are several terms used indicating primal religious practices, beliefs and traditions, such as "Animism", "Primitive", "Pre-literate", "Tribal" and so on, but many scholars identified that these terms have been used in terms of inferior to so-called classical or great religious traditions, therefore opposed to use these terms. Primal Religion is the term used in the sense of all the beliefs and practices are at primal stage, not inferior, but distinctive.[1] Primal religion is the priori,

[1] For more clarification refer, H.S., Pressler, *Primitive Religion of India;* Jonathan H. Thumra, "The Primal Religious Tradition," in *Religious Traditions of India*, edited by P.S. Daniel, David C. Scott and G.R. Singh (Delhi: ISPCK, 2011),, T. Swami Raju, "Adima matamulut" in *Manamatamulu Mukhyalakshnamulu.*

the root, the base of all religions. It is the most authentic and purest form of human interaction with the creator and the creation expressed in everyday life. This relationship is what a mother is to the child; this relation encompasses every aspects of human life from birth to afterlife on earth. Unlike the modern religion that comes with set of principles, dogmas and creeds, to the Primal, the consciousness of the Supreme Bing is written in the heart of every being, it is intrinsic, innate. The Stars, the Moon, the Groves, the Birds, the spring, the River to name a few are their family member and teachers. Few of the distinct characteristic of Primal religious tradition are the belief in Supreme Being, the belief in Spirit (malevolent and benevolent), the belief in Mana, the power of Fetish, the observance of Taboo, the relational Totems, the belief in Omen, the practice of Divination, the practice of Magic, the power of Evil Eye and others.

The practitioners or the communities who were once primal in their religious outlook were many in numbers especially the so-called tribal[2] community. This chapter shall therefore confine mainly on the indigenous community[3] of the north east India.[4] The reason for the decline of primal religion is the onset of Christianity and modernity in the middle and late nineteenth century and early 20th century. Although, most of the north eastern India who were primal in their origin were mostly Christianised/modernised, the influence of primal culture, religion, practices and worldview are still very close to the people. Today, it is also the struggle of the indigenous community to reclaim their past.

2) The Primal Religious Worldview

The primal worldview is based on a kind of triangular relationship, where human needs to have good relation with both creator and creation. Razouselie Lasetso while citing Renthy Keitzar expressed similar opinion that the primal worldview is the "God-Human-Creation relationship". The indigenous has their own way of

---

[2] See, "State/Union Territory-wise List of Scheduled Tribes in India," in *Ministry of Tribal Affairs – Government of India*, http://tribal.nic.in/content/list%20of%20scheduled%20tribes%20in%20India.aspx (16-08-2016).

[3] The presenter as long as possible prefers to use the term Indigenous community or names of the particular community in place of tribal. Tribal as a term is derogative; it is undefined in the constitution of India; this term was never used by the indigenous community; also article 342 the "scheduled tribe" in the Indian constitution explicitly fail to define who and what the tribals are, instead vesting power upon the President of India in consultation with the Governor is bestowed the power to deem/demit a community as a tribal. See, "The Constitution (Scheduled Tribes) Order 1950," http://lawmin.nic.in/ld/subord/rule9a.htm (12-08-2016).

[4] Although as per the constraint of the sources, few communities' practices have been mentioned or cited time and again, it is the understanding of the presenter that the cited communities' practices are more or less the same if not a representation inasmuch as North East India's indigenous community is concerned.

practically relating themselves to nature, natural forces and supernatural powers.[5] This wholistic worldview of the Tribal certainly explains the inter-connectedness of creation that humanity is incomplete without the rest of the creation because it is only through the creation that humankind finds the meaning and purpose of its existence. All the indigenous/tribal identity is radically related to the land, to mountains, rocks, the entire cosmic universe and everything therein. Even the Sacred Power is understood in relation to land/space. The experience of time and history is also related to land.[6]

A) Intra Kinship Relation: Vision of Indigenous Cosmology

Renthy Keitzar is of opinion that there are "Intra Kinship Relations" between human being, creation and the creator.[7] Indigenous cosmological kinship is one whole creation in an organic whole, integrated and coherent.[8] It is, indeed, an acknowledgement of non-dichotomy in the outlook towards creation in terms of sacred and secular, physical and secular, earthly and heavenly; this is what Yangkahao Vashum call it as "Undifferentiated Unity."[9] Human being is one among the many creatures; all created beings are derived from the same source of one creator; this creator too is one part of the cosmic life.

There are few of these similar terms used to denote Indigenous cosmological vision such as human-nature-spirit,[10] and God-self-world.[11] Vashum in laying forth the foundational "Undifferentiated Unity" of the Primal Ecological Vision also reaffirm M.M. Thomas' primal vision which reads,

[5] Razouselie Lasetso citing Renthy Keitzar; see, Razouselie Lasetso, "Tribal Theology and the Bible: A Contextual Reading of the Bible," in *Tribal Theology - A Search for Quality Theological Education and Relevant Ministry*, edited by Yangkahao Vashum (Jorhat: Tribal Study Series, 2009), 40.

[6] Wati Longchar, "Green Theology: Resources from Primeval Traditions" in *The Journal of Theologies and Cultures in Asia,* vol. 11, edited by A. Wati Lonchar (Kolkata: PTCA, 2012), 161.

[7] Renthy Keitzar, *In Search of a Relevant Gospel Message* (Guwahati: CLC, 1995), 21-25.

[8] Wati Longchar, "Ecumenical Responses to Ecological Crisis: A Critique from the Indigenous Peoples' Perspective," in *The Journal of Theologies and Cultures in Asia*, vol. 11, edited by A. Wati Longchar (Kolkata: PTCA, 2012), 153, 154.

[9] Yangkahao Vashum, "Theology of Land: A Naga Perspective," in *The Tribal Worldview and Ecology*, edited by A. Wati Longchar and Yangkahao Vashum (Jorhat: Tribal Study Centre, 1998), 70.

[10] The term employed by Nirmal Minz in his article, Nirmal Minz, "Primal Religious Perspectives on Ecology," in *Ecology and Development: Theological Perspective*, edited by Daniel D. Chetti (n.p: GLTC, 1991), no page no. cited by Vashum, "Theology of Land: A Naga Perspective,"..., 70.

[11] This is a term used by K. Thanzauva in K. Thanzauva, "Theological Basis for Social Transformation: Methodological Implications of Third World Liberation Theology in the Context of Mizoram, North East India" (Unpublished Ph. D Dissertation, Melbourne, 1993), 300, cited by Vashum, "Theology of Land: A Naga Perspective,"..., 70.

> In it there is the vision of the spiritual continuum with which the dead and the living, natural objects, spirits and gods, the individual, clan and tribes, animals, plants, minerals and humans form an unbroken hierarchical unity of the spiritual forces; and the human self is not an individual self but an extended universal self present and actively participating in an all parts of the totality.[12]

B) The Relation of the Earth, the Sky and the Indigenous

In the olden days, a high valuation for the eco-system was found among many indigenous communities. The sky is seen as the male and the earth the female. The health of either was considered of paramount importance for life's sustenance. It is a belief that if this mother earth is harm through deforestation the sky will be injured. If the sky does not provide due rainfall and sunshine the mother earth will be injured. Therefore, keeping both the mother earth and the male sky healthy was a beautiful cosmology.[13]

3) Indigenous Understanding of Land: An Ecological Resource

The land in the Primal religious tradition is the wholeness of life; it is the source of life and it is part of their life. The land therefore is sacred; it is not treated as an object because human beings are not the real owner of land; it is rather the land that owns the community and gives the identity. It is a symbol of unity of all living creatures, the spirit(s); it is a basis that enables them to co-exist with other living beings, their ancestors and the Creator.[14] Therefore, land is a symbol of pride, identity and prosperity, it is undisputable property; and it cannot be commercialized.[15]

A) Land as "The Gift of God"

The Land for the indigenous people is not a means of production but a means of livelihood. It is not greed based but need based. The use of land among the Nagas/ indigenous people is worth noting. There is a certain fixed time and mode of cultivation in the land. Certain months are usually set aside for cultivation while

---

[12] M.M. Thomas, "Primal Vision and Modernization," A Paper Presented in the National Seminar on Theological Implications of the Primal Vision Sponsored by BTESSC/GLTC, September 9-12, 1993 at GLT College, Madras, 3, cited by Vashum, "Theology of Land: A Naga Perspective,"..., 70.

[13] Razouselie Lasetso, "Exploring Ecological Values from Tribal Resources" in *Tribal Ecology*, edited by Razouselie Lasetso, Marlene Ch.Marak and Yangkahao Vashum (Jorhat: ETC Programme Coordination, 2012), 2.

[14] Wati Longchar, *Returning to Mother Earth: Theology, Christian Witness and Theological Education, an Indigenous Perspective* (Taiwan: Programme for Theology and Culture in Asia, 2012), 29.

[15] Lasetso, "Exploring Ecological Values from Tribal Resources" in *Tribal Ecology*...," 3.

the rest of the month are aside for the land to rest and rejuvenate. Moreover, using the land for beyond one's need is considered as greed and a sign of pride. Thus, the gift of God through land is for sustenance.[16] Now since the land is a gift from God, the land is older than humanity, it is sacred; the land does not belong to humankind. It is for this reason land is not supposed to be sold[17] because it is not a commodity; rather it is an identity on which a person is defined. For instance among most tribes of the north eastern part of India, an individual's identity is known by asking the name of the village from which the person comes from, never by the person's name.[18]

B) Land as "Sacred"

The Land is the gift of God, hence it is sacred. It is the belief of indigenous people that the land is the dwelling place of divine powers/gods/spirits. The land is sacred, for in it is the moral remains of their ancestors whom the indigenous people greatly revere. Now may observe that the land as the meeting point or the place of union among human, gods, the death and the rest of the creation. One is not expected to dig or till the land before invoking the will of God.[19] The land is a temple;[20] the earth therefore is sacred and animated by spirit. It is for these reasons ceremonial rites of purification for the soil at the beginning of agricultural cultivation is performed. There is also a primal practice among the Tangkhul Nagas in which in cases relating to land disputes, a lump of soil/earth of the disputed earth is eaten by the chiefs of the two contending parties. Whoever dies first is understood to be considered as the guilty person/party. The point is this: the land is always considered as older than humankind; that the land is sacred therefore one must not lie against land.

---

[16] Vashum, "Theology of Land: A Naga Perspective,"..., 73.

[17] Further explanation is needed here. This concept of land is slowly dying out due to the wave of comerciali- zation and capitalism. There has been a misconception (especially among the non-tribals) as to why indige- nous land is immune from land ownership by the non-tribals in indigenous areas. See, Forest Right Acts 2006 also amended on 6-9-2102 which gives special provision to the protection of tribal land by the tribals in, "Forest Rights Acts 2006," *Ministry of Tribal Affairs – Government of India*, http://www.tribal.nic.in/ Content/ ForestRight ActOtherLinks. aspx (16-08-2016). But to the indigenous, land is more than a mass of soil, it is their identity, their birthright. It is for this reason one witness revolution, uprising in the name of land.

[18] K. Thanzauva, *Theology of Community – Tribal Theology in the Making* (Bangalore: Asian Trading Corporation, 2004), 226.

[19] Vashum, "Theology of Land: A Naga Perspective,"..., 74.

[20] As per the Primal spirituality, their religion is not centered on a temple or church or mosque or particular shrine. Rather, the earth as a whole is the temple/place of devotion and spirituality. See, Thanzauva, *Theology of Community* ..., 218.

C) Land as "Mother Earth"

The Land is not just a mass of earth to be stamped upon by the inhabitants of this world. The Primal understanding of land as the mother earth that gives life and sustains inhabitants of the world is in fact a significant kinship of humankind with the mother earth. For instance, the Ao Naga has a tradition that holds that the Aos came out of six stones, *Longtrok*;[21] Chang Naga legend understands the existence of human on earth emerged from a big hole on earth;[22] or that of the Tangkhul Nagas folk tale in which the origination of the community was understood to be from the bowel of earth called *Miwurlung*.[23] Two important points can be drawn from these traditions: the mother earth as the mother that gave birth to the people and the mother earth as the source of life and sustenance to the people. After all, the earth nourishes and nurtures the whole creation. This mother-child relation is closely existent in the heart of every Primal religious tradition.

D) God-Human-Land Relationship

Indigenous community, particularly Nagas, has a Primal religious tradition that relates an organic unity among God and Human and land. Local people believe that the earth is the mother and the spirit of god dwells on that mother earth. This symbiotic relationship does not end up in this world but extents even to the next world. Such is the proximity of people with the land. For example, the understanding of *Kazeiram*,[24] a place where in is the land of the dead, the dead continue to sustain their life by tilling the ground as dead do while on earth. This place is not just confined to human beings but that of the domestic animals.[25] We may observe here two things: one is the unending relationship of human with the animal creations and other is the relationship of human and animals with land. As mentioned elsewhere that it is the land which is the mother, it is land that sustains and nourishes and one goes back to that mother (land).

---

[21] These traditions although common among many indigenous settings, one finds special mention among the Sangtam Naga and Ao Nagas. See, Vashum citing Panger Imchen in, Panger Imchen, *Ancient Ao-Naga Religion and Culture* (New Delhi: Haranad Publications, 1993), 20 cited by Vashum, "Theology of Land: A Naga Perspective,"..., 74. Also refer, Thanzauva, *Theology of Community* ..., 218.

[22] Folk Tales from Nagaland Part I and II (Kohima: Directorate of Art and Culture, Nagaland, 1989), 151 cited by Vashum, "Theology of Land: A Naga Perspective,"..., 74.

[23] According to this folk tale of the Tangkhul Nagas, the community was understood to have came upon the earth led by a person called as *Phungshoka* (name of a person, meaning: the one who led) to come and settle in their present place. The Nagas, Mizos, Garos and others consider their ancestral origination from the earth and the stone. See, Vashum, "Theology of Land: A Naga Perspective,"..., 74-75; also refer, Thanzauva, *Theology of Community* ..., 219.

[24] It is a term of the Tangkhul Nagas signifying a place where the dead goes after their life on earth. It is neither hell nor heaven but a place where one can find the extension of life after death on earth.

[25] Vashum, "Theology of Land: A Naga Perspective,"..., 84-85.

4) The Place of Supreme Being in Creation Narratives

There are several myths and folk tales in Primal Religious Traditions among indigenous people that the god/supreme being actively involved in creation and re-creation process. The following examples illustrate the same.

A) *Lijaba*: Supreme Being's entrance into the Earth

As per the practice of the *Ao Nagas* every year in honour of *Lijaba,*[26] a *genna* (a public observation that is binding especially religiously significant) is observed known as *Lijaba za mong*. On this day *Lijaba* is believed to enter the earth/soil like a seed that enters the soil, buried to be germinated again. This *genna* observes that *Lijaba* enter the earth with the soil and rises again along with the crops. *Lijaba* is the one who gives the vegetation in the land, *Lijaba* is the creator but also the active life giving crate who is always re-creating as the earth continue to be the constant source of fertility for the growth of all vegetations thereby providing food both for animal and human.[27] What we observe here is the Supreme Being creating and re-creating, the unmistakable and unbreakable relationship between God, human and nature.

B) A *Tangkhul Naga* Creation Myth

It is a creation myth which vividly expose in the Primal religious understanding that humanity as a part of creation family. The animated discussion, consultation, consensus and the wisdom of *Kasa Akhava*[28] presents creation one plane. The cause and effect of one creature to the other in creation effects the whole creation. *Kasa Akhava* is the renewer of creation who at the same time judge upon the manipulator of the flow of life, one that uphold the moral law; a judge both now and afterlife.[29]

i) Creation in Dialogue

There was a great assembly of the whole creation. It reads,

> The assembly was convened by Kasa Akhava to determine the duration of day and night. The Kasa Akhava invited the opinion of the assembled

---

[26] *Lijaba* is an *Ao Naga* name for the Supreme Being. The lexical meaning of Lijaba is "the one who enters the earth. Li meaning "earth," while zaba or jaba meaning "enter;" thus the one who enters the earth. It is better translated as the Supreme Being who indwells the earth. See, A. Wati Longchar, "Lijaba – The Earth Entering Supreme Bieng : The Ao-Naga Concept of God and Ecology," in *The Tribal Worldview and Ecology* ..., 29.

[27] Longchar, "Lijaba – The Earth Entering Supreme Being ..." 29.

[28] *Kasa Akhava* literally translated as *Kasa* (creator), *Akhava*(owner) is understood among the Tangkhul nagas to be the Supreme Being. The Supreme Being is also known with the name *Uri Ura/Varivara*. See, Jonathan H. Thumra, "The Primal Religious Tradition," in *Religious Traditions of India*, edited by P.S. Daniel, David C. Scott and G.R. Singh (Delhi: ISPCK, 2011), 48.

[29] Thumra, "The Primal Religious Tradition"..., 48.

> creatures. After a spell of silence, the mole came out with a suggestion to have one year each as day and night. This suggestion was rejected by all sue to its impracticability. The discussion prolonged, but no acceptable proposal was forthcoming. The cock was then left with the responsibility to determine an answer. The cock should crow when he is exhausted and needed rest. This would signal the end of the day. Again, the cock should crow after he had sufficiently rested in the night, heralding the dawning of the day. The cock, hence, became the time keeper of the world.[30]

ii) The Flow/Chain of Creation

In another myth of creation it reads,

> A scene was created by a hungry fox disturbing the peaceful sleep of the fellow creature at night. He was seated on a tree enjoying the walnut. By mistake a walnut fell off from his hands and hit the crab lying below. The crab filled with fury destroyed the nest of the giant ants who in turn stung a sleeping wild boar. The agonized boar went wild and destroyed the banana trees. This disturbed the tiny bat sleeping peacefully on the leaf of the banana. The angry bat sped about wildly and landed in the nostril of a sleeping elephant. The agitated elephant went wild resulting in the death of man. Kasa Akhava called all creatures for an explanation ... the flying fox was punished by the amputation of one of his legs....[31]

5) Eco-cantered Primal Religious Traditions

The basic characteristics of primal religious traditions closely connected to eco-friendly spirituality, which indeed provides resources to honour the nature and protects the environment.

A) *Taboo*:

In Primal Religious Traditions *taboo*[32] is an important belief of indigenous community and its basic characteristic. There are several kinds of *taboos* have been observed by local folk.

---

[30] A slightly different version of this story exists in a number of communities of the Nagas and other tribal community although the intended meaning of the myth is the same. See, Yangkahao Vashum, "A Tangkhul Creation Myth: Implication for Holistic View of Human Rights," in *The Tribal Worldview and Ecology* ..., 34-35; Also refer, A. Wati Longchar, "Myth: A Source for Conceptualizing Tribal Theology," in *An Exploration of Tribal Theology*, edited by A. Wati Longchar (Mokokchung: TzÜdikong Baptist Church, 1997), 85-86.

[31] Vashum, "A Tangkhul Creation Myth ..." 35.

[32] It means prohibition or forbidden activity, something that is against the social norms. This practice of Taboo covers all aspects of tribal life. See, Thumra, "The Primal Religious Tradition" ..., 54; also refer, Wati Long char, "Green Theology: Resources from Primeval Traditions," in *Green Theology*, edited by Wati Longchar (Kolkata: SCEPTRE, 2014), 231.

i) *Taboos* in Relation to Killing Animals

Taboos are observed with the awareness that negligence in observing certain prohibition cause suffering not only to human beings but to the whole creation. Few of the taboos in relation to human relation with animals are: the village is not allowed to kill animals on restricted season, especially in the season of breeding. It is also the case of taboo against killing or hunting pregnant animals or animals in the company of their young ones. The use of poisonous leaf to fish in the rivers or spring to fish is prohibited. Moreover, supposing if a domesticated animal is born in a family for instance, calf, piglets, chicks or puppies, the family is expected to observe taboo of three to six days[33] in which none of the new members of the family should be touched or disturbed in their cradle of the new life lest they die.

ii) *Taboos* in Relation to Plant

Trees are prohibited from being felled unless accorded with proper rituals performed by the village priest for sustaining agricultural purpose. There are also big, huge, old trees and sacred groves considered to be the abode of the spirits.[34] They should in no way be felled lest one invite the wrath of the spirit. A *taboo* could be period of one single day, days, week or more observed by an individual or the whole of the village or community. Trees such as Banyan and Oak were prohibited from being planted by young people. The reason is one's consciousness of the trees outgrowing the good fortune of the planted. After all tress are understood to be possessing life. During these days all routine work comes to a standstill; it is a time of rest or restraint, rest for the land, domestic animals and the family. This *taboo* is necessary as it provide period of revitalisation of the earth.[35]

B) *Totem*[36] in Relation to Creation

Totem is another important characteristic of Primal Religious Traditions, which is also connected to natural objects of universe such as animals, insects, plants, birds and so on are the sources to reflect on present day eco-concerns.

i) *Totem* of the Highlanders (North East India)

Primal religious traditions totemic relationship with animals, plants, insects or birds support an authentic unbroken relation between human and the creation. For instance, among the *Tangkhul Nagas* in Manipur Lunghar Village there is

[33] Longchar, "Green Theology ..." 232.

[34] Although not all trees are understood to be the abode of spirit the point presented here is the respect towards trees and forest which is the only means of sustenance for the tribals. See, Thumra, "The Primal Religious Tradition" ..., 54.

[35] A. Wati Longchar, *The Tribal Religious Traditions in North East India – An Introduction* (Jorhat: A. Wati Longchar, 2000), 45-46.

[36] Derived from the Ojibway Indian Tribe of North America, it means "brother-sister kin." As referred in Thumra, "The Primal Religious Tradition" ..., 56.

a clan known as *Harvanao* which means children of the cock; the *Keishings* in Manipur trace their ancestry to Baffalo;[37] for the *Ao Nagas* in Nagaland *OzÜkum* means born out of bird;[38] for the *Thadous Mithun* is the totem; *Fanai* (Mizos) have Tiger as their totem; for *Sangmas* (A 'chik in Meghalaya) owl is considered as their totem;[39] likewise the number of totemic relation can go on and on. The point to be noted is the Primal relationship with the creature which bind them in close affinity with their totemic ancestry thereby manifesting the sacred worldview ascribed to the creation.

ii) Totem in the Plain Areas (Outside North East)

Nirmal Minz discusses the totemic relationship of the primeval traditions in plain area by reflecting on the relationship of tress, plants, animals, insects and others as relatives to human beings. For instance, Minz draws this totemic relationship by citing these indigenous names[40] Lakras, Kujurs, Khakhas, Ekkas and Minz meaning Tiger, Creeper, Crow, Tortoise, and Fish respectively. Minz asserts human, nature, animals and insects similar ancestral roots hence the personal and social relationship. To the indigenous community therefore each item of nature has spirit. For instance, the spirit may be present in the stones, trees, and waters. Minz further asserts that the living consciousness of spirits in nature draws the community most closely to the environment; and as such there is no sacred and secular dichotomy, "for all existence is spiritual for us."[41]

C) Omen

Omens[42] are connected to nature and foretelling future happenings and indicate bad and good outcome. To the indigenous people the creations are sings. They

---

[37] Thumra, "The Primal Religious Tradition" ..., 58. The presenter's surname "Thumra" has a totemic relation in which the ancestor of this title was understood to have raised a hen out of which thirty chicken were born, hence the title. Thumra means thirty in English.

[38] Longchar, *The Tribal Religious Traditions in North East India* ..., 56.

[39] A. Wati Longchar, *The Traditional Tribal Worldview and Modernity* (Jorhat: N. Limatula Lkr, 1995), 59.

[40] These are titles of the Oraon tribals residing mostly in Chota Nagpur (Bihar) Madhya Pradesh, Orissa and West Bengal speaking a Dravidian language known as Kurukh. Although a small minority of the tribe are Christians, the great majority follow a Hindu form of worship. Their main deities are local, non-Sanskritic ones, such as Chandi, Chauthia, Dadgo Burhia, Gaon Deoti, and Jair Budhi, See, "Oraon,"http://www.everyculture. com/South-Asia/Oraon. html#ixzz4HP6GDZUX (15-08-2016); also see, "Totems," in *Tribal Zone*, http://www. tribalzone. net/history/totems.htm (15-08-2016).

[41] George E. Tinker, "Spirituality, Nature and American Personhood, Sovereignty and Solidarity," in *Voices from the Third World*, vol. xv, no. 1, 1998, cited by Nirmal Minz, "Tribal Perspective on Ecology," in *The Tribal Worldview and Ecology* ..., 3.

[42] Omen is of two kinds: good and bad. Omens are indications, warnings manifested through the sings of creation. See, Thumra, "The Primal Religious Tradition" ..., 59.

are foretellers of the near future. The creations are important not just because they give indigenous community the signs of time but they are relational, they are our friends and therefore sacred. The signs of the teacher (creation) are often sought in times of embarking for a journey, war, hunting and others. For instance if a lightning strikes on the rice field it is an indication of an impending sickness against the particular household; if a dog barks circling around with its tail straightened up and cured, it indicates an impending death in the family; if fishes float together in vigorous movement while fishing it is a sign of heavy rain;[43] if a snake comes inside a house it indicates death of family members; if a cock crow at odd time it is a sign on impending trouble in the village; if in a dream one dreams catching a lot of small fishes it indicates the flow of richness in the person.[44] Likewise there are several other of these omen that teaches, instruct and warn human beings of both a good time and bad times according to the omens received. It is unthinkable therefore for the indigenous to subdue the importance of creations; the creations are our brothers and sisters.

D) Divination[45]

Divination is an important method of seeking signs by indigenous people about their future. They observe several kinds of divinations as follows.

i) Divination by Cock

Among the *Tangkhul Nagas* a handsome well structured rooster without any blemishes is strangulated to read the signs. If the right leg of cock is paced over the left with the excreta out, it indicates good fortune; the vice-versa is bad. If the legs are parallel while the excreta are out it is also bad sign. Worst is if both the legs' position are in disorder.[46] The rooster teaches and prepares the people for any bad events that may occur on the person performing it or for whom it is performed. The indigenous live according to the voices and ways of the creation.

ii) Divination by bamboo

Primal tribes followed divination by splitting a piece of bamboo. The piece of bamboo is cut in the middle a little, then it is pulled by both sides of the hand until it is split and the fibres come out. At he time of pulling, the Tangkhull Nagas say like this, "phameilo, yachuilo" (meaning "Let the omen be good,, let the right side be higher or longer"). Then the positions of the fibres are observed. If the right side fibre is higher than that of the left it is a good omen, but if it is vice-versa

---

[43] Longchar, *The Tribal Religious Traditions in North East India* ..., 35-36.

[44] Thumra, "The Primal Religious Tradition" ..., 61.

[45] Divination is derived from the latin word "deus" or "divus" meaning god or divine. In divination human try to seek the sign of time through animals and plants. See, Longchar, *The Traditional Tribal Worldview* ..., 48; also see, Thumra, "The Primal Religious Tradition" ..., 61.

[46] Thumra, "The Primal Religious Tradition" ..., 61.

the omen is bad. If the piece of bamboo is split without any fibre coming out it is a bad omen.[47]

iii) Divination by frog

In many villages people used frog to divination about rain fall. Usually children followed this divination, by hanging a frog to a yoke and visited houses in their village, or thanda begging arms from householders. At every house they poured water on the frog and offered food and gifts to children. People believed that by rain will come. Sometimes it was happened. This is also nature friendly divination/ omen.

iv) Divination by egg breaking

It is another popular practice among primal tribes. This divination is commonly performed to know whether this year they will have rain or draught; or pests or natural calamities that spoil the crops. For this purpose, the village priest prepares a heap of rice-husk on a board or a floor. The egg with its top opened is placed at the centre of it, and it the divination is for the village, lines are drawn towards the direction where cultivation for that particular year is to be done, but if it is for the whole of the Tangkhul area, the lines are drawn in four directions - north, east, west and south. Then the tribal priest sets fire the husk and let it burn slowly. If the egg boils over completely, the year is not good. If the egg flows in the east direction that is would be good and the rest would be bad. If it does not flow out some evil will come to the village or the land.[48] There are several other similar traditions among tribes popularly known as eco-friendly in nature.

6) A Creation-Centred History and Time

In the Primal religious tradition the concept of time and history is in relation to the life cycle of events associated with creation.[49] Time and events are circular, for it is the sun, the season that instruct them about time and events. For instance, the activity of a tribal society in a day can be brought out this way: the rooster wakes the indigenous up from the sleep; the sun rises bright to remind them of the events ahead of the day; the sun above their head is a time for rest; the sun setting is the time to go home; and when it is dark they rest along with the sleep of the sun.

Likewise the events of the season set the activity of an indigenous life. For example, the onset of new buds on the tress (spring) prepares them to sow their seeds; the onset of rainy season (summer) prepares them to cultivate their

---

[47] Thumra, "The Primal Religious Tradition" ..., 61.

[48] P.R.T. Gurdon, *The Khasis,* (Cosmo Publications, Delhi) reprint 1976); 65-66, see Appendix C for the Khasi egg-breaking tradition.

[49] Longchar, *The Traditional Tribal Worldview* ..., 83.

yearly harvest; the onset of autumn marked by the falling of tree leafs ushered in harvest; while the coldness of the air, the dry wind was mostly a time of rest. In addition every onset and end of every season is marked by agricultural festivities in remembrance of the Supreme Being, in thanksgiving, in search for bountiful harvest. For illustration every indigenous community in north east India has seed sowing festivals, harvest festivals associated with every season of agricultural cycles. These cycles of nature gives identity to the people. For example, names such as Lushomla and Lahala[50] are given after seasons of the year.

Having discussed all these resources to protect our environment, one may come to the conclusion that when humanity gets back to the priori one will reclaim the innocence of humanity lost. To conclude one may reaffirm the intra kinship relation vision of indigenous cosmology, where the stars are the guide at night, the sun that gives us light in the day time and the forest that sustains the people. To the indigenous people therefore the land is not just a junk or mass of earth but it is the gift of God; the lands are our big brothers, the rivers our sisters and the earth our mother. The land therefore is sacred to the indigenous people; it is their identity. It is for this reason the land is protected from any outside influence. For this reason battles have been fought and it continues to be so. The sacredness of land and its identity thereof is still a struggle yet to be materialised. This wealth of knowledge and eco-spirituality rooted in the primal religious traditions are of immense importance if one has to reclaim this broken world.

The Primal religious tradition is indispensable in our ecological search for healing of the world. It is in the spirituality of the primal tradition one finds a continuum of God-Human-Land Relationship; a relation even beyond this life. Primeval resources speak of the Earth entering Supreme Being, a response to the abuse of land for commercialisation, industrialisation for profit. This is important so long as human need to see the earth as not the means to wants but means to fulfil the needs. The Primal resources speak for the ecological chain of creation, the family like relationship. If and only when the world wakes up to the understanding of Oikos, the member of the household of creation, the earth will be relived.

The ecological disasters today are in need of dialogue with the creation. This dialogue again is where one finds in the primeval tradition. The created beings, the human and God is in the same plane of dialogue. They share life experiences, they together decides what is best for them. It was never human being who decides for the welfare of human at the expenses of the rest of the creation. Observe the totemic relation of human with the creation, the divination in and through the

---

[50] A person is called as Lushomla ("Lushom" literally translated as sowing and "la" a suffix indicating feminine gender) because she was born in the season of sowing; Lahala ("laha" literally translated as paddy straw and "la" a suffix on names indicating feminine gender) because she was born in harvest season.

creation and the taboos related with creation. They give us a good example of how creation has always been our teachers, subject of reverence, guide and a sign for humanity. Therefore, the place and status of creation is highly exalted.

Today time has come to dictate the life of human beings. People work as though there is no tomorrow. The mother earth can no longer bear the demand of time; she needs rest, she demanded to be understood. Looking back to the primal religious tradition one is reminded that seasons are the natural course of action. The earth too rest in the season of Jubilee. The season of Jubilee, a time of rest, rejuvenation, refreshment is therefore the need of the hour. All these resources of primal religious traditions from the experience of the indigenous life, help us today to build up "eco-spirituality" that protects and promote the healthy environment.

Chapter 5

Hinduism and Eco-Spirituality

Hinduism treats that all living beings are sacred because they are parts of God, and should be treated with respect and compassion. This is because the soul can be reincarnated into any form of life. Hinduism is full of stories that treat animals as divine, such as how Krishna used to herd cows, or how the monkey Hanuman was a faithful servant of the Rama. Most Hindus are vegetarian because of this belief in the sanctity of life. Even trees, rivers and mountains are believed to have souls, and should be honoured and cared for.

Hindus revere sacred rivers, mountains, forests and animals, and love to be close to nature. For example, many Hindu villages have a sacred lake, and around it a grove of trees to catch rainfall and protect the banks from erosion. The lake and its grove store rainfall to irrigate surrounding fields and supply village wells with drinking water. These lakes and groves are places of tranquillity and sanctuaries for wildlife, but in recent times the neglect of these simple techniques for gathering and protecting clean water has led to serious water shortages and advancing desertification in many parts of India. This is a common story in India: traditional Hindu practices of caring for nature are being forgotten and as a result human survival is becoming more difficult. This chapter is brief attempt of Hindu Religious Traditions from the time of Indus Valley Civilization to present day activities that are closely related to ecological concerns and environmental promotion.

1) The Indus Valley Civillization and Eco-Spirituality

The Indus people had a primitive type of religious system though they had more developed civilization of the time. We have very little information about the religious life of Indus Valley Civilization. During it's hey days Indus Valley Civilization (IVC) covered an area in the Indian subcontinent that was the larger then present Europe. This civilization flourished roughly between 3500 BCE and 2000 BCE. IVC was essentially an urban civilization, characterized by well planned cities. The discovery of IVC brought the Indian subcontinent into limelight as home to one of the most ancient human civilizations. Whatever may be truth, the Indus Valley people built a vast civilization that disappeared mysteriously by 1800 BCE and was replaced by Aryan/Vedic culture in parts of India. They had the knowledge of written script which is yet to be deciphered that they used in their seals. The seals, along with other artefacts such stone statues and terracotta figures, provide some clues about their religious beliefs and practices that help us to know their attitude towards environment.

A) Major Religious Beliefs

As it is found in archaeological investigations at Harappa and Mohenjo-Daro by John Marshal, scholars opined that Indus Valley people may have the following beliefs:

i) The Indus Valley people may be worshiped "Mother Goddess", in addition to other little male and female deities.
ii) They worshiped a father God who might be a progenitor of the race and probably a prototype of Siva as the Lord of the animals.
iii) People were familiar to certain form of yoga and meditation.
iv) They believed in some kind of tree of life, which is symbolised in seals as a Pipal or Acasia tree.
v) They worshiped fertility symbols as round stones symbolized female sex organ, and pierced stones symbolizing male sex organ, a practice probably preceded the worship of Siva and Parvathi in the form of Sivalinga.
vi) They might have also believed some kind of magical rituals, charms, amulets and so also in spirits and demons.
vii) They mostly cremated the dead providing place for ancestral worship after the departure souls.
viii) The great bath of Mohenjo-Daro, or much larger one found recently at the Dholavira site in Kutch, was probably a prototype "Kovali" or sacred tank, which are found in the ancient temples of South India, where devotees have been taken ritual baths for spiritual purification.

B) Eco-friendly Irrigation

It was found that Indus valley people developed environmental friendly irrigation system. To overcome arid environments and make them suitable for farming, large scale irrigation systems were created. Numerous irrigation canals linked to rivers have been discovered. A canal system would consist of a main canal, which received water directly from the river that would branch off as smaller canals distributing the water to different areas.[1] These canals filled up with water whenever the rivers swelled, carrying water throughout. In Kutch, water management in the form of reservoirs and dams have also been found.

People are not only dependent on the environment for survival, but it also plays a role in the development of their world view. Rivers are important for irrigation, for transportation, and as a source of food. The environment dictates the diet on which people depend, their lifestyles, the resources available to them, the physical location where to settle, and the tools which they will need to overcome these obstacles. Therefore, it's no surprise that physical surroundings also shape a society's culture. This is no different within the Indus Valley civilization. Both their religious ideas and technological developments represent this influence, and therefore can be seen in the artefacts discovered at various sites.

2) The Nomadic Life of Aryans and their Influence

India was invaded around 1500 BCE by a group of people known as the Aryans. They conquered the primary inhabitants of India, who were knows as the *Dasyus*[2] (slaves). The Aryans were comprised of quite different physical and cultural features in contrast to the *Dasyus*; the Aryans were a white race and the *Dasyus* were a dark race.[3] The primal Indians in the north believed in supreme gods and spirits and never believed in idolatry.[4] The Aryans spoke a different language, worshipped different gods, had different cultural practices and their influence in India was prominent as the majority of Indians today speak and value the Indo-Aryan language and culture.[5]

The Aryans had a rich culture that still influences India today. The Aryans were primarily warrior-nomadic people and their main source of wealth was cattle.[6] However, after the migration into India there was a greater urgency to retain copper, iron ore, and minerals for profits. During this time, the head of the household had gained respect primarily through trade, manufacturing, or farming.[7] The Aryan society was patriarchal and much of the importance was placed on the male, therefore an abundance of Aryan gods were males. The women in the Aryan culture were usually housewives and the women were said

---

[1] Chakrabarti, *The Oxford Companion to Indian Archaeology: The Archaeological Foundations of Ancient India Stone Age to 13th Century*, (New Delhi; New York: Oxford University Press, 2006), 144.

[2] Sharma, A, (2005) "Dr. B. R. Ambedkar on the Aryan Invasion and the Emergence of the Caste System in India", *Journal of the American Academy of Religion*, *73*(3), 2005, 844.

[3] *Ibid*, 846.

[4] Snaitang, O. L, *Asia Journal of Theology*, (Vol. 18, Issue 2, October 2004), 398-411.

[5] Habib, Irfan *A Peoples History of India 2: The Indus Valley Civilization*. (New Delhi: Tulika Books, 2002), 99.

[6] Kosambi, D. D, *The Culture and Civilisation of Ancient India in Historical Outline,* (New Delhi: Vikas Publishing House Pvt. Ltd, 1996), 76.

[7] *Ibid,* 101.

to be very skilled in weaving. In technological advancements, the Aryans were mostly interested in making chariots, tools and weapons and did not concentrate many efforts into building anything else.[8] The Aryans annexed various tribes and communities on their journey towards India and were successful because they were nomadic people and their food supply of cattle was easy to transport. They had mastered the art of using horse-chariots for war and they also held great knowledge of heavy transportation using ox-carts.[9]

The unique language of the Aryans was a key factor in distinguishing them from other races. Aryan is a term that can define a linguistic group, which is a group of people classified as speaking the same language, or can be defined as a race, which is a group of people who comprise of specific and distinct characteristic.[10] The prevalent evidence throughout history suggests that Aryan was referred to as a unity of language and people. For example, the emperor Darius refers to himself as an 'Aryan of Aryan descent', the Vedas speaks of the Aryans as a race that worshipped the gods mentioned in the Vedas and the Medes, ancient Iranian people, used to bear the name Aryans.[11] The language spoken by the Aryans came from the classical Aryan language which is a tree that consists of three important branches. These are Sanskrit, Greek and Latin; Sanskrit being the bearer of the Indo-Aryan Language which was spoken by the Aryans. The earlier derivatives of Sanskrit used by the Aryans are called "*Pali*" or "*Magadhi*" and "*Prakrits.*"[12] The Dravidians of India, however communicated in their own language which is not a part of the classical Aryan language tree. Later on, during the Rig-Vedic period, Sanskrit was the predominant language. The text and verbal communication were all practiced in Sanskrit.[13] The Aryans' language was very influential, however their religious and social beliefs crafted the way we see India today.

The Aryans were the warrior nomadic people that migrated to the Indian subcontinent with their influential culture, religion and language. On further inspection we can see that the Aryan culture played a vital role in sculpting Hinduism by influencing the religion with their epics, texts and religious ideologies. The Aryans mixed with the Dravidians to create the complex religion of Hinduism. The emergence of this religion and the Aryans seeking higher recognition in contrast to the commoners led to the creation of the caste system. The caste system divided the people into various sects, mainly as *Brahmins, Kshatriyas, Vaisyas and Sudhras,* who were responsible for different duties within

---

[8] Ibid, 80.

[9] *Ibid*, 76.

[10] *Ibid.* 72.

[11] *Ibid*, 75.

[12] *Ibid*, 73.

[13] *Ibid*, 84.

the frameworks of society; such as religious priesthood and worship; ruling the people and administration; trading and agriculture; and cleaning and serving.

3) Environmental Science of Vedic Age: Cosmotheandric Vision of Vedic Aryans

As per the belief of Hindus, the Vedas are the first texts in the library of human literary history. They are universally acknowledged to be the most precious Indian Heritage. The antiquity to the Vedic civilization is debated to greater extent and understood that there is no civilization known to humanity with such antiquity as Vedic Aryan Civilization. The so-called Aryans would have originated in the Aryavarta. N. J. Lockyer is of opinion: "The Vedas, in fact, is the oldest book in which we can study the first beginnings of our language and of everything which is embodied in all the languages under the sun."[14]

The Vedas deal with the knowledge both physical and spiritual. They are source of all knowledge according to Manusmriti "सर्व वेदात् प्रसद्धिती" (*sarva vedath prasishyati*).[15] Especially, the Vedic views revolve around the concept of nature and life. The symbolical pictures projected there remain close to life and nature. The most authoritative among the four Vedas is called the Rigveda. Generally, *Rishis* are supposed to be the recipient of knowledge revealed in the verses and *Devatas* are supposed to be the gods in whose praise verses are revealed. The oldest and simplest form of Nature-worship finds expression in Vedic texts. Many scholars have come to the conclusion that the Vedas are primarily concerned with cosmology, however, they are not in a position to show that Vedic cosmology has the solutions to the most difficult problems of modern cosmology.[16] Some say, like dramas are played to remember history, the process of various *shrauta yajnas* describes the science of Cosmology.[17]

In recent days, environmental science and ecology are disciplines of modern science under which study of environment and its constituents is done with minute details. As Science, they are established in 20th century, but their origin can be seen long back in the Vedic and ancient Sanskrit literature. The concepts of environment differ from age to age, since it depends upon the condition, prevalent at that particular time. It is an effort to find out the awareness of the environment among ancient Indian people. As Sanskrit literature is so wide we refer here mainly to Vedic texts, particularly the Vedic Samhitas.

---

[14] N.J. Lockyer, *The dawn of Astronomy,* (Massachusetts, Institute of Technology), 432.

[15] Manusmriti 2.7.

[16] Cf. Raja Ram Mohan Roy, *Vedic Physics, Scientific Origin of Hinduism*, (Golden Egg Publishing, Toronto, 1999), 6; M. Vannucci, *Ecological Readings in the Veda*, [New Delhi, D.K. Print World, 1994); Wati Longchar (ed.), *Green Theology*. (Kolkata: SCEPTRE, 2014).

[17] Yudhishthira Mimansaka, *Vaidika Siddhanta Mimansa*, (Sonipata, 1976), 40.

The Environment (Protection) Act, 1986 defines the environment as follows: "Environment includes water, air and land and the inter-relationship which exists among and between water, air and land and human beings, other living creatures, plants, micro organisms and property."[18] From the above definition, it can be briefly said that environment consists of two components namely biotic (living organisms) and abiotic (non-living materials) factors. The living organisms can be grouped into three types - those living mainly on land, in water and in air. The non-living materials of the environment are land, air, water, property and so on.

In modern Sanskrit, the word पर्यावरण *(paryavarana)* is used for environment, meaning which encircles us, which is all around in our surroundings. But in the Atharvaveda words equivalent to this sense are used; such as वृतव्रित *(vritavrita)*,[19] अभिवर: *(abhivarah)*,[20] आवृत: *(avritah)*,[21] परिवृता *(parivrita)*[22] and so on. Vedic view on environment is well-defined in one verse of the Atharvaveda where three coverings of our surroundings are referred as *Chandamsi*: 'Wise utilize three elements variously which are varied, visible and full of qualities. These are water, air and plants or herbs. They exist in the world from the very beginning. They are called as " चन्दन्सि" *(chandansi)* meaning 'coverings available everywhere'.[23]

It proves the knowledge of Vedic seers about the basic elements of environment. According to one indigenous theory established in the Upanishads, the universe consists of five basic elements, such as, 1) earth or land, 2) water, 3) light or lustre, 4) air, and 5) ether.[24] The nature has maintained a status of balance between and among these constituents or elements and living creatures. A disturbance in percentage of any constituent of the environment beyond certain limits disturbs the natural balance and any change in the natural balance causes lots of problems to the living creatures in the universe. Different constituents of the environment exist with set relationships with one another. The relation of human being with environment is very natural as he/she cannot live without it. From the very beginning of creation he/she wants to know about it for self protection and benefit.

A) Vedic Aryans' attitude to Environment

The Vedic Aryans were lovers of nature. Sand-storm and cyclone, intense lightening, terrific thunderclaps, the heavy rush of rain in monsoon, the swift

---

18 A.R. Panchamukhi, *Socio-economic Ideas in Ancient Indian Literature*, (Rashtriya Sanskrit Sansthan, Delhi, 1998), 467.

19 *Atharvaveda* 12.1.52.

20 *Ibid.*, 1.32.4.

21 *Ibid.*, 10.1.30.

22 *Ibid.*, 10.8.31.

23 *Ibid.*, 18.1.17.

24 *Ibid.*, 18.1.17.

flood in the stream that comes down from the hills, the sweltering heat of the sun, the cracking red flames of the fire, all witness to power beyond human power. The Vedic sages felt the greatness of these forces. They adored these activities, appreciated these forces, worshiped and prayed these powers due to regard, surprise and fear. They realized instinctively that action, movement, creation, change and destruction in nature are the results of forces beyond human control, hence, they attributed divinity to nature.

(i) **Divinity to Nature**: Rigvedic hymns could be divided into many parts, but their main part belongs to Natural hymns, the hymns related with natural forces. Yet, Vedic gods are explained in different ways by the scholars of India and West, but speaking generally, the hymns addressed to deities – god/goddess (*deva/ta*) are under the influence of the most impressive phenomenon of nature and its aspects. The word *deva/ta* means divine, dignity which is bright, strong, donor, and powerful. In these hymns we find prayers for certain natural elements such as air, water, earth, sun, rain, dawn and so on. The glorious brightness of the sun, the blaze of the sacrificial fire, the sweep of the rain-storm across the skies, the recurrence of the dawn, the steady currents of the winds, the violence of the tropical storm and other such natural energies, fundamental activities or aspects are glorified and personified as divinities (*deva/ta*). The interaction with nature resulted in appreciation and prayer but, indeed, after a good deal of observation. Attributes assigned to deities fit in their natural forms and activities, as Soma is green, fire is bright, air is fast moving and sun is dispenser of darkness. The characteristics of these forces described in the verses prove that Vedic seers were masters of natural science.[25]

In Vedic view, this world consists of Agni, i.e., fire or heat and Soma, i.e., water.[26] Sun (Surya) is the soul of all which is moving and also of which is not moving.[27] Indra is most powerful god who kills *Vritra*, the symbol of cloud to free waters. *Vritra* means one who covers and is derived from the root vri, to cover. Raja Ram Mohan Roy is of opinion that the main force of expansion in the Vedic cosmology is Indra, and his chief adversary, the main force of contraction, is *Vritra*.[28] Maruts are Indra's associates. Vedic seers pray boldly to these natural forces and aspects for bestowing plenty and prosperity on them. Aditi is praised as *devamata*, the mother of all natural energies and she symbolizes the Nature. A famous geologist S.R.N. Murthy has written on the earth sciences in the Vedas. He has somehow a different opinion about Vedic gods and hence states, 'the

[25] *Aitareya Upanishad*, 3.3.

[26] Cf. Shashi Tiwari, "Origin of Environmental Science from Vedas" , 156-167 http://www.sanskrit.nic.in/svimarsha/v2/c17.pdf , (accessed on 28-06-2017).

[27] अग्निसिमात्मकं जगत्

[28] Rigveda 1.115.1 (सूर्य आत्मा जगतस्तस्तस्थुषस्चा)

natural geological aspects have been described as Indra, Agni, Vayu, Varun, Usas and so on.[29]

(ii) **Cosmic Order 'Rita' and Varuna**: In the Vedas, the order of the Universe is called '*Rita.*' Rita reduces chaos to cosmos, and gives order and integration to matter. It also gives symmetry and harmony in the environment. Hence, the conception of *Rita* has an aesthetic content too; it implies splendour and beauty. It is for this reason that the Vedic gods, upholding *Rita*, are all lawful, and beautiful and good. Their beauty is a significance attribute. *Rita* is defined variously by scholars in different Vedic contexts, but in general sense it has been elaborated as great 'cosmic order' which is the cause of all motion and existence, and keeps world in an order. No one can ignore it,[30] even gods are abided by the '*Rita*' and they are born of *Rita*. It is controlling and sustaining power. It sustains sun in the sky.[31] *Rita* as Universal Law governs everything in the cosmos. H.W. Wallis is of opinion:

> The principle of the order of the world, of the regularity of cosmic phenomena, was conceived by the *Rishis* to have existed as a principle before the manifestation of any phenomena. The phenomena of the world are shifting and changeable, but the principle regulating the periodical recurrence of phenomena is constant; fresh phenomena are continually reproduced, but the principle of order remains the same; the principle, therefore, existed already when the earliest phenomena appeared.[32]

In the Vedas, Varuna is depicted as the Lord of *Rita*, the universal natural order. He is sovereign god, great king, law-maker and ruler of cosmos and even of the gods. Basically, he is regarded as the Lord of water and ocean but chiefly he controls and keeps the world in order. From his throne on high he looks down upon all that happens in the world, and into the heart of man.[33] 'By the law of Varuna heaven and earth are held apart. He made the golden swing, the sun to shine in heaven. He has made wide path for the sun. By his ordinances the moon shining brightly moves at night, and the stars placed up on high are seen at night but disappear by day. He causes the rivers to flow. As a moral governor Varuna stands far above any other deity.[34] Therefore, the concept of Varuna represents the consciousness of Vedic seers in respect to controlling and balancing the natural forces in environment.

(iii) **Division of Universe**: Vedic seers have a great vision about universe. The universe is made on scientific principles, and that's why it is well measured.

[29] Raja Ram Mohan Roy, *Vedic Physics, Scientific Origin of Hinduism,* 58.

[30] S.R.N. Murthy, *Vedic View of the Earth*, (D.K. Print World, New Delhi, 1997), 12.

[31] *Taittiriya Brahmana* 1.5.5.1.

[32] *Rigveda* 10.85.1.

[33] H.W. Wallis, The *Cosmology of the Rigveda*, (Cosmo Publications, 1999), 94-95.

[34] *Ibid*, 91-101; *Rigveda* 1.25.7,9,11,

The universe consists of three intertwined webs, *Prithivi, Antariksha* and *Dyau.* Vedic scientists divided even the length in three calling them upper, medium and lower. The tripartite division of the universe into three regions - *Prithivi,* (the earth); *Antariksha* (the aerial or intermediate region) which is between heaven and earth; and *Dyau,* (the heaven or sky) is very well established in the Vedic literature. *Prithavi* can be given a scientific name 'observer space.' It is our space, the space in which we live and die whatever we can see and observe. A verse from the *Yajurveda* states that the division of universe was done on a subtle level, and not on gross level.[35] Here; in reference to environmental study, we regard the division of the universe as the most important concept of the Vedas. Though a large number of gods are described in the Vedic hymns, and it is very difficult to arrange them in different classes, but they were classified as three gods based on regions: Agni in earth, Vayu or Indra in atmosphere and Sun in heaven. Each one of them is known by various names depending on the different actions performed. These three gods are three major forms of energy, fire on earth, air in intermediate space and light in upper region. Other energies of those regions are related to or under them. So generally gods are classified in three groups called upper, middle and lower, and, therefore, provide a system to study atmosphere and its all aspects. Regarding global harmony, Vedic seers always pray for the welfare of all creatures and all regions.

B) Aryans Approach to "*Prithivi*" the Earth

The concept of the form of the earth in the *Rigveda* is the most fascinating. It is mostly addressed along with the heaven into a dual conception (*Rodasi, Dyavaprithivi*). There is one small hymn addressed to *Prithivi,* while there are six hymns addressed to *Dyavaprithivi. Prithivi* is considered the mother and *Dyau* is considered the father in the Vedas, and they form a pair together.[36] One of the most beautiful verse of the *Rigveda* says, 'Heaven is my father, brother atmosphere is my navel, and the great earth is my mother.'[37] Heaven and earth are parents: *Matara, Pitara, Janitara*[38] in union while separately called as father and mother. They sustain all creatures. They are parents of all gods. They are great (*Mahi*) and widespread. Earth is described as a goddess in *Rigveda.* In the *Atharvaveda,* the earth is described in one hymn of 63 verses. This famous hymn called as *Bhumisukta* or *Prithivisukta* indicates the environmental and ecological concerns of Vedic seers. The seers appear to have advanced understanding of the earth through this hymn. She is called *Vasudha* for containing all wealth, *Hiranyavaksha*

[35] A.A. MacDonnell, *A History of Sanskrit Literature,* (MLBD, 1965), 61-62.

[36] *Yajurveda* 7.5.

[37] Cf. Shashi Tiwari, "Origin of Environmental Science from Vedas", 161.

[38] *Rigveda* 1.164.33.

for having gold bosom and *Jagato Niveshani* for being abode of whole world. She is not for the different races of human alone but for other creatures also.[39]

She is called *Visvambhara* because she is representative of the universe. She is the only planet directly available for the study of the universe and to realize the underlying truth. This is wide earth which supports varieties of species such as plants, birds, animals, herbs; oceans, rivers, mountains, hills and so on. She has at places different colours as dark, tawny, white. She is raised at some place and lowered at some places. The earth is fully responsible for our food and prosperity. She is praised for her strength. She is served day and night by rivers and protected by sky. The immortal heart of earth is in the highest firmament (*Vyoma*). Her heart is sun. 'She is one enveloped by the sky or space and causing the force of gravitation. She is described as holding Agni. It means she is described as the geothermal field. She is also described as holding Indra, i.e., the geomagnetic field. The earth is described then as being present in the middle of the oceans (sedimentary rocks) and as one having magical movements.'[40] 26 The hymn talks about different energies which are generated from the form of the earth.[3]'O *Prithvi*! thy centre, thy navel, all forces that have issued from thy body- Set us amid those forces; breathe upon us.'[41] Thus, the earth holds almost all the secrets of nature, which will help us in understanding the universe. She is invested with divinity and respected as mother. 'The earth is my mother and I am her son.'[42] The geographical demarcations on this earth have been made by human beings and not by nature.

C) '*Apah*'- Water in Vedic Texts

Water is essential to all forms of life. According to Rigveda the water as a part of human environment occurs in five forms: 1) Rain water (*Divyah*), 2) Natural spring (*Sravanti*), 3) Wells and canals (*Khanitrimah*), 4) Lakes (*Svayamjah*), 5) Rivers (*Samudrarthah*).[43] There are some other classifications also in the *Taittiriya Aranyaka* (1.24.1-2), *Yajurveda* (22.25), and *Atharvaveda* (1.6.4) as drinking water, medicinal water and stable water. *Chandogya Upanishad* describes about qualities of water 'The water is the source of joy and for living a healthy life. It is the immediate cause of all organic beings such as vegetations, insects, worms, birds, animals, men, etc. Even the mountains, the earth, the atmosphere and heavenly bodies are water concretized.'[44] The cycle of water is also described in

---

[39] *Rigveda* 1.159,160.

[40] *Atharvaveda* 12.1.15;12.1.45.

[41] S.R.N. Murthy, *Vedic View of the Earth,* 87.

[42] Atharvaveda 12.1.12.; RTH Griffith, *The Hymns of the Atharvaveda*, (D.K. Publishers, Delhi, 1995), 95.

[43] *Atharvaveda*, 12.1.12.

[44] *Rigveda*, 7.49.2.

Vedic literature: 'From ocean waters reach to sky and from sky come back to earth'.[45] Rain waters are glorified. The rain-cloud is depicted as *Parjanya* god.

The fight between Indra and *Vritra* is a celebrated story from the *Rigveda*. It is explained in many ways. According to one view it is a fight for waters. Indra is called *Apsu-jit* or conquering the waters, while *Vritra* is encompassing them. *Vritra* holds the rain and covers waters and thus being faulty is killed by *Indra* through his weapon called *Vajrayuda,* i.e., thunderbolt. The Indra-Vritra fight represents natural phenomenon going on in the aerial space. By the efforts of Indra all the seven rivers flow. The flow of water should not be stopped and that is desired by humanity. The significance of water for life was well known to Vedic seers. They mention – 'waters are nectars'.[46] Waters are source of all plants and giver of good health.[47] Waters destroy diseases of all sorts.[48] Waters are for purification.[49] It seems that later developed cultural tradition of pilgrimage on the river-banks is based on the theory of purification from water. The ancient Indians knowing water as a vital element for life, were very particular to maintain it pure and free from any kind of pollution. The *Manusmriti* (4.56) stresses on many instances to keep water clean. The *Padma Purana* condemns water pollution forcefully saying, 'the person who pollutes waters of ponds, wells or lakes goes to hell.'[50]

D) "*Vayu*" – Air in Vedic Texts

The observer space is the abode of matter particles, light space is the abode of energy and the intermediate space '*Antariksha*' is the abode of field. The principal deity of *Antariksha* is *Vayu*. Jaiminiya Brahmana quotes,' *Vayu* brightens in *Antariksha*.'[51] Field is another form of energy and, therefore, Yajurveda says,' *Vayu* has penetrating brightness.'[52] The meaning of *Vayu* is made clear in Satapatha Brahmana in the following Mantra, 'Sun and rest of universe is woven in string. What is that string, that is *Vayu*.' This verse clearly shows that here *Vayu* cannot mean air alone.[53] Apparent meaning of *Vayu* is air. The Vedic seers knew the importance of air for life. They understood all about air in the atmosphere and also about the air inside the body. The *Taittiriya Upanishad* throws light on five

[45] *Chandogya Upanishad*, 7.10.1.

[46] *Atharvaveda,* 4.27.4

[47] *Satapatha Brahmana,* 1.9.3.7.

[48] *Rigveda*, 1.23.20.

[49] *Rigveda* 10.87.6

[50] *Satapatha Brahmana,* 1.1.1.1.

[51] *Padmapurana, Bhimi* 96.7.8.

[52] *Jaiminiya Brahmana*. 1.192.

[53] *Yajurveda*, 1.24.

types of wind inside the body: *Prana, Vrana, Apana, Udana* and *Samano.* Air resides in the body as life.[54]

Concept and significance of air is highlighted in Vedic verses. *Rigveda* mentions 'O Air! You are our father, the protector.'[55] Air has medicinal values.[56] 'Let wind blow in the form of medicine and bring me welfare and happiness.'[57] Medicated air is the international physician that annihilates pollution and imparts health and hilarity, life and liveliness to people of the world. Hilly areas are full of medicated air consisted of herbal elements. Another verse describes characteristics of air 'The air is the soul of all deities. It exists in all as life-breath. It can move everywhere. We cannot see it. Only one can hear its sound. We pray to air God.[58] Ancient Indians, therefore, emphasized that the unpolluted, pure air is source of good health, happiness and long life. Vedic seers prayed *Vayu deva* to blow the air with its medicinal qualities. One of the major ecological problems of our contemporary world is "air pollution", which polluted the healthy environment and resulting hazardous diseases.

E) '*Akasha*' – Ether in Vedas

Modern environmentalists are very much concerning about sound or noise pollution. There is a relation between ether and sound. The sound waves move in sky at various frequencies. Scientist could see the sky which exists only in the vicinity of earth, but *Taittirya Upanishad* throws light on two types of ether i.e: one inside the body and the other outside the body.[59] The ether inside the body is regarded as the seat of mind. An interesting advice to the mankind is found in the *Yajurveda*, 'Do not destroy anything of the sky and do not pollute the sky. Do not destroy anything of *Antariksha*.'[60] Sun shines in *Dyuloka* and we get light from sky. The sunrays strengthen our inner power and are essential for our life. Thus importance and care for ether is openly mentioned in the Vedas.[61]

F) Care for Birds and Animals in Vedic Texts

Animals and birds are part of nature and environment. It is natural, therefore, that Vedic seers have mentioned about their characteristics and activities and have desired their welfare. *Rigveda* classifies them in three groups -sky animals

---

[54] *Satapatha Brahmana*, 8.7.3.10; Raja Ram Mohan Roy, *Vedic Physics, Scientific Origin of Hinduism*, (Golden Egg Publishing, Toronto, 1999), 84.

[55] *Taittiriya Upanishad*, 2.4.

[56] *Rigveda* 10.186.2.

[57] *Ibid*, 1.37.2.

[58] *Ibid*, 10.186.1.

[59] *Ibid*, 10.168.4.

[60] *Taittiriya Upanshad*, 1.6.1; 1.5.1.

[61] *Yajurveda*, 5.43.

like birds, forest animals and animals in human habitation.[62] All the three types of living creatures found in the universe have distance environment and every living creature has an environment of its own. But when we look from human's perspective all of them constitute his environment. There is a general feeling in the Vedic texts that animals should be safe, protected and healthy.[63] Domestic animals, as well as wild animals along with human beings should live in peace under the control of certain deities like Rudra, Pushan, etc. Vedic people have shown anxious solicitude for welfare of their cattle, cows, horses and so on. The cow as the symbol of wealth and prosperity, occupied a very prominent place in the life of the people in Vedic times.[64]

G) Herbs (*Oshadhi*) and Trees in Vedic Literature

The knowledge about the origin and significance of plants/trees can be traced out from Vedic Literature in detail. In *Rigveda* one *Aranyani sukta* is addressed to the deity of forest.[65] *Aranyani,* queen of the forest, received high praise from the sage, not only for her gifts to humans, but also for her charm. Forests should be green with trees and plants. *Oshadhi Sukta* of *Rigveda* addresses to plants and vegetables as mother, 'O Mother! Hundreds are your birth places and thousands are your shoots.'[66] The plants came to existence on their earth before the creation of animals.[67] *Chandogya Upanishad* elaborates water have generated plants which in turn generated food.[68] The *Atharvaveda* mentions certain names of *Oshadhis* with their values. Later this information became important source for the *Ayurveda,* which became the most ancient and popular medicine of India. The *Rigveda* instructs that forests should not be destroyed.[69]

The *Atharvaveda* talks about the relation of plants with earth, 'The earth is keeper of creation, container of forests, trees and herbs.'[70] *Brihadaranyaka Upanishad claims that* plants/trees are to be lived.[71] There is an important quotation in a *Purana* which says, 'One tree is equal to ten sons.'[72] There is a prayer in *Atharvaveda* for continuous growth of herbs,'O Earth! What on you, I dig out, let

---

[62] Cf. Nandita Singhavi, *Vedame Paryavarana,* (Sonali Publications, Jaipur, 2004), 313-356.

[63] *Rigveda,* 10.90.8.

[64] *Yajurveda* 19.20, 3.37; *Atharvaveda* 11.2.24.

[65] Cf.N.M. Kansara, *Agriculture and Animal Husbandry in the Vedas,* (Nag Publishers Delhi, 1995), 126-138.

[66] *Rigveda,* 10.146.

[67] *Rigveda,* 10.97.2.

[68] *Rigveda,* 10.97.1.

[69] *Chandogya Upanishad,* 6.2.4.

[70] *Rigveda,* 8.1.13.

[71] *Atharvaveda,* 12.1.57.

[72] *Brihadaranyaka Upanishad,* 3.9.28.

that quickly grow over.'[73] And another prayer says, 'O Earth! Let me not hit your vitals.'[74] The '*Avi*' element referred in the *Atharvaveda*, as the cause of greenness in trees,[75] is considered generally by Vedic scholars as 'Chlorophyll.' The term '*Avi*' is derived from the root '*Av*' and thus gives the direct meaning of 'protector.' Hence, plants were studied as a part of environment and their protection was prescribed by the Vedic seers.

It is clear from the above detailed discussion; some light is thrown on the awareness of our ancient seers about the eco-spirituality, and its constituents. Modern Indian Scientists should be astonished and also feel proud of our ancestors for their knowledge and views about environment. Ancient seers knew about various aspects of environment, about cosmic order, and also about the importance of co-ordination between all natural powers for universal peace and harmony. When they pray for peace at all levels in the '*Shanti Mantra*' they side by side express their belief about the importance of coordination and interrelationship among all natural powers and regions. The prayer says that not only regions, waters, plants trees, natural energies but all creatures should live in harmony and peace. Peace should remain everywhere. The *mantra* takes about the concord with the universe's peace of sky, peace of mid-region, peace of earth, peace of waters, peace of plants, peace of trees, peace of all-gods, peace of Brahman, peace of universe, peace of peace; May that peace come to me![76]

It is clear that the Vedic vision to live in harmony with environment was not merely physical but was far wider and much comprehensive. The Vedic people desired to live a life of hundred years[77] and this wish can be fulfilled only when environment will be unpolluted, clean and peaceful. The knowledge of Vedic sciences is meant to save the human beings from falling into an utter darkness of ignorance. The unity in diversity is the message of Vedic physical and metaphysical sciences. Essence of the environmental studies in the Vedas can be put here by quoting a partial *Mantra* of the Ishavasyopanishad 'One should enjoy with renouncing or giving up others part'. Vedic message is clear that environment belongs to all living beings, so it needs protection by all, for the welfare of all.

4) The Hindu Dharma on Environment

Hindu dharma mentioned here is in the sense of comprehensive nature of Hinduism and "dharma" is indeed used by Hindus for their religion. Hinduism contains numerous references to the worship of the divine in nature in its Vedas,

[73] *Padmapurana,* 1.44.455.

[74] *Atharvaveda,* 12.1.35.

[75] *Ibid.*

[76] *Atharvaveda,* 10.8.31; Kapil Dev Dwivedi, *Vedic Sahitya Avam Sanskriti,* (Varanasi, 2000), .337

[77] *Yajurveda,* 36.1; *Atharvaveda,* 19.9.94; A.C.Bose, *The Call of the Vedas,* (Bhartiya Vidya Bhavan, Mumbai, 1999), 281.

Upanishads, Puranas, Sutras and its other sacred texts. Millions of Hindus recite Sanskrit mantras daily to revere their rivers, mountains, trees, animals and the earth. Although, the Chipko (tree-hugging) Movement is the most widely known example of Hindu environmental leadership, there are examples of Hindu action for the environment that are centuries old. Hinduism is a remarkably diverse religious and cultural phenomenon, with many local and regional manifestations. Within this universe of beliefs, several important themes emerge. The diverse theologies of Hindu dharma suggest that:

- The earth can be seen as a manifestation of the goddess, and must be treated with respect.
- The five elements — space, air, fire, water and earth — are the foundation of an interconnected web of life.
- Dharma — often translated as "duty" — can be reinterpreted to include our responsibility to care for the earth.
- Simple living is a model for the development of sustainable economies.
- Our treatment of nature directly affects our karma.

Gandhi exemplified many of these teachings, and his example continues to inspire contemporary social, religious and environmental leaders in their efforts to protect the planet. The following are some of the important concerns of Hindu teachings on the environment:

A) *Pancha Mahabhutas*

The five great elements – space, air, fire, water and earth, are considered as *Pancha Mahabutas* by Hindu dharma, which create a web of life that is shown forth in the structure and interconnectedness of the cosmos and the human body. Hinduism teaches that the *Pancha Mahabutas* that constitute the environment are all derived from *prakriti* (nature), the primal energy. Each of these elements has its own life and form; together the elements are interconnected and interdependent. The *Upanishads* explains the interdependence of these elements in relation to *Brahman*, the supreme reality, from which they arise: "From Brahman arises space, from space arises air, from air arises fire, from fire arises water, and from water arises earth." Hinduism recognizes that the human body is composed of and related to these five elements, and connects each of the elements to one of the five senses. The human nose is related to earth, tongue to water, eyes to fire, skin to air and ears to space. This bond between our senses and the elements is the foundation of our human relationship with the natural world. For Hinduism, nature and the environment are not outside us, not alien or hostile to us. They are an inseparable part of our existence, and they constitute our very bodies.[78]

[78] *Atharvaveda*, 19.67.1.

B) *Ishavasyam* — Divinity is Omnipresent and takes infinite Forms

Hindu texts contain many references to the omnipresence of the Supreme divinity, including its presence throughout and within nature.[79] Hindus worship and accept the presence of God in nature. For example, many Hindus think of India's mighty rivers — such as the Ganges, the Krishna and the Godavary — as goddesses. In the *Mahabharata*, it is noted that the universe and every object in it has been created as an abode of the Supreme God meant for the benefit of all, implying that individual species should enjoy their role within a larger system, in relationship with other species.

C) Protecting the Environment is part of Dharma

Dharma, one of the most important Hindu concepts, has been translated into English as duty, virtue, cosmic order and religion. In Hinduism, protecting the environment is an important expression of dharma. In past centuries, Indian communities, like other traditional communities, did not have an understanding of "the environment" as separate from the other spheres of activity in their lives. A number of rural Hindu communities such as the Bishnois, Bhils and Swadhyaya have maintained strong communal practices to protect local ecosystems such as forests and water sources. These communities carry out these conservation-oriented practices not as "environmental" acts but rather as expressions of dharma. When Bishnois are protecting animals and trees, when Swadhyayis are building *Vrikshamandiras* (tree temples) and *Nirmal Nirs* (water harvesting sites) and when Bhils are practicing their rituals in sacred groves, they are simply expressing their reverence for creation according to Hindu teachings, not "restoring the environment." These traditional Indian groups do not see religion, ecology and ethics as separate arenas of life. Instead, they understand it to be part of their dharma to treat creation with respect.

D) Our Environmental Actions affect our Karma

Karma, a central Hindu teaching, holds that each of our actions creates consequences, good and bad, which constitute our karma and determine our future fate, including the place we will assume when we are reincarnated in our next life. Moral behaviour creates good karma, and our behaviour toward the environment has karmic consequences. Because we have free choice, even though we may have harmed the environment in the past, we can choose to protect the environment in the future, replacing environmentally destructive karmic patterns with good ones.

---

[79] Refer for clarity, Pankaj Jain, "10 Hindu Environmental Teachings", http://www.huffingtonpost.com/pankaj-jain-phd/10-hindu-environmental-te_b_846245.html (accessed on 04th July, 2017).

E) The earth as "Mother Goddess"

There is good place to "Mother Goddess" worship in Hindu dharma. Hindus worship earth as goddess - *bhudevi*. Many Hindu rituals recognize that human beings benefit from the earth, and offer gratitude and protection in response. Many Hindus touch the floor before getting out of bed every morning and ask Devi to forgive them for trampling on her body. Millions of Hindus create *kolams* daily-artwork consisting of bits of rice or other food placed at their doorways in the morning. These *kolams* express Hindu's desire to offer sustenance to the earth, just as the earth sustains themselves. The *Chipko* movement made famous by *Chipko* women's commitment to "hugging" trees in their community to protect them from clear-cutting by outside interests represents a similar devotion to the earth.

F) Tantric and Yogic Traditions

Hindu dharma affirms the sacredness of material reality and contains teachings and practices to unite people with divine energy. Hinduism's Tantric tradition teaches that the entire universe is the manifestation of divine energy. Yoga, derived from the Sanskrit word meaning "to yoke" or "to unite," refers to a series of mental and physical practices designed to connect the individual with this divine energy. Both these traditions affirm that all phenomena, objects and individuals are expressions of the divine. And because these traditions both envision the earth as a goddess, contemporary Hindu teachers have used these teachings to demonstrate the wrongness of the exploitation of the environment, women and indigenous peoples.

G) Belief in Reincarnation

This belief supports a sense of interconnectedness of all creation. Hindus believe in the cycle of rebirth, wherein every being travels through millions of cycles of birth and rebirth in different forms, depending on their karma from previous lives. So, a person may be reincarnated as a person, animal, bird or another part of the wider community of life. Because of this, and because all people are understood to pass through many lives on their pathway to ultimate liberation, reincarnation creates a sense of solidarity between people and all living things, therefore respect the environment. Through belief in reincarnation, Hinduism teaches that all species and all parts of the earth are part of an extended network of relationships connected over the millennia, with each part of this network deserving respect and reverence.

H) '*Ahimsa*' (non-violence)

Ahimsa is one of the greatest principles of Hindu dharma. Ahimsa to the earth improves one's karma. For observant Hindus, hurting or harming another being damages one's karma and obstructs advancement toward *moksha* — liberation. To prevent the further accrual of bad karma, Hindus are instructed to avoid activities associated with violence and to follow a vegetarian diet. Based on this doctrine of ahimsa, many observant Hindus oppose the institutionalized breeding and killing of animals, birds and fish for human consumption. This concept/principle, indeed, helps to protect ecological destruction and promote healthy environment.

I) *Sanyasa* (asceticism)

Hindu dharma upholds "*sanyasa*" as one of the basic components of *ashrama* dharma of devoted Hindu life, which also represents a path to liberation and is good for the earth. Hinduism teaches that asceticism - restraint in consumption and simplicity in living, represents a pathway toward *moksha* (liberation), which treats the earth with respect. A well-known Hindu teaching "*Tain tyakten bhunjitha*" has been translated, "Take what you need for your sustenance without a sense of entitlement or ownership." One of the most prominent Hindu environmental leaders, Sunderlal Bahuguna, inspired many Hindus by his ascetic lifestyle. His repeated fasts and strenuous foot marches, undertaken to support and spread the message of the *Chipko,* distinguished him as a notable ascetic in our own time. In his capacity for suffering and his spirit of self-sacrifice, Hindus saw a living example of the renunciation of worldly ambition exhorted by Hindu dharma texts.

J) Gandhi's Exemplary Life

Gandhi's entire life can be seen as an ecological treatise. This is one life in which every minute act, emotion or thought functioned much like an ecosystem: his small meals of nuts and fruits, his morning ablutions and everyday bodily practices, his periodic observances of silence, his morning walks, his cultivation of the small as much as of the big, his spinning wheel, his abhorrence of waste, his resorting to basic Hindu and Jain values of truth, nonviolence, celibacy and fasting. The moralists, nonviolent activists, feminists, journalists, social reformers, trade union leaders, peasants, prohibitionists, nature-cure lovers, renouncers and environmentalists all take their inspirations from Gandhi's life and writings.

5) Hindus Commitment to Eco-Concerns Today

A) Hinduism and Ecology: Future Prospects

What can be expected in the development of a Hindu-inspired environmentalism? This collection of information suggests that several avenues can be pursued to lift up Hindu religious imagery and symbolism in the name of environmental protection.[80] However, any visitor to India will see that it is just as likely that the same religious symbols might be used to promote the latest consumer

[80] Cf. *The Bhagavad Gita* (7.19, 13.13) and the *Bhagavata Purana* :2.2.41, 2.2.45.

product. As Vasudha Narayanan has noted, "A burgeoning middle class in India is now hungry for the consumer bonbons of comfortable and luxurious living."[81] Nonetheless, despite the onslaught of advertising and industrialization, ecological consciousness is growing in India today. Public urgency has caused wide public discussion of ecological degradation. Some visible changes have been made to improve the state of the environment. For instance, three-wheeled taxis have been banned from the New Delhi airports because they create a great deal of pollution. Narayanan pointed out:

> With the growing awareness of our ecological plight, Hindu communities are pressing into us the many dharmic texts and injunctions, using the texts from Hindu scriptures as inspiration in planting gardens, and reviving customary lore on the medicinal importance of trees and plants. Women, through song and dance, communicate the assaults on women and nature.[82]

Narayanan describes a dance performed by Usha Vasanthkumar and Sudha Vijayaraghavan titled *Pancha Bootangal,* the Five Elements, that dramatically enacts humanity's greedy attack on the elements, resulting in ecological havoc. Swami Agnivesh of the Arya Samaj order of monks works extensively with the poor and disenfranchised of India, seeking economic justice, protection of children, and universal education. Like Gandhi, he suggests that the village model provides for an ecologically sound lifestyle. He states that simplicity and contentment are needed to counter the juggernaut of industrial development and consumerism that leads to pollution and environmental degradation.

The swami's comments reflect a general distrust throughout India of modern life patterned on the Western paradigm. The rise to power of the Bharatiya Janata Party (BJP) during the 1990s came about in part due to a wariness of this cultural shift throughout India. Thomas Blom Hansen is of opinion:

> The entire problematic of consumption of "Western" products—food, styles of dress, electronic gadgets, music—is among Hindu nationalists (and others) linked to the contamination, exposure, and corruption of the body . . . [A]ccess to electronic implements, motorized transport, and excessive watching of TV divert the attention away from healthier and more physically demanding pursuits.[83]

Nonetheless, the task of stopping or even slowing the spread of consumerism and industrialization seems quite impossible. It seems that the Nehruvian vision

---

[81] For more details visit http://fore.yale.edu/publications/books/cswr/hinduism-introduction/ (accessed on 6th July, 2017).

[82] Vasudha Narayanan, "'One Tree Is Equal to Ten Sons': Hindu Responses to the Problems of Ecology, Population, and Consumption," *Journal of the American Academy of Religion,* 65, no. 2 (1991): 321.

[83] *Ibid.*

for India has prevailed and that such Gandhian notions as nonviolence *(ahimsa)* and nonpossession *(aparigraha)* are insufficient to bring about the changes needed to make India more environmentally conscious.

Anil Agarwal is rightly pointed out that this current urban ecological crisis took India by surprise. In his personal life, he has struggled with environmentally induced cancer. In 1994 he was diagnosed with lymphoma and has received extensive treatments in the United States for his condition. He expressively writes:

> The elite of our nation [India] have failed to internalize the ecological principle that every poison we put out into our environment comes right back to us in our air, water, and food. These poisons slowly seep into our bodies and take years to show up as cancer, as immune system disorders, or as hormonal or reproductive system disorders-affecting even the fetus . . . [T] he Indian people must not remain ignorant and nonchalant about the acute threats they face to their own health and to the health of their children.[84]

As the general population of India becomes more aware of the great harm and difficulty inflicted by industrial pollution and inappropriate use of resources, it will begin to awaken to the need for voluntary compliance with much-needed clean-up campaigns. Despite the good intentions of government agencies and the passage of various pieces of antipollution legislation, Indians have a long history of ignoring government regulations. Public advocacy, perhaps inspired by the memory of cleaner times, will eventually prompt the government and industries of India to be more attentive to the destructive nature of its current techno-industrial complex. The Hindu religion, with its vast storehouse of text, ritual, and spirituality, can help contribute both theoretical and practical responses to this crisis.

B) Awareness and Commitment to Environmental Issues Today

Long term plan

In November 2009 Hindus launched their "Nine Year Plan" to protect the living planet. Amongst more than 30 faith plans they celebrated the launch at Windsor Castle in the presence of HRH The Prince Philip, founder of Alliance of Religions and conservation (ARC), and UN Secretary General Mr Ban Ki-moon who, during his speech, reminded the faith representatives that "You can, and do, inspire people to change."[85]

---

[84] Thomas Blom Hansen, *The Saffron Wave: Democracy and Hindu Nationalism in Modern India,* (Princeton, N.J.: Princeton University Press, 1999), 233.

[85] Anil Agarwal, "My Story Today, Your Story Tomorrow: An Environmentalist Searches for the Genesis of His Own Cancer," *Down To Earth,* 5, no. 13 (30 November, 1996), 30–37.

The Bhumi Project and Nine Year Plan

Inspired by ARC and facilitated by the Oxford Centre for Hindu Studies (OCHS), the Bhumi project is an initiative aimed at educating, inspiring, informing, and connecting Hindus interested in service to Mother Earth ("Bhu devi"). The project aims at long-term sustainable plans, and the first of these is their Nine Year Plan. The Plan focuses on three main areas:

i) Networking: Working to promote the work of individuals and communities that are presently engaged in environmental action, the Nine Year Plan also aims to bring those with similar aims and ideals together to learn from each other and teach others, so that more and more Hindu eco-action can happen. This section of the plan places emphasis on the following areas:

- **Websites:** As the projects contained within the plan evolve and grow they will require their own websites. The aim of these websites will be to educate and inform. They will provide the facility for users to interact with one another and share their experiences and success stories.
- **Major conservation projects**: The Bhumi project aims to partner with major conservation projects which are already operating so that they can bring their good work to the attention of a broader audience, and provide examples of good practice and dharmic living.
- **Green pilgrimage**: Most Hindu pilgrimage sites are in India. As the Hindu diaspora and Indian middle class have grown, such sites are seeing a growth in their number of pilgrims. To reduce the environmental impact of the pilgrimages, the Plan aims to develop a set of guidelines that will encourage Hindu devotees to see all aspects of pilgrimage as sacred. This includes the means of transport, accommodation, and use of resources at holy sites.

ii) Action: An essential element of the Nine Year Plan is a call to arms. Without encouraging action – thoughtful, informed, and enthusiastic – the best formed Plan will be more suited to an archive than an impetus for change. This section of the Plan, then, promotes the following actions amongst many others:

- **Hindu labelling scheme**: The Hindu community has purchasing power. The Bhumi project wants to develop a set of standards based on the principle of ahimsa (non-violence) that will assist the community in ethical buying in line with its ethos and values.
- **Cruelty-free milk**: The Bhumi project will work closely with the lotus trust, which wishes to pioneer the production of cruelty-free milk for the Hindu community where no animals are sent for slaughter.
- **Green festivals and gatherings**: From travel to the temple to the plates on which food is served – all can have a significant impact on

the environment. A team will be formed to help each Hindu festival to incorporate a protective attitude towards the planet. Sustainable practices will include: using recycled paper for printing promotional materials; using bio-degradable plates, cups and cutlery for serving food; promoting greener ways of transport to the festival; and ensuring all energy is used efficiently.

There are also plans to throw the Bhumi Festival in Summer 2011, which promises to attract thousands upon thousands of young people from the Hindu community as well as other faith and secular groups. The plan is for the festival to be ecologically sound as possible, and as such a great testament to Hindu environmentalism.[86]

iii) Education: Effective education is key to all aspects of the Plan and is aimed at effecting a generational change in the Hindu community. Educational aims include:

- **Training for priests**: Hindu priests are influential in the daily running of their temples and in the performance of ceremonies. Crucial to effecting a positive change in the environmental choices of the Hindu community therefore is the education and training of temple priests. Establishing ecological awareness and standards in temple worship will, over time, influence and change the practice of those who worship at home.
- **Online course:** Not all Hindus live near a temple, or are able to attend a place of worship or gathering on a regular basis. To reach these people, and others, a short course on Hindu approaches to the environment will be developed by the OCHS to be delivered online. The course will run over a four-week period, two–three times a year. It is hoped that by the end of nine years, over 25,000 people will have taken it.
- **Summer camps:** Many temples and organisations run summer camps for the youth of their communities. Such events are an ideal way to educate young people on environmental issues and teach best practice. The *Bhumi* project will produce resources which these summer camps can use.

[86] http://environment-ecology.com/religion-and-ecology/283-what-does-hinduism-teach-us-about-ecology.html (accessed on 6th July, 2017).

Chapter 6

Jainism/Buddhism and Environmental Concerns

The main aim of "Ecology and Indian Religious Traditions" is to search for ecological resources from Indian religions and explore the possibility to develop sustainable eco-spirituality. The "Religions of the World and Ecology" project brings the rich historical and contemporary resources of the world's religions into critical dialogue with the global environmental crisis.[1] In particular, it seeks to broaden and deepen the symbolic, conceptual, and practical dimensions of their distinctive holistic worldviews for an understanding of human flourishing, community, the natural environment, and their interactions. The project also seeks to influence both social behaviour and public policy by encouraging ongoing collaboration among various interdisciplinary arcs that must be forged if the environmental crisis has any hope of being resolved.[2] This chapter explores ways in which the Buddhist and Jain traditions might contribute to this discussion and to the practice of a more ecologically aware lifestyle. Buddhism and Jainism, both are ancient religious traditions which had originated in India and comprise the oldest religions that continually observed religious traditions of the Indian subcontinent along with Hinduism. Both have spread beyond the subcontinent to virtually many parts of the world, though most adherent to these faiths claim Indian ancestry.

---

[1] For more details, refer Donald K. Swearer, "Buddhism and Ecology: Challenge and Promise" in http://fore.yale.edu/religion/buddhism/ accessed on 6th July, 2017 and also his recent publications: *The Buddhist World of Southeast Asia* (SUNY, 1995/rev. ed. Silkworm Books, 2007); *The Legend of Queen Cama* (SUNY, 1998); *Becoming the Buddha: The Ritual of Image Consecration in Thailand* (Princeton, 2004); and *The Sacred Mountains of Northern Thailand and their Legends* (Silkworm Books, 2004).

[2] Cf., James Gustafson, *A Sense of the Divine,* (Cleveland, Ohio: Pilgrim Press, 1994).

1. Ecological Concerns of Buddhism

Buddhism is a path of practice and spiritual development leading to Insight into the true nature of reality. Buddhist practices meditation as a means of changing themselves in order to develop the qualities of awareness, kindness, and wisdom. The experience developed within the Buddhist tradition over thousands of years has created an incomparable resource for all those who wish to follow a path - a path which ultimately culminates in Enlightenment or Buddhahood. An enlightened being sees the nature of reality absolutely clearly, just as it is, and lives fully and naturally in accordance with that vision. It is the goal of the Buddhist spiritual life, representing the end of suffering for anyone who attains it. Because Buddhism does not include the idea of worshipping a creator god, some people do not see it as a religion in the normal Western sense. The basic tenets of Buddhist teaching are straightforward and practical: nothing is fixed or permanent; actions have consequences; change is possible. So, Buddhism addresses itself to all people irrespective of race, nationality, caste, sexuality, or gender. It teaches practical methods which enable people to realise and use its teachings in order to transform their experience, to be fully responsible for their lives.[3]

A) Buddhism's Holistic Worldview

Despite significant variations among the different Buddhist traditions that have evolved over its 2,500 year journey throughout Asia and now in the West, Buddhists see the world as conjoined on four levels: existentially, morally, cosmologically, and ontologically. Existentially, Buddhists affirm that all sentient beings share the fundamental conditions of birth, old age, suffering, and death. The existential realization of the universality of suffering lies at the core of the Buddha's teaching. Insight into the nature of suffering, its cause and its cessation, and the path to the cessation of suffering constitutes the capstone of the Buddha's enlightenment experience *(Mahasacakka Sutta, Majjihma Nikaya)* as well as the content of the four noble truths, the Buddha's first teaching. That the Buddha decides to share this existential insight into the cause and cessation of suffering is regarded by the tradition as an act of universal compassion. Buddhist environmentalists assert that the mindful awareness of the universality of suffering produces compassionate empathy for all forms of life, particularly for all sentient species. They interpret the *Dhammapada's* ethical injunction not to do evil but to do good as a moral principle advocating the nonviolent alleviation of suffering, an ideal embodied in the prayer of universal loving-kindness that concludes many Buddhist rituals: "May all beings be free from enmity; may all beings be free from injury; may all beings be free from suffering; may all beings be happy." Out of a concern for the

---

[3] "The Buddhist Centre: Buddhism for today", https://thebuddhistcentre.com/buddhism, 23/08/16.

total living environment, Buddhist environmentalists extend loving-kindness and compassion beyond people and animals to include plants and the earth itself.

The concepts of *karma* and rebirth *(samsara)* integrate the existential sense of a shared common condition of all sentient life-forms with the moral dimension of the Buddhist cosmology. Not unlike the biological sciences, rebirth links human and animal species. Evolution maps commonalities and differences among species on the basis of physical and genetic traits. Rebirth maps them on moral grounds. Every form of sentient life participates in a karmic continuum traditionally divided into three world-levels and a hierarchical taxonomy of five or six life-forms. Although this continuum constitutes a moral hierarchy, differences among life-forms and individuals are relative, not absolute. Traditional Buddhism may privilege humans over animals, animals over hungry ghosts, male gender over the female, monk over laity but all forms of karmically conditioned life - human, animal, divine, demonic—are related within contingent, *samsaric* time: "In the long course of rebirth there is not one among living beings with form who has not been mother, father, brother, sister, son, or daughter, or some other relative. Being connected with the process of taking birth, one is kin to all wild and domestic animals, birds, and beings born from the womb" *(Lankavatara Sutra).*

Nirvana, the Buddhist highest good, offers the promise of transformation from karmic condition into an unconditioned state of spiritual liberation, a realization potentially available to all forms of sentient life on the karmic continuum. That plants and trees or the land itself have a similar potential for spiritual liberation became an explicit doctrine in Chinese and Japanese Buddhism but may even have been part of popular Buddhist belief from earliest times—in sum, a realization that all life-forms share both a common problematic and promise. Although, the Buddhist doctrines of *karma* and rebirth link together all forms of sentient existence in a moral continuum, Buddhist ethics focus on human agency and its consequences. The inclusion of plants and animals in Buddhist soteriological schemes may be important philosophically because it attributes inherent value to nonhuman forms of life. Nonetheless, humans have been the primary agents in creating the present ecological crisis and will bear the major responsibility in solving it.

The myth of origins in the Pali canon describes the deleterious impact of human activity on the primordial natural landscape. Unlike the garden of Eden story in the Hebrew Bible where human agency centre on the God-human relationship, the Buddhist story of first origins describes the negative impact of humans on the earth created by selfishness and greed. In the Buddhist mythological Eden, the earth flourishes naturally, but greedy desire leads to division and ownership of the land that in turn promotes violent conflict, destruction, and chaos. In short, in the Buddhist myth of first origins, human agency destroys the natural order of things. Though change is inherent in nature, Buddhists believe that natural processes are directly affected by human morality.[4]

Within the Buddha's enlightenment vision *(Nirvana)* all the major dimensions of the Buddhist worldview are found. Tradition records that during the night of this experience the Buddha first recalled his previous lives within the karmic continuum; then he perceived the fate of all sentient beings within the cosmic hierarchy; finally he fathomed the nature of suffering and the path to its cessation formulated as the four noble truths and the law of interdependent carousing. The Buddha's enlightenment evolved in a specific sequence: from an understanding of the particular (his personal karmic history), then to the general (the karmic history of humankind), and finally to the principle underlying the cause and cessation of suffering. Subsequently, this principle is further generalized as a universal law of causality: "On the arising of this, that arises; on the cessation of this, that ceases."

Buddhist environmentalists find in the causal principle of interdependence an ecological vision that integrates all aspects of the ecosphere—particular individuals and general species—in terms of the principle of mutual co-dependence. Within this cosmological model individual entities are by their very nature relational, thereby undermining the autonomous self over against the "other," be it human, animal, or vegetable.

Buddhist environmentalists see their worldview as a rejection of hierarchical dominance of one human over another or humans over nature, and as the basis of an ethic of empathetic compassion that respects biodiversity. In the view of the Thai monk, Buddhadasa Bhikkhu, "The entire cosmos is a cooperative. The sun, the moon, and the stars live together as a cooperative. The same is true for humans and animals, trees, and the earth. When we realize that the world is a mutual, interdependent, cooperative enterprise . . . then we can build a noble environment. If our lives are not based on this truth, then we shall perish." A Western Buddhist, observing that the Buddhist worldview or *dharma* not only refers to the teachings of the Buddha but also to all things in nature, characterizes Buddhism as a "religious ecology."[5]

In later schools of Buddhist thought the cosmological vision of interdependent causality evolved into a more substantive sense of ontological unity. Metaphorically, the image of Indra's net found in the Hua Yen (Jp. *Kegon)* tradition's *Avatamsaka Sutra* has been especially important in Buddhist ecological discussions. For Gary Snyder the image of the universe as a vast web of many-sided jewels each constituted by the reflections of all the other jewels in the web and each jewel being the image of the entire universe symbolizes the world as

[4] Lily de Silva, "The Hills Wherein My Soul Delights," in *Buddhism and Ecology,* Martine Batchelor and Kerry Brown, eds., (London: Cassell, 1992).

[5] Martine Batchelor and Kerry Brown, (eds.), *Buddhism and Ecology,* (London: Cassell, 1992).

a universe of bioregional ecological communities. Buddhist environmentalists argue, furthermore, that ontological notions such as Buddha-nature or Dharma-nature (e.g., *buddhakaya, tathagatagarbha, dharmakaya, dharmadhatu)* provide a basis for unifying all existent entities in a common sacred universe, even though the tradition privileges human life vis-a-vis spiritual realization. For T'ien-t'ai monks in eighth century China, the belief in a universal Buddha-nature blurred the distinction between sentient and non-sentient life-forms and logically led to the view that plants, trees, and the earth itself could achieve enlightenment. Kukai (774–835), the founder of the Japanese Shingon school and Dogen (1200–1253), the founder of the Soto Zen sect, described universal Buddha-nature in naturalistic terms, "If plants and trees were devoid of Buddhahood, waves would then be without humidity" (Kukai); "The sutras [i.e., the *dharma]* are the entire universe, mountains, and rivers and the great wide earth, plants and trees" (Dogen). Buddhist environmentalists cite Dogen's view as support for the preservation of species biodiversity.

Two types of criticism have been levelled against Buddhist environmentalists (sometimes characterized as Eco-Buddhists or Green-Buddhists); scholars who argue that ecologizing the Buddhist worldview distorts the philosophical and historical integrity of the tradition; and, practioners who see a tendency in Green-Buddhism to reduce the tradition to a one-dimensional teaching of simple interrelatedness at the expense of its classical emphasis on the development of spiritual and ethical transformation. The four dimensions of the Buddhist worldview as proposed above offer a framework for understanding both the advocates of Buddhist environmentalism and their critics.

B) Teaching and traditions of Buddhism related to Eco-concerns

Buddhism teaches that the idea of separateness is an illusion. The health of the whole is inseparably linked to the health of the parts, and the health of the parts is inseparably linked to the health of the whole. This means that caring for the environment begins with caring for oneself:

i) **Respect for life:** Buddhist practice makes one feel one's existence is no more important than anyone else's. If one treats nature as a friend and teacher, one can be in harmony with other creatures and appreciate the interconnectedness of all that lives.[6]

ii) **Simplicity and moderation:** Buddha taught people to live simply and appreciate the natural cycle of life. Craving and greed only bring unhappiness, since demands for material possessions can never be

[6] Lynn A. de Silva, "The Buddhist Religious Tradition." edt. P.S. Daniel, David C. Scott, G. R. Singh (New Delhi: ISPCK, 2011), 211.

satisfied and people will always demand more, so threatening the environment. This is why the real solution to the environmental crisis begins with the individual. Buddhists in Japan tell a story. The Buddha once received a donation of 500 new robes for his followers. So he considered what to do with the old ones. They would be used for bed-sheets, he decided. And the old sheets would become towels. And the old towels would be used as cleaning rags. Everything should be used and reused.[7]

iii) **Right livelihood:** According to Buddhism from *Sutra-pitaka* of the *Tripitaka*, the way you earn your livelihood – not killing, not stealing, not taking more than you need – all these are part of the Buddhist way of life. A livelihood that avoids harming others, such as trading in weapons, meat, alcohol or poisons – is in harmony with nature.[8]

iv) **The Noble Eight Fold Path:** The noble eight fold path consists of right vision, right thought, right speech, right action, right livelihood, right efforts, right mindfulness and right concentration. Treatises could be written on the relevance of each of these to the human future. On right livelihood for example Buddhist teaching requires every person to consider the manner in which the performance of his duties as employee would impact on society and the future. Employment, for example, in the armaments industry, which imperils the human future, would be a violation of the path of right livelihood. Any employment which causes damage to the environment such as manufacturing of toxic substances, felling of forests and the adverse exploitation of marine resources would also be a violation of right livelihood. Any employment which involves damage to the environment such as working in the nuclear industry, manufacturing toxic substances, and the exploitation and depletion of marine resources would be included in this prohibition.[9]

v) **The Buddhist Scriptures on ecology/environment:** The vastness of the volume of Buddhist scriptures needs to be appreciated. The Buddha's discourses, delivered during the 45 years of his ministry, were memorised by his followers and later reduced to writing. A notable compilation is that which was affected in the first century prior to the Christian era by a group of 500 monks at Aluvihare in Sri Lanka. This is one of the most monumental processes of recording in world history,

---

[7] http://www.arcworld.org/faiths.asp?pageID=3," "What does Buddhism teaches about ecology?" Faith and Ecology", accessed on 07/07/17.

[8] http://buddhism.about.com/od/theeightfoldpath/a/rightlivelihood.htm, "Right Livelihood: The Ethics of Earning a Living", 27/08/16.

[9] Walpola Sri Rahula, *What the Buddha Taught* (London: Gordon Fraser Gallery Ltd., 1978), 45-46.

amounting in bulk to several multiples of Justinian's codification - long celebrated as one of the outstanding compilations of all time[10].

a) **Buddhism is eco-centric:** Buddhism is completely averse to the notion that nature and all created things exist for the benefit of mankind. Mankind is part of the entire cosmic order but not in a position of dominance. Humans are just as much subject to the natural order of the universe as any other form of sentient existence. "Buddhism is eco-centric rather than anthropocentric since it views humans as an integral part of nature.

b) **Coexistence rather than Conquest:** The aim that Buddhism instils in every individual mind is emancipation from suffering. The route to that emancipation is not the pursuit of power and possessions but the very opposite – the rejection of the pursuit of those materialistic goals which are so greatly imperilling the human future. Conquest of the natural environment, of other species or of other groups of the human family is hence the very reverse of the ideals which Buddhism teaches. Co-existence is vital and this requires a recognition and respect of those other species and groups and not an attempt at dominance.

c) **Principles of Trusteeship:** Buddhist philosophers and scholars have expanded on these concepts in a manner which makes them intensely relevant to the subject under discussion. Historical examples of such teaching abound, of which one of the best known

---

[10] Judge Weeramantry, http://www.asiantribune.com/index.php?q=node/6210, 12/07/16. The details of Buddhist scriptures is as follows: The Pali Canon, called the *Tripitaka* or the three baskets, arranges its subject-matter in three collections called the *Vinaya Pitaka* (the basket of discipline), the *Sutta Pitaka* (the basket of discourses), and the *Abidhamma Pitaka* (the basket of higher doctrine). The basket of discourses is immense and contains sermons and didactic stories embodying a vast range of principles of justice – individual, national and international. Comparatively little legal effort has been expended on quarrying from this vast mass of material the legal principles latent within them. This vast literature consists of five collections, known as *Nikayas* – the *Dirgha Nikaya* (34 long discourses), the *Majjhima Nikaya* (152 middle length discourses), the *Samyutta Nikaya* (2,889 short discourses), the *Anguttara Nikaya* (2,308 short sayings, often in the form of maxims or aphorisms), and the *Khuddaka Nikaya* (over a thousand sayings in the form of stanzas or aphorisms, covering the whole range of Buddhist philosophy). Perhaps the most popular collection of these short sayings, which has been translated into practically every major language, is the *Dhammapada,* a collection of 423 stanzas. The basket of higher doctrine *(Abhidamma)* contemplates the human condition at the most advanced philosophical level. It is replete with insights bearing on the long term future. Some idea of the volume of all this literature can be gathered from the translations of the Pali Text Society, which include the *Anguttara Nikaya* (5 vols.), the *Dirgha Nikaya* (3 vols.), *Digha Nikaya* Commentary (3 vols.), the *Dhammapada* Commentary (4 vols.), the *Jataka* (6 vols.), the *Majjhima Nikaya* (3 vols.), the *Majjhima Nikaya* Commentary (5 vols.), the *Samyutta Nikaya* (5 vols.) and the *Vinaya Pitaka* (5 vols.).

illustrations is the sermon preached by the arahat Mahinda, son of the Emperor Asoka, to the King of Sri Lanka when the monk accosted the King who was enjoying a hunt in the royal forest. The monk's sermon included a reminder to the King that although he was the King of the country, he was not the owner but the trustee of the land on which he was hunting.

d) **Practical Activism:** Buddhism has been the inspiration in recent times for much practical work on environmental protection. It is often ranged against governments which seek to improve their economies by rapid "development" which often takes the form of damaging the environmental heritage. The practical movements Buddhism has inspired in several countries are of importance to the rest of the world. Buddhism teaches that one does not have to traverse the length and breadth of the Universe to gain knowledge of what is right or wrong. All this knowledge is latent within oneself. Applying this to environmental protection, what is required is an internal change of attitude. This strikes a resonant chord with the deep ecologists, for deep ecology requires changes of attitude, changes within oneself, as the secret of reversing the environmental crisis. It is not sufficient to correct the external environment. One must begin the process by correcting the attitudes of the individual.[11]

C) Religious Ecology in Buddhism

Buddhism is rightly considered to be the ecological religion or religious ecology. Buddhist ecology includes both living and non-living aspect of nature. The love of nature is so deep rooted that cannot overlook the attractive aspect particularly when the entire world is experiencing ecological crisis. However, Buddhism views the environment from the perspective of the holistic and moralistic understanding. It lay emphasis on the purity of motive and fairness of the conduct. Buddhism wants to purify the mind and fill it with noble ideas, in order to find the best from the natural environment. At the same time, peace and tranquillity is not possible in an atmosphere when environment is upset. In order to protect the environment, one must protect oneself by opposing selfishness with generosity, ignorance with wisdom, hatred with loving kindness. Selflessness, mindfulness, compassion and wisdom are the essence of Buddhism.[12] From the analysis, we can assume the following points regarding the Buddhist ecology as below:

---

[11] Judge Weeramantry, http://www.asiantribune.com/index.php?q=node/6210.

[12] Mritunjay Kumar, "Religious Ecology in Buddhism", *Ecological Perspective in Buddhism*, edt. K. C. Pandey (New Delhi: Readworthy Publications Pvt. Ltd., 2008), 51-54.

Men/women, like other creatures are co-sharers of natural resource, hence they have no rights to consume and exhaust these at a faster rate for their own benefit alone.

Buddhist wisdom necessarily points to be suitable use of nature, keeping in mind the interest of next generation and other living beings.

Universal responsible motivated by love and compassion for all is considered key to Buddhist ideal which is quite significant for eco-ethics.

Buddha's own life is deeply associated with flora and fauna. He always inspires his followers to conserve and preserve wildlife and honour all form of life.

Buddha's moral teaching contains seeds of environmental ethics. His notions of ahimsa, compassion and middle path have all the essentials of environmental ethics. Right conduct and right livelihood are the mainstay of ecological pursuit, which we trace in the four noble truth.

Buddhist notions of incarnation theory and rebirth may be focused to arouse consciousness among masses for eco-conservation.

Buddhism lays stress on the excellence of morality which helps in creating a pleasant and healthy environment. Thus, environment and morality seem to be interlinked as per Buddhist teaching.[13]

D) Philosophical Criticism

Buddhadasa Bhikkhu called his forest monastery in south Thailand "the Garden of Empowering Liberation," observing: "The deep sense of calm that nature provides through separation from the stress that plagues us in the day-to-day world protects our heart and mind. The lessons nature teaches us lead to a new birth beyond suffering caused by our acquisitive self-preoccupation." For Buddhist environmentalists, centres like Buddhadasa's Garden of Empowering Liberation also present an example of a sustainable lifestyle grounded in the values of moderation, simplicity, and non-acquisitiveness. Technology alone cannot solve the eco-crisis. More importantly, it requires a transformation of values and of lifestyle.

Buddhadasa intended the Garden of Empowering Liberation not as a retreat from the world but as a place where all forms of life—humans, animals, and plants—live as a cooperative microcosm of a larger ecosystem and as a community where humans can develop an ecological ethic. Such an ethic highlights the virtues of restraint, simplicity, loving-kindness, compassion, equanimity, patience, wisdom, nonviolence, and generosity. These virtues represent moral ideals for all members of the Buddhist community— religious practioner, lay person, political

[13] Mritunjay Kumar, "Religious Ecology in Buddhism", *Ecological Perspective in Buddhism*, edt. K. C. Pandey (New Delhi: Readworthy Publications Pvt. Ltd., 2008), 59.

leader, ordinary citizen, male, female. For example, political leaders who are mandated to maintain the peace and security of the nation, are also expected to embody the virtue of nonviolence. In this connection, King Asoka is cited for his rejection of animal sacrifice and protection of animals. The twin virtues of wisdom and compassion define the spiritual perfection of the *bodhisattva* (saint) but these prized moral qualities, associated especially with the Buddha or monks, are represented in narrative and didactic literature by a variety of human and animal life-forms. For contemporary engaged Buddhists—the Dalai Lama especially—a sense of responsibility rooted in compassion lies at the very heart of an ecological ethic: "The world grows smaller and smaller, more and more interdependent . . . today more than ever before life must be characterized by a sense of universal responsibility, not only . . . human to human but also human to other forms of life."[14]

For many Buddhist environmentalists compassion necessarily follows an understanding of all life-forms as mutually interdependent. Others argue that a mere cognitive recognition of interdependence is a necessary but not a sufficient condition for an ecological ethic. These critics emphasize the centrality of practice in Buddhism and the tradition's insistence on training in virtue and the threefold path to moral and spiritual excellence (morality, mindful awareness, wisdom). Among contemporary engaged Buddhists, the Vietnamese monk, Thich Nhat Hanh, has been the most insistent on the central role of mindful awareness in the development of a peaceful and sustainable world.

Critics of the ethical saliency of the traditional Buddhist vision of human flourishing argue that philosohical concepts such as not-self *(anatman)* and emptiness *(sunyata)* undermine human autonomy and the distinction between self and other, essential aspects for another-regarding ethic. What are the grounds for an ethic or laws that protect the civil rights of minorities or animal species threatened with extinction when philosophically Buddhism seems to undermine their significance by deconstructing their independent reality as an epistemological fiction? Furthermore, they point out that the most basic concepts of Buddhism—Nirvana, suffering, rebirth, not—self, and even causality - were intended to further the goal of the individual's spiritual quest rather than engagement with the world. They conclude, therefore, either that Buddhism serves primarily a salvific or soteriological purpose or that the attempt to ecologize the tradition distorts the historical and philosophical record.

Buddhist environmentalists respond that their tradition brings to the debates about human rights and the global environment an ethic of social and environmental responsibility more compatible with the language of compassion based on the mutual interdependence of all life-forms than the language of rights.

[14] Nancy Nash, "The Buddhist Perception of Nature Project," in *Buddhist Perspectives on the Ecocrisis,* Klas Sandell, ed., (Buddhist Publication Society, 1987).

Furthermore, to apply Buddhist insights to a broad ecology of human flourishing represents the tradition at its best, namely, a creative, dynamic response to its contemporary context.

A related but more sympathetic criticism from within the Buddhist environmental movement suggests that for Buddhism to be an effective force for systemic institutional change, the traditional Buddhist emphasis on individual moral and spiritual transformation must be adjusted to address more forcefully the structures of oppression, exploitation, and environmental degradation. While preserving the unique Buddhist emphasis on the practice of mindful awareness and a lifestyle of simplicity, today's engaged Buddhist activists are, indeed, addressing head-on international issues ranging from the disposal of nuclear waste to human rights violations in Myanmar and a just and peaceful resolution of the Chinese occupation of Tibet. The most internationally visible leaders in this movement are the Dalai Lama and Thich Nhat Hanh but they are joined by many others from around the globe including Sulak Sivaraksa, Ahangamage T. Ariyaratna, Joanna Macy, and Kenneth Kraft.

Furthermore, in recent years some Buddhists have been among the leading voices trumpeting the need for ecological awareness and action. For example, the Council of All Beings, a ritual in which one places oneself as in a trance in the position of another species in order to appreciate the impact of ecological decline on it, was designed by Buddhists and has become popular among environmentalists of all persuasions. Also, there are several examples of Buddhist movements establishing environmentally sustainable rural communities in America, and the group known as "engaged Buddhists," many of whom are associated with the Buddhist Peace Fellowship, have consistently led protests against the misuse of nuclear power and a host of other issues. At the same time, it must be acknowledged that there has always been another side of Buddhism, which after all is largely a monastic tradition for home-leavers -- a side that is hermetic, withdrawing, and socially and environmentally disengaged and, at times in history, corrupt, at least as a by-product of benign neglect.

The question is, which side of Buddhism will prevail in the discourse concerning environmental issues? Will it be the one emphasizing how to analyze and act on the ecological crisis based on the inseparability of all forms of existence? Or will it be the face of Buddhism that may appear disconnected with and neglectful of current social issues in focusing exclusively on the individual quest for enlightenment or, as was the case in medieval China, on the growth of powerful, independent temple complexes? While several of the contributions to eco-concerns of Buddhism rather uncritically celebrate the former side of Buddhist discourse, the more constructive contributions make it clear that a notion of Buddhist engagement with the environment must be grounded in a careful, thoroughgoing understanding of the history of Buddhist thought and the impact of Buddhist institutions in society.[15]

2. Environmental Concerns of Jainism

Jainism is one of the oldest living religions of India. It predates chronicles as per recordings in the Hindu Holy Scriptures. Jainism is a religious faith of strictly human origin and is preach and practiced by one who have achieved ideal knowledge, Nirvana and self-control by his/her own individual efforts and has been released from the shackles of corporeal existence, the cycle of birth and death. The idea of God as a creator, protector, and destroyer of the world doesn't exist in Jainism. In short Jainism does not believe in creator God, but it is not an atheist religion because they believe in many gods who are self-realised persons and achieved nirvana. Jainism is basically a religious faith of *Tirthankars.*[16] Jainism has come from the word "Jin" which means the one who has vanquished their passion. It basically means the conquest of one's own self bondage. A *tirthankar* is one who has built a ford which takes one across the ocean of bondage and suffering.[17] According to the *Tattvartha Sutra* there are 8,400,000 species of living things – each of which is part of the cycle of birth, life, death, and rebirth, and is therefore precious. R. P. Chandaria is of opinion that "Lord Mahavira preached about the environment in the first book of '*Acharanga Sutra*', which is accepted, as His direct words. The elements of nature were described as living beings and under the fundamental principle of AHIMSA these were to be protected in all ways - no waste, no overuse, no abuse, no polluting. If we follow these principles, then we would stop destroying our environment as well as preserve the resources that are available for all to share. If there are more resources available for all, then the poor will also get a fair share thereof."[18]

A) Basic teaching of Jainism on Ecology

i) **Ahimsa:** The first and foremost principle of Jainism was Ahimsa or non-injury to anyone. The non-violence is found very clearly *in Tattvartha sutra* 7:1 and *Acaranga Sutra* are exclusively concerned with observance of

---

[15] Mary Evelyn Tucker and Duncan Ryuken Williams (eds.), "Buddhism and ecology: The Interconnection of Dharma and Deeds", Reviewed by Steven Heine, in *Philosophy East & West,* Vol. 51, No. 1, (January 2001), 136-138; http://ccbs.ntu.edu.tw/FULLTEXT/JR-PHIL/ew032953.htm, accessed on 7th July, 2017.

[16] Tirthankarais a Sanskrit word which means "Ford-maker" also called Jina which means"Victor", in Jainism, a saviour who has succeeded in crossing over life's stream of rebirths and has made a path for others to follow. Mahavira (6th century bce) was the last Tirthankara to appear. https://www.britannica.com/topic/Tirthankara, 27/08/16.

[17] Arun Kumar Jain, *Faith and Philosophy of Jainism* (Delhi: Kalpaz Publications, 2009), 18.

[18] *Quotation from R. P. Chandaria, Chairman of the Institute of Jainology,* 15 August 2008. Link to *Institute of Jainology*.

non-violence and interrelationship of all living beings, in this way many of the Jains walk bare-footed, filter water before drinking and even tie a band of cloth round their mouth so that they may not kill small insects.[19] They even take care not to injure any plant or tree, not to speak of causing pain to men, birds and beasts. This principle was against the rising rate of animal sacrifice in the *yajnas*.[20] The teaching of ahimsa refers not only to wars and visible physical acts of violence but to violence in the hearts and minds of human beings, their lack of concern and compassion for their fellow humans and for the natural world. Ancient Jain texts explain that violence (*ahimsa*) is not defined by actual harm, for this may be unintentional. It is the intention to harm, the absence of compassion that makes action violent. Without violent thought there could be no violent actions.[21] This central teaching of Jainism was made famous in recent times by Mahatma Gandhi, who was greatly influenced by Jain ideas. He made *ahimsa* the guiding principle of his struggle for social freedom and equality. *Ahimsa* means more than not hurting others, it means not intending to cause harm, physical, mental or spiritual, to any part of nature, for, in the words of Mahavira: 'You are that which you wish to harm.'[22]

ii) **Interdependence**: This ancient Jain principle teaches that all of nature is bound together, and says that if one does not care for nature one does not care for oneself. Mahavira proclaimed a profound truth for all times to come. According to him "One who neglects or disregards the existence of earth, air, fire, water and vegetation disregards his own existence which is entwined with them". The ancient Jain scriptural aphorism *Parasparopagraho Jivanan* (All life is bound together by mutual support and interdependence). It means that all aspects of nature belong together and are bound in a physical as well as a metaphysical relationship. Life is viewed as a gift of intimacy, accommodation and assistance in a universe crowded with interdependent constituents.[23]

iii) ***Jiva-karunya* (compassion, empathy and charity):** The word *Jiva-karunya* or *Jiva-daya* means caring for and sharing with all living beings, tending, protecting and serving. It entrails universal '*maitry*' (friendliness), universal '*kshama*' (forgiveness) and universal '*abhaya*' fearlessness. Jains, whether

[19] Nathmal Tatia, "The Jain Worldview and Ecology," *Jainism and Ecology: Nonviolence in the web of Life*, Edt.,Christoper Key Chapple (New Delhi: Motilal Banarsidass Publishers Pvt. Ltd., 2006), 6.

[20] Yajna- It is the ritual of sacrifice which gives the meaning to a prayer, praise or worship.

[21] "The Jain Teaching", http://www.jainworld.com/jainbooks/Books/Jaindecl.htm, 27/08/16.

[22] "What does Jainism teaches about ecology?" in http://www.arcworld.org/faiths.asp?pageID=7 accessed on 07-07-2017.

[23] "The Jain Teaching", http://www.jainworld.com/jainbooks/Books/Jaindecl.htm, 27/08/16.

monks, nuns or householders, therefore, affirm prayerfully and sincerely, that their heart is filled with forgiveness for all living beings and that they have sought and received the forgiveness of all beings, that they crave the friendship of all beings, that all beings give them their friendship and that there is not the slightest feeling of alienation or enmity in their heart for anyone or anything. They also pray that forgiveness and friendliness may reign throughout the world and that all living beings may cherish each other.[24]

iv) ***Samyaktva* (equanimity):** The discipline of non-violence, the recognition of universal interdependence and the logic of the doctrine of manifold aspects, leads inexorably to the avoidance of dogmatic, intolerant, inflexible, aggressive, harmful and unilateral attitudes towards the world around. It inspires the personal quest of every Jain for *samyaktva* (equanimity) towards both *jiva* (animate beings) and *ajiva* (inanimate substances and objects). It encourages an attitude of give and take and of live and let live. It offers a pragmatic peace plan based, not on the domination of nature, nations or other people, but on equanimity of mind devoted to the preservation of the balance of the universe.[25]

B) Eco-spirituality of Jain Tradition

i) Spirituality is essentially an individual endeavour. Individuals create collectively on the basis of discipline and practice. Every basic reality of the universe is integral. Jainism reconciled the parts of reality with the whole by means of the relativistic approach. Spiritual relationships, from an ecological perspective, can be understood with the help of some of the basic tenets of Jainism; 1) Injure no creatures; 2) Do not command any creature; 3) Do not own any creature; and 4) Do not employ one as the servant.

ii) Jain ecology is based on spirituality and equality. Each life form, plant, or animal, has an inherent worth and each must be respected. Within Jainism, the term for ecology might be *Sarvodayavada*, or the concern for lifting up all life forms, as articulated by Samantabhadra (third c. C.E.), the prominent Jain philosopher. Acarya Jinasena explained the same view of social equality by saying that the entire human world is one because of the interconnectedness of different aspects of the human community. Seeing other people as connected with oneself develops the spiritual perspective through which all life takes on sanctity that can and must be protected by observing the principles of ecology. The real task of religion consists in removing bitterness between people, between races, between religions,

[24] Jeffery D Long, *An Introduction to Jainism* (London/New York: I.B. TAURIS, 2010), 90.

[25] Jeffery D Long, *An Introduction to Jainism*..., 91-92.

and between nations. That nature of religion has been discussed in Jain scriptures in various ways in the form of Non-violence (*Ahimsa*).

iii) Jainism holds that the entire world, including plants, trees, birds, animals, water, and so forth, is possessed of life. It is our prime duty to protect all this. We are to treat others, as we want to be treated, and this refers not only to other people but also to the entirety of our planet. One is therefore expected to respect the land and its natural beauty. Jainism does so philosophically by accepting the principle of the interdependent existence of nature and *jivas*.

iv) Non-violence creates identity between self and self. Therefore Mahavira says, "Kill no creature", One has to experience personally the consequences of one's own Karmas. Through this unitized experience, the existence of souls is established. Mahavira goes on to say that one who is afflicted with lust is bereft of knowledge and perception. Truth will always baffle such a person. He indulges himself in action, causing violence to the beings of earth body, water body, fire body, vegetable body, and others. These beings have consciousness.

v) The vivid description is found in Jain scripture as to how plants and other beings can and should be saved by a Jain. These are very important principles laid down by Jainism to avoid harm to water, air, fire, and all forms of life and to minimize such evils as sound pollution, and thus to balance the community and ecosystem. To keep silence, to observe carefulness in speaking, to protect the forest and plants- these are religious rules that apply even to the Jain laity. Jain cosmology gives paramount importance to mountains, rivers, trees, and other natural resources. In its opinion, nonviolence should be observed strictly, at any cost to protect the ecological atmosphere.

vi) Nonviolence, the humanistic element is based on the principles of equality and equanimity as applied in society. Nonviolence still may allow for the theory of caste, but one based on one's own deeds and not on one's birth. Jainism tries to shape our attitude toward nature by prescribing humane and nonviolent approaches to everyday behaviour. Jainism inspired its followers to safeguard what in contemporary discourse would be called the ecological perspective. Jainas even today practice these principles and religious traditions prescribed for the protection of nature. Through its philosophy, its ascetic practices, and in its narrative arts and architecture, Jainism and its leaders have made efforts to create the society dedicated to love for all creatures. Jain Philosophy and Psychology.[26]

---

[26] Bhagchandra Jain Bhaskar, "Ecology and Sprituality in the Jain Tradition", *Jainism and Ecology: Nonviloence in the Web of Life,* edt. Christopher Key Chapple, vol. XXII (Delhi: Motilal Banarsidass Publishers, 2006), 170-178.

vii) The global ecological crisis cannot be solved until spiritual relationship is established between humanity as the whole and its natural environment. Jainism has been staunch protector of nature since inception of the Jain faith. The religion of nature, Jainism paves the way to understanding nature's utility and the essential nature of plants, worms, animals, and all sorts of creatures that have their own importance for maintaining ecological balance. Jainism therefore says that the function of souls is to help one another.

viii) This principle is connected to the whole of life. It includes humans and other creatures. The plant, animal, and human populations are merely part of the landscape. For Jainism, the landscape is itself lives and breathes and merits protection.

ix) Ecology sees the individual as interconnected with both nature and the fabric of society. Ecological theory considers the community the supra-organism, the complex social organism. Therefore, the Jain tradition instructs the Jain laity to keep the community very pure and pious. They are supposed not to indulge in obnoxious habits, which make life disastrous. A Jain should be a strict vegetarian. He should not indulge in professions related to violence, such as dealing in weapons. Jain laymen also practice the twelve types of *Vratas,*[27] which assist in eliminating corruption from society and in purifying ourselves in the process.[28]

Let me sum up the preceding discussion and evaluate the connectivity of both Buddhism and Jainism to environmental concerns. Buddhism and Jainism emerged as the most potent religious reform movements. Post-Vedic society was clearly divided by *varna dharma (*caste system) into *Brahmanas, Kshatriyas, Vaishyas,* and *Shudras.* Each *varna* was assigned well-defined functions. The Jains believed that Vardhamana Mahavira had twenty-three predecessors who were called *tirthankaras*. Jainism taught to not commit violence, not tell a lie, not steal, not hoard and observe continence. Mahavira organized an order of his followers in order to spread the teachings of Jainism. He preached his teachings in Prakrit. Gautama Buddha was a contemporary of Mahavira. He undertook long journeys and carried his message far and wide. He recommended an eightfold path (*ashtanga marga*) for the elimination of human misery. The rules and

[27] Vrata-The word Vrata (Vows) is derived from the verb word "Vru" meaning to select. Therefore, the Vrata means the type of the selection for renunciation. 'Vrata' is approximately translated by the English word 'vow'. Literally, a Vrata means a kind of choice. The twelve types of vrata are non-violence, truthfulness, non-stealing, celibacy, non-possessiveness, restraints of geographical limitations, consumption restraints, avoidance of purposeless activities, 48 minutes of meditation and equanimity, stricter geographical limitations, practicing the life of a monk, discipline of share and care. http://www.jainbelief.com/PPOJ/20.htm, 27/08/16.

[28] http://www.jainworld.com/jainbooks/asceticism/ch8.asp.

teachings of Buddha took full account of the new changes in the material life of the time and strengthened them ideologically. Buddhism created and developed a new awareness in the field of intellect and culture. There is a religious climate in Buddhism and Jainism to affirm the oneness of life on this planet. This calls forth a vision of human wholeness which includes not only our relationship with one another but with all *jivas* in the nature. The bio-cosmology of Jainism presents a world view that stresses the interrelatedness of life form. Both traditions include a strong emphasis on asceticism that might discourage some adherent from placing too much value on earthly concern, but as we have seen, both Buddhism and Jainism contain concept that can lead to the enhancement of core human earth relation. Both traditions upholds *ahimsa* and interrelatedness which inevitably creates an awareness of environmental concern. "Self-restraint" is the ideology of both religious traditions. An important principle is not to waste the gifts of nature, and even to reduce one's needs as far as possible. There is enough in this world for human needs, but not for human wants.

Chapter 7

Ecological Concerns in Sikhism

The word "Sikh" is derived from the Sanskrit term '*shishya*' meaning disciple. Sikhs are the disciples of their ten Gurus.[1] Sikh religious traditions are founded by the teachings of these ten gurus. Their perpetual "living" Guru, is the "Guru Granth Sahib". There are over 23 to 25 million Sikhs in the world today, the vast majority live in the north Indian state of Punjab. Sikhism or *Sikhi* is the latest religion of Indian origin during the life time of ten gurus and the fifth largest organised religion in the world. The aim of this chapter is not dealth with the detailed history of the origin and development of Sikhism as a distinctive religious tradition, but it's focus is to attempt "ecological concerns" of Sikh religious tradition. This chapter is, perhaps, a tentative endeavour to reconstruct the ecological wisdom, embedded in the Sikh tradition as a viable response to global living, in the context of environmental crisis, for if ecological crisis is defined as the alienation/estrangement of human life from Mother Nature, it is the responsibility of humans, to establish again, filial relationship with Her, which, in turn, will develop into a certain subjective, emotional attitude towards Nature. How and in what sense Sikhism, as a religion, may be considered eco-sophical? Whether the Sikh Scriptual tradition (Sri Guru Granth Sahib) has the potential to promote deep ecological consciousness? These are some of the inter-related queries that I have tried to expound in this chapter.

[1] 1) Guru Nanak (1469-1539)' 2) Guru Angad Dev (1504-1552), 3) Guru Amar Das (1479-1574), 4) Guru Ram Das (1534-1581), 5) Guru Arjan (1563-1606), 6) Guru Hargobind (1595-1644), 7) Guru Har Rai (1630-1661), 8) Guru Har Krishan (1656-1664), 9) Guru Tegh Bahadur (1621-1675) and Guru Gobind Singh (1666 -1708).

THE REASON FOR ECO-CRISIS

There is a sense of crisis in all parts of the world, in various countries and among various peoples. The demands of national economic growth and individual needs and desires are depleting the natural resources of the earth. There is serious concern that the earth may no longer be a sustainable bio-system. The major crises facing the earth—the social justice crisis and the environmental crisis—together are heading the earth toward a disastrous situation. The social justice crisis is caused by humanity's confrontation with itself and the environmental crisis is caused by humanity's confrontation with nature.[2]

The social justice crisis is that poverty, hunger, disease, exploitation, and injustice are widespread. There are economic wars over resources and markets. The rights of the poor and the marginal are violated. Women, constituting half the world's population, have their rights abused. The environmental crisis caused by humanity's exploitation of nature is leading to the depletion of renewable resources, destruction of forests, and overuse of land for agriculture and habitation. Today pollution is contaminating air, land, and water. Smoke from industries, homes, and vehicles is in the air. Industrial waste and consumer trash is affecting streams and rivers, ponds and lakes. Much of the waste is a product of modern technology; it is not biodegradable and not reusable, and its long-term consequences are unknown. The viability of many animal and plant species, and possibly that of the human species itself, is at stake.[3]

The Sikh scripture, Guru Granth Sahib, declares that the purpose of human beings is to achieve a blissful state and to be in harmony with the earth and all creation. It seems, however, that humans have drifted away from that ideal. The earth is today saturated with ecological problems. It is agonizing over the fate of its inhabitants and their future! It is in peril as never before. Its lakes and rivers are being choked, killing its marine life. Its forests are being denuded. A smoky haze envelops the cities of the world. Human beings are exploiting human beings. Human mind, by being self-conceited, loses communion with Nature, and ultimately with God. This causes him misery and it is the repeated assertion of Sikhism: The thief of self conceit (domination) is robbing the house (oikos) [..] now he finds no place to rest (Sri Guru Granth Sahib (SGGS): p. 752). By affirming the immanence of God and His presence in the Creation, the Sikh religion imparts the spirit of self-righteousness to the entire subject of Nature.[4]

---

[2] http://www.arcworld.org/faiths.asp?pageID=73 accessed on 14-07-17

[3] http://www.sikhiwiki.org/index.php/Sikhism_and_the_environment accessed on 13-07-17

[4] For details, S. Lourdunathan, "Ecosophical Concerns in the Sikh Tradition" a Faculty member of Arul Anandar College, India, presented as a paper at a conference Sikhism and Global Living, organized by Guru Nanak Devji Chair, School of Religions, Philosophy and Humanistic Thought, Madurai Kamaraj University, Madurai, April 1996. http://www.ecosikh.org/wp-content/uploads/2011/09/Ecosophical-Concerns-in-the-Sikh-Tradition.pdf accessed on 13-07-17

Solution to the Eco-crisis from Sikhism

This crisis cries out for an immediate and urgent solution. The crisis requires going back to the basic question of the purpose of human beings in this universe and an understanding of ourselves and God's creation. We are called to the vision of Guru Nanak which is a World Society comprising God- conscious human beings who have realized God. To these spiritual beings the earth and the universe are sacred; all life is unity, and their mission is the spiritualization of all. Guru Nanak in his philosophy states that the reality that humans create around themselves is a reflection of their inner state. The current instability of the natural system of the earth—the external environment of human beings—is only a reflection of the instability and pain within humans. The increasing barrenness of the earth's terrain is a reflection of the emptiness within humans. The gulf between the material and the spiritual is in the minds of humans only. It is a limitation of the human condition that spirit and matter appear as duality, and their unity is not self-evident.

CREATION OF GOD

The material universe is God's creation. Its origin was in God and its end is in God, and it operates within God's hukam. Guru Nanak declares that God alone knows the reasons for and the moment of earth's creation. The origin of the universe is unknowable. The act of creation itself, the creation of the primeval atom, was instantaneous, caused by the Will of God. The Sikh Guru reveals that real peace can only be found when desire and greed are subdued and diminished. This will only happen when the individual realises that God is found in all the elements including water, earth and the woods and he stops damaging these elements purely to satisfy his material greed (SGGS. P 617). Further descriptions of the universe and its creation in Sikh scripture are remarkably similar to recent scientific speculation about the universe and its origin. One of the basic hymns in the Sikh scripture, which may be called the Hymn of the Genesis, describes the indeterminate void before the existence of this universe. "There are planets, solar systems and galaxies. If one speaks of them, there is no limit, no end. There are worlds upon worlds of His Creation. As He commands, so they exist. He watches over all, and contemplating the creation, He rejoices. O Nanak, to describe this is as hard as steel!" (SGGS page 8). Guru Nanak speaks of innumerable galaxies, of a limitless universe, the boundaries of which are beyond human ability to comprehend. God alone knows the extent of creation.

God created the universe and the world, for reasons best known to Him. And being the results of God's actions all parts of the universe are holy. God is an all-pervasive being manifest through various elements of creation. Having created this universe and the world, God directs them. All actions take place within God's hukam. God alone knows how and why. God, however, not only directs this vast and massive theatre, but also watches over with care and kindness—the benign, supportive parent! This illustrates the following quotation from Guru Grandh Sahib:

> "Men, trees, pilgrimage places, banks of sacred streams, clouds, fields. Islands, spheres, universes, continents, solar systems. The sources of creation, egg-born, womb-born, earth-born, sweat-born, oceans, mountains and sentient beings. He, the Lord, knows their condition, O Nanak. Nanak, having created beings, the lord takes care of them all. The Creator who created the world, He takes thought of it as well. "(SGGS 466)

The world, like all creation, is a manifestation of God. Every creature in this world, every plant, every form is a manifestation of the Creator. Each is part of God and God is within each element of creation. God is the cause of all and He is the primary connection between all existence:

> "The Creator created himself ... And created all creation in which He is manifest. You Yourself the bumble-bee, flower, fruit and the tree. You Yourself the water, desert, ocean and the pond. You Yourself are the big fish, tortoise and the Cause of causes. Your form cannot be known." (SGGS 1016)[5]

In the world God has created he has also provided each species and humans with means of support and nurturing. In Sikh beliefs, a concern for the environment is part of an integrated approach to life and nature. As all creation has the same origin and end, humans must have consciousness of their place in creation and their relationship with the rest of creation. Humans should conduct themselves through life with love, compassion, and justice. Becoming one and being in harmony with God implies that humans endeavour to live in harmony with all of God's creation.

THE IDEA OF GOD: (ECO-SPIRITUALITY)

Apart from the transcendental idea of God, Sikhism lays emphasis on the immanent nature of God. God, for Sikhism, is a 'Living Truth', the Creator and the Sustainer of the Universe. He is ik-oan-kar, meaning that God manifests Himself as a determinate Infinity in the dimension of Time and History. He is the manifesting material Reality. He is conceived to be the Creator-Person (karta-purakhu), He is immanent in the cosmic form (moorati). The act of creation of God, for Sikhism, is a never-ending process, that He is the continuous life-giving principle. He creates, animates, sustains Nature. Nature is the dwelling place of God, and hence reverence to Nature is a must. SGGS reads: "He, the Creator, Himself creates the world....and watches all....He alone imparts understanding" (SGGS: p.767).

---

[5] Quoted in "Sikhism and Environment", http://www.sikhiwiki.org/index.php/Sikhism_and_the_environment accessed on 13-07-17

Where is this Creator-God?

The Lord, (it is said) is contained in spaces and inter-spaces. He cherishes all beings (SGGS: p.760). The Lord has made this world an arena of symphonic dance. Creating the entire creation He has placed in various forms and colours (SGGS: p.746). The Lord abides amongst all (SGGS: p.748). The devotee remains pleased with their Lord and sees Him, in water, land, nether regions and firmament (SGGS: p.748). God, who has created, sustains the creation; He gives sustenance to all....thine Benefactor (SGGS: p.751). There are innumerable texts that reflect the mind of Sikhism, that God is the source of cosmic formation, and He manifests in it, and hence, Nature is not a mere object that could be utilised to human ends - but it has intrinsic dignity and value.

Spiritual Discipline

Sikhs believe in practicing a highly disciplined life, while remaining active in the world, which leads to further spiritual progression. It is important that Sikhs retain the primacy of spirit over matter, while it is desirable that they do not deny matter or material existence. It is not required that humans renounce the world. They must maintain their life in the world and uphold all responsibilities in the world. Humans should be renouncers of plenty and maintain a simple life. Further spiritual progress fundamentally starts with an individual conquering himself/herself with the guidance of the Guru. The emphasis is on mastery over the self and the discovery of the self, not mastery over nature, external forms, and beings. Sikhism teaches against a life of conspicuous, wasteful consumption. The Guru recommends a judicious utilization of material and cultural resources available to humans. The Gurus taught humans to be aware of and respect the dignity in all life, whether human or not. Such a respect for life can only be fostered where one can first recognize the Divine spark within oneself, see it in others, cherish it, nurture and fulfil it.

Humans have the capability to further their spiritual progression through conscious choice and it is important to identify the method by which they might do so. The method suggested by Guru Nanak is one of spiritual discipline, meditation and prayer, and sharing. Sikhism emphasizes mastering five negative forces: Lust, Anger, Worldly or Materialistic Attachment, Conceit, and Greed. These together constitute what Sikhs term Haumai—"I am-ness." Mastering Haumai is achieved by developing five positive forces: Compassion, Humility, Contemplation, Contentment, and Service (seva) without expecting any material or spiritual reward. The guiding principles are Love and Forgiveness. Every decision in life has to be based on rationality and a personal code of ethics. Guru Nanak's philosophy of values inspires the individual to transcend his/her existence through this spiritual discipline. Sikh religion preaches strong family involvement.

A person pursuing this spiritual discipline must also work to create an atmosphere for other members of the family to progress spiritually.

THE IDEA OF WORLD

In contrast to philosophies that encourage world denial, Sikh tradition affirms the reality/authenticity of the world/body. Body, is the mediation to the attainment of the Lord. The earth and the "here and now" is the space for liberation of life: engrossing into duality leads to forgetfulness of the dwelling God (SGGS: p.757). In the body are the invaluable wealth and the brimful treasures of Lord's mediation[..] Within the body abide all, the continents, the worlds and the nether regions. In the body dwells the Beneficent Lord, the life of the world Who cherishes all. Ever illustrates is the body-bride....meditates on the Name (SGGS: p.754).

Body symbolically stands for earth in Sikhism. Nature, Cosmos, through her (bridegroom) attainment of the Lord (peace) is possible. In the eco-sophical language, the Sikh religion with its affirmation of the earth as Divine, calls for continuous consciousness of its harmony and unity. The earth cannot be consumed for selfish purposes, but conserved - on the basis of need and not greed.

THE EARTH AS DHARAMSAL

Amidst (creation) He fixed the earth, a place for righteous action" (Japuji: SGGS-7). According to the SIkh belief the world is Holy, and one's relation to it must also be holy. The whole world is Holy. Be you in its purity absorbed. By discarding of egoism does one find acceptance at God's portal (SGGS: p.142). By this portrayal of the world (earth) as a place for righteousness and purity, Guru Nanak insists that we relate with others with equality and justice. And that there is a possibility of a future for the history of Nature, for it has a spiritual meaning. The monistic denial of the "reality" of the world, for the Sikh religious mind, is inadequate and un-Godly.

An intense desire to do good

The true end of human beings is in their emergence as God-conscious beings, who remain aware of the earth and operate in the mundane material world, with the object of transforming and spiritualizing it into a higher plane of existence. In this spiritual state individuals are motivated by an intense desire to do good, transforming their surroundings. Through a life based on the method prescribed by the Gurus humans may achieve a higher spiritual state. Such truly emancipated, valiant, and enlightened spirits (*jivan-mukta, brahma-jnani*) become the true benefactors of humanity and the world around them. Such an individual would not exploit another human or sentient being, as each is a manifestation of the eternal and the supreme. In this God-conscious state they see God in all and everything. "I perceive Thy form in all life and light; I perceive Thy power in all spheres and sight." (SGGS. 464)

Spiritualization is liberation from material compulsions and attractions. It means an awareness of the Cosmic Order and striving toward the execution of divine will. So, the spiritualized human is creative and constructive. Therefore, a Sikh life is a life of harmony with environment, other individuals, other beings, and other forms. For an enlightened individual the world has only one purpose: to practice spirituality – that does not limit to worship divine or meditate the scripture, but also "eco-spirituality" – that maintain harmonious and sustainable relations with nature and environment. That is the ultimate objective of all humans. Such a person is involved in human problems and society and has to prove his or her effectiveness there. Such a person lives with a mission—and works for the emancipation of all. A true Sikh is for individual human rights, the environment, and justice for all. "The God-conscious person is animated with an intense desire to do good in this world." (SGGS. 273)

THE SIKH-PROTEST AGAINST INJUSTICE

The history of Sikhism is a history of 'class struggle' that fought against all forms of political imperialism, economic exploitation and caste inequality, and religious hypocrisy: If the mighty molest the mighty no feeling of protest rises in my mind; But should a ferocious tiger (the greedy caste-men) attack the feeble herd (Nature, women and the downtrodden), I would question even my Lord (Guru Nanak). For bhagat Kabir, "I can't keep on meditating on a hungry stomach, here, have Thy rosary back, my Lord." Protesting the theory and practice of pollution (untouchability) - (environmental pollution refers to water, air, etc. But ecological pollution refers to all forms of discrimination) Guru Nanak says: Caste is hollow, fame is hollow and the One Saviour protects all.

Guru Nanak advises the caste ridden Indian mind not to practice it, and for him the one who is proud of his caste and practices it, causes pollution of the other. The question he raised, 'Is the Brahmin really born of Brahma?. For the Sikh Guru, the source of pollution is primarily in the mind of man (haumai) which is self-centred. Removal of the self-centeredness of the technocratic humanity would contribute to peace and justice. It is but the liberation of life in its totality, from false consciousness and unequal social structures. *Sangat*, the basic Sikh community, may be viewed as the basic eco-sophical community that intensively reflect and live a life of harmony with nature. It is a community of equals. *Khalsa*, is the congregation, whose members when initiated into the Order, are baptised by water, symbolic to reveal that the mystery of parthenogenetic creation of the first human society in the world history, organised with the deliberate object of and pledged to - bring about an ecumenical (eco-sophical) human society. (Phenomenology of Sikhism, p.77).

The idea of Guru or Gurmukh, implies that the Guru (liberated one) is a realized person of the fundamental unity of God with the creation, man with other creations. He strives to foster ecological harmony, by being cosmic-God conscious. He is a true *yogin*, who treats all the creation equally, and hence asceticism is discouraged in Sikhism, because detachment from everyday life is a form of escapism, or denial of earth/world, that amounts to the denial of God, the Creator person, who abides in life. His dedication to God, is his devotion to the well being of all life.

Practicing the Philosophy

Integrated approach: Care of the environment without social justice is not possible as per belief of devoted Sikhs. Environmental concerns may be viewed as part of the broader issue of human development and social justice. Many environmental problems, particularly the exploitation of environmental resources in developing nations, are due to the poverty of large parts of the population. Therefore, an integrated approach is necessary. Sikhism opposes the idea that the struggle of the human race is against nature and that human supremacy lies in the notion of "harnessing" nature. The objective is harmony with the eternal—God—which implies a life of harmony with all existence. Striving for a life of harmony, therefore, also implies a life of supporting individual rights and environmentalism—a life that works against injustice toward anybody and anything.[6]

The tenth Guru in 1699 founded the Order of the *Khalsa*, whose members practice the spiritual discipline of Sikhism and are committed to ensure the preservation and prevalence of a World Society. Over the last three centuries the members of the *Khalsa* order have stood up for the rights of the oppressed and the disenfranchised even at the cost of their own lives. The *Khalsa* vision of the World Society is: "Henceforth such is the Will of God: No man shall coerce another; No person shall exploit another. Each individual has the inalienable birthright to seek and pursue happiness and self-fulfilment. Love and persuasion is the only law of social coherence" (SGGS. 74). The *Khalsa* has opposed any force that has threatened the freedom and dignity of human beings. For the *Khalsa*, justice requires the participation and inclusion of all in obtaining and enjoying the fruits of God's creation. Justice achieved through cooperative effort is desirable. The ideal for the *Khalsa* is to strive for justice for all, not merely for themselves. The relationship between human beings and the earth is increasingly complicated and urgent. Every day there are stories about pollution, global warming and animal species facing extinction. Religion is responding with views on the environment and our responsibility for it.

---

[6] http://www.sikhiwiki.org/index.php/Sikhism_and_the_environment accessed on 17-07-17

Sikh belief about the Environment

Although, human beings are seen as the most intelligent life form on earth, they are responsible for almost all the damage done to the planet. If we imagined the earth is aged 46, all the damage done has taken place in the last 60 seconds of the earth's life. Sikhism is very much concerned with the relationship between humanity and the environment. They believe that *Waheguru* created the world as a place where every type of plant and animal could live so that all life could have the chance to prove that it was good enough to reach *mukti* (liberation from the cycle of birth and death, reincarnation).

Guru Nanak taught, "Nature we see Nature we hear Nature we observe with awe, wonder and joy Nature in the nether regions Nature in the skies Nature in the whole creation...Nature in species, kinds, colours Nature in life forms Nature in good deeds Nature in pride and in ego Nature in air, water and fire Nature in the soil of the earth All nature is yours, O powerful Creator You command it, observe it and pervade within it" (SGGS). The lives of the Gurus are full of stories of their love for nature. Sikhs are forbidden to kill for the sake of killing or to eat to excess. In Sikh hymns *Waheguru* is said to be the provider of all life. There is no difference between the world of humans and the world of nature. Both of these are equally important and must be treated with respect. The Gurus have strongly made us aware of our responsibility towards this earth. Sikhs believe that the environment can only be preserved if the balance created by *Waheguru* is maintained.

The Assisi Declarations on Nature, 1986

In 1986, HRH Prince Philip, then President of the WWF International invited five leaders of five of the major religions of the world - Buddhism Christianity, Hinduism, Islam and Judaism - to meet to discuss how their faiths could help save the natural world. The meeting took place in Assisi in Italy, because it was the birth place of St Francis, the Catholic saint of ecology. From this meeting arose key statements by the five faiths outlining their own distinctive traditions and approach to the care for nature. In the Assisi Declarations on Nature the Sikh statement was:[7]

- Since the beginning of the Sikh religion in the late fifteenth century, the faith has been built upon the message of the 'oneness of Creation'. Sikhism believes an almighty God created the universe. He himself is the creator and master of all forms of the universe, responsible for all modes of nature and all elements of the world. Sikhism firmly believes God to be the source of the birth, life and death of all things.

---

[7] "Sikhism: beliefs about care of the planet" http://www.bbc.co.uk/schools/gcsebitesize/rs/environment/sikhstewardshiprev2.shtml accessed on 14-07-2017.

- Sikhism teaches that the natural environment and the survival of all life forms are closely linked in the rhythm of nature. The history of the Gurus is full of stories of their love and special relationship with the natural environment-, with animals, birds, vegetation, earth, rivers, mountains and the sky. There is also a very strong vegetation tradition.
- It is for this reason that in Sikhism those who kill for lust of hunting, eating or to make sacrifices are condemned. In Sikh hymns God is often referred to as the provider for all life which God loves and is loved by. God as both father and mother guarantees equality to man and woman in faith and compassion towards all beings and nature.

Sharing of Resources

Traditional modes of farming and traditional modes of life in northern India have been dependent upon limited resources. As there exist circumstances where large numbers of people depend upon relatively scarce resources, the traditional lifestyle ensures use of the least resources, considerable reuse, and recycling. In a culture based on organic materials, recycling is an intrinsic and natural part of the resource cycle. There are strong traditions of sharing. There have been traditional practices that maintained lands and forests as community property within proximity of human habitation. For instance, in traditional rural India and Punjab, two of the most important centers of human activity have been the Sikh Gurudwara and a source of water—pond, tank, pool, or running water. Both of these sites were surrounded by community land, not owned by anyone and not used for agriculture. This was where there were trees and plants, such as groves or small forests. They provided shade and shelter, and were a source of firewood within easy reach of habitation.

The Gurus established towns and cities, each created around a religious center. The focus was on a lifestyle based on sharing: a lifestyle that promoted equity among people, and optimum utilization of resources. Even today, rural Punjab families share resources with their neighbours. This is particularly evident on large family occasions such as weddings, when the entire village may play host to guests and share living space, beds, and so on. Most Gurudwaras in India were specifically designed to have a water tank, or were near running water (rivers or pools), which were always considered a community resource. For instance, Amritsar grew up around the Harimandir (ordinarily referred to as the Golden Temple) and the Amrit Sarovar (the pool of nectar, that is, the water). The cities and towns that grew around Gurudwaras were ideally centered on a spiritual lifestyle based on sharing.

Since the time of the Gurus, Sikh Gurudwaras have included institutionalized practices that emphasize sharing of resources. Gurudwaras, in addition to being places where people congregate for prayer and meditation, are a place to stay for travellers and others; a community kitchen (Langar); a place for dispensing medication and medical care; and a place to impart education to the young. Gurudwaras have always been places of shelter for travellers and visitors, and most major Gurudwaras have rooms where visitors may stay. In addition Sikh Gurudwaras stock extra beds, sheets, pots and pans, etc. At weddings and other family events, the Gurudwaras are a source for borrowing these items. There has always been great emphasis on avoiding waste. Traditionally, the community kitchen served food on plates made from leaves and cups made from clay. Today they tend to use steel plates and utensils that are reused. The kitchens have always been stocked by ordinary people—farmers, traders, others in the community—on a voluntary basis. It is the belief of Sikh community that all these practices help to foster a healthy environment.

The ideal for Sikhism is a society based upon mutual respect and cooperation and providing an optimal atmosphere for individuals to grow spiritually. Sikhism regards a cooperative society as the only truly religious society, as the Sikh view of life and society is grounded in the worth of every individual as a microcosm of God. Therefore, an individual must never be imposed upon, coerced, manipulated, or engineered: "If thou wouldst seek God, demolish and distort not the heart of any individual" (SGGS. 1384). All life is interconnected. A human body consists of many parts; every one of them has a distinct name, location, and function; and all of them are dependent upon each other. In the same way, all the constituents of this universe and this earth are dependent upon each other. Decisions in one country or continent cannot be ignored by others. Choices in one place have measurable consequences for the rest of the world. It is part of the same system. Life, for its very existence and nurturing, depends upon a bounteous nature. A human being needs to derive sustenance from the earth and not deplete, exhaust, pollute, burn, or destroy it. Sikhs believe that an awareness of that sacred relationship between humans and the environment is necessary for the healthy planet – the mother earth, and for our survival. A new "environmental ethic" dedicated to conservation and wise use of the resources provided by a bountiful nature can only arise from an honest understanding and dedicated application of our old, tried and true spiritual heritage.

Chapter 8

Christian Attitude towards Environment

The issues like "eco-concern" and "environmental protection" have been special focus of our contemporary world. Christian views on environmentalism vary among different Christians of various denominations. Major Christian denominations endorse the Biblical view of our stewardship of God's Creation and our responsibility for its care. Some of this church policy is relatively recent and may not be followed by some parishioners. Many Christians, however, are environmental activists and promote awareness and action plans at the church, community, and national levels. Green Christianity is a broad field that encompasses Christian theological reflection on environment. Christian liturgical and spiritual practices centered on environmental issues, as well as Christian-based activism in the environmental movement. Within the activism arena, green Christianity refers to a diverse group of Christians who emphasize the biblical or theological basis for protecting and celebrating the environment. The term indicates not a particular denomination, but a shared territory of concern.

Christians, indeed, have special concern on this contemporary issue and they are searching for resources from the Bible and Christian ecclesiological traditions to reflect relevantly on present eco-crisis and actively involved in bringing awareness on eco-concern and environmental protection. Christian attitude towards environment is distinctively unique in it's world view, theological response and plan of activities. This chapter is an attempt to find out Christian attitude towards environment searching resources from Biblical attitude in protecting environment; Christian perspective on environment; Christian theological world view of eco-concern and Christian theological response to eco-crisis.

1) Biblical Attitude on Environmenal Protection

Caring for the world around you is an important aspect of Biblical faith. The Bible is very clear on the conservation/preservation of the environment since it is the creation of God the creator, hence he is the only owner of this whole universe. Human beings are not rulers in the strict sense to misuse or abuse the sources of God's creation, but only stewards to take care of ecological sources and protect the environment from any kind of degradation. The following Bible verses[1] strongly support this view providing right sources for eco-spirituality of Christian community:

Caring for the Environment:

God entrusted the whole creation to the careful stewardship of human beings. Most Christian teens can easily bring up Genesis first chapter when discussing Bible verses about the environment and protecting it. Yet, there are so many other scripture verses that remind us that God not only created the Earth, but also calls on us to protect it. The Bible verses declare that God created the earth, indeed, every creature and everything is part of Gods creation. The Bible reveals that God not only created the Earth, but also uses it to teach lessons to human beings. The Bible shows that God asks human beings to take care of His creation. Let us examine some important Biblical verses related to environmental concerns.

The Book of Genesis: God's creation is good, he created everything with goodness Genesis 1:1-31".

- "In the beginning, God created the heavens and the earth. The earth was without form and void, and darkness was over the face of the deep. And the Spirit of God was hovering over the face of the waters. And God said, "Let there be light," and there was light. And God saw that the light was good. And God separated the light from the darkness. God called the light Day, and the darkness he called Night. And there was evening and there was morning, the first day (Genesis 1:1-5).
- "Then God said, "Let us make man in our image, after our likeness. And let them have dominion over the fish of the sea and over the birds of the heavens and over the livestock and over all the earth and over every creeping thing that creeps on the earth." So, God created man in his own image, in the image of God he created him; male and female he created them. And God blessed them. And God said to them, "Be fruitful and multiply and fill the earth and subdue it and have dominion

[1] Kelli Mahoney, "Caring for the World Around You is an Important Part of Your Faith" in *Bible Verses About Protecting the World,* https://www.thoughtco.com/bible-verses-about-protecting-the-environment-712753 accessed on 17-07-17.

over the fish of the sea and over the birds of the heavens and over every living thing that moves on the earth." (1:26-28)

- God saw everything that he had made, and indeed, it was very good. And there was evening and there was morning, the sixth day" (Genesis 1:31).
- "The LORD God took the man and put him in the Garden of Eden to till it and keep it" (Genesis 2:15).
- The main reason for ecological degradation on this earth globe is recorded in first book of the Bible:

> And to Adam he said, "Because you have listened to the voice of your wife and have eaten of the tree of which I commanded you, 'You shall not eat of it,' cursed is the ground because of you; in pain you shall eat of it all the days of your life (Genesis 3:17).

- "The Lord saw that the wickedness of humankind was great in the earth, and that every inclination of the thoughts of their hearts was only evil continually. And the Lord was sorry that He had made humankind on the earth and it grieved Him to His heart. So the Lord said, 'I will blot out from earth the human beings I have created – people together with animals and creeping things and birds of the air, for I am sorry that I have made them. But Noah found favour in the sight of the Lord" (Genesis 6:5-8).
- And God blessed Noah and his sons and said to them, "Be fruitful and multiply and fill the earth. The fear of you and the dread of you shall be upon every beast of the earth and upon every bird of the heavens, upon everything that creeps on the ground and all the fish of the sea. Into your hand they are delivered (Genesis 9:1-2).
- Then God said to Noah and to his sons with him, "Behold, I establish my covenant with you and your offspring after you, and with every living creature that is with you, the birds, the livestock, and every beast of the earth with you, as many as came out of the ark; it is for every beast of the earth. I establish my covenant with you, that never again shall all flesh be cut off by the waters of the flood, and never again shall there be a flood to destroy the earth." (Genesis 9:8-11)

The Book of Exodus

- "Now therefore, if you obey my voice and keep my covenant, you shall be my treasured possession out of all the peoples, indeed, the whole earth is mine, but you shall be for me a priestly kingdom and a holy nation. These are the words that you shall speak to the Israelites" (Exodus 19-5-6).

- "When you come upon your enemy's ox or donkey going astray you shall bring it back. When you see the donkey of one who hates you lying under its burden and you would hold back from setting it free, you must help to set it free" (Exodus 23: 4-5).
- "For six years you shall sow your land and gather in its yield, but the seventh year you shall let it rest and lie fallow, that the poor of your people may eat; and what they leave the beasts of the field may eat. You shall do likewise with your vineyard, and with your olive orchard (Exodus 23:10-11).

The Book of Leviticus:

- "When you reap the harvest of your land, you shall not reap your field right up to its edge, neither shall you gather the gleanings after your harvest. And you shall not strip your vineyard bare, neither shall you gather the fallen grapes of your vineyard. You shall leave them for the poor and for the sojourner: I am the LORD your God" (Leviticus 19:9-10).
- The LORD spoke to Moses on Mount Sinai, saying, "Speak to the people of Israel and say to them, When you come into the land that I give you, the land shall keep a Sabbath to the LORD. For six years you shall sow your field, and for six years you shall prune your vineyard and gather in its fruits, but in the seventh year there shall be a Sabbath of solemn rest for the land, a Sabbath to the LORD. You shall not sow your field or prune your vineyard. You shall not reap what grows of itself in your harvest, or gather the grapes of your undressed vine. It shall be a year of solemn rest for the land (Leviticus 25:1-5).
- "The land shall not be sold in perpetuity, for the land is mine. For you are strangers and sojourners with me. Throughout the country that you hold as a possession, you must provide for the redemption of the land" (Leviticus 25:23-24).

The Book of Numbers:

- "You shall not pollute the land in which you live, for blood pollutes the land, and no atonement can be made for the land for the blood that is shed in it, except by the blood of the one who shed it. You shall not defile the land in which you live, in the midst of which I dwell, for I the LORD dwell in the midst of the people of Israel. (Numbers 35:33-34)"

The Book of Deuteronomy:

- "Behold, to the LORD your God belong heaven and the heaven of heavens, the earth with all that is in it" (Deuteronomy 10:14).

- "A land that the LORD your God cares for. The eyes of the LORD your God are always upon it, from the beginning of the year to the end of the year" (Deuteronomy 11:12).
- "When you besiege a city for a long time, making war against it in order to take it, you shall not destroy its trees by wielding an axe against them. You may eat from them, but you shall not cut them down. Are the trees in the field human, that they should be besieged by you?" (Deuteronomy 20:19)
- "If you come across a bird's nest in any tree or on the ground, with young ones or eggs and the mother sitting on the young or on the eggs, you shall not take the mother with the young. You shall let the mother go, but the young you may take for yourself, that it may go well with you, and that you may live long. (Deuteronomy 22:6-7)

The Book of I Chronicles:

- Then shall the trees of the forest sing for joy before the LORD, for he comes to judge the earth (I Chronicles:16: 33).

The Book of Nehemiah:

- "You alone are the LORD. You made the heavens, even the highest heavens, and all their starry host, the earth and all that is on it, the seas and all that is in them. You give life to everything, and the multitudes of heaven worship you" (Nehemiah (**9:6**).

The Book of Job:

- "But ask the beasts, and they will teach you; the birds of the heavens, and they will tell you; or the bushes of the earth, and they will teach you; and the fish of the sea will declare to you. Who among all these does not know that the hand of the LORD has done this? In his hand is the life of every living thing and the breath of all mankind (Job 12:7-10).
- "Listen to this, Job; stop and consider God's wonders. Do you know how God controls the clouds and makes his lightning flash? Do you know how the clouds hang poised, those wonders of him who is perfect in knowledge? You who swelter in your clothes when the land lies hushed under the south wind; can you join him in spreading out the skies, hard as a mirror of cast bronze?" (Job 37:14-18)

The Book of Psalms:

- "LORD, our Lord, how majestic is your name in all the earth! You have set your glory above the heavens. Out of the mouth of babies and infants, you have established strength because of your foes, to still the enemy and the avenger. When I look at your heavens, the work of your fingers, the moon and the stars, which you have set in place, what is man that you are mindful of him, and the son of man that you care for him? Yet you have made him a little lower than the heavenly beings and crowned him with glory and honour. You have given him dominion over the works of your hands; you have put all things under his feet, all sheep and oxen, and also the beasts of the field, the birds of the heavens, and the fish of the sea, whatever passes along the paths of the seas. O Lord our Sovereign, how majestic is your name in all the earth!" (Psalm 8:1-9).

- "The heavens declare the glory of God, and the sky above proclaims his handiwork. Day to day pours out speech, and night to night reveals knowledge. There is no speech, nor are there words, whose voice is not heard. Their voice goes out through all the earth, and their words to the end of the world. In them he has set a tent for the sun" (Psalm 19"1-4).
- "The earth is the LORD's and the fullness thereof, the world and those who dwell therein, for he has founded it upon the seas and established it upon the rivers (Psalm 24:1-2).
- "I will not accept a bull from your house; or goats from your folds. For every wild animal of the forest is mine, the cattle on a thousand hills. I know all the birds of the air; and all that moves in the field is mine" (Psalm 50:9-11).
- "You visit the earth and water it, you greatly enrich it; the river of God is full of water, you provide the people with grain, for so you have prepared it. You water its furrows abundantly, settling its ridges, softening it with showers, and blessing its growth...the meadows clothe themselves with flocks, the valleys deck themselves with grain they shout and sing together for joy" (Psalm 65:9-13).
- Let heaven and earth praise him, the seas and everything that moves in them (Psalm 69:34).
- The heavens are yours; the earth also is yours; the world and all that is in it, you have founded them (Psalm 89:11).
- The sea is his, for he made it, and his hands formed the dry land (Psalm 95:5).
- "Say among the nations, "The LORD reigns." The world is firmly established, it cannot be moved; he will judge the peoples with equity. Let the heavens rejoice, let the earth be glad; let the sea resound, and all that is in it; let the fields be jubilant, and everything in them. Then all the trees of the forest will sing for joy; they will sing before the LORD, for he comes, he comes to judge the earth. He will judge the world in righteousness and the peoples in his truth" (Psalm (96:10-13).

- Bless the LORD, O my soul! O LORD my God, you are very great! You are clothed with honour and majesty, covering yourself with light as with a garment, stretching out the heavens like a tent. He lays the beams of his chambers on the waters; he makes the clouds his chariot; he rides on the wings of the wind; he makes his messengers winds, his ministers a flaming fire. He set the earth on its foundations, so that it should never be moved. (Psalm 104:1-5)
- There is the sea, vast and spacious, teeming with creatures beyond number— living things both large and small. There the ships go to and fro, and the leviathan, which you formed to frolic there. These all look to you to give them their food at the proper time. When you give it to them, they gather it up; when you open your hand, they are satisfied with good things. When you hide your face, they are terrified; when you take away their breath, they die and return to the dust. When you send your Spirit, they are created, and you renew the face of the earth (Psalm 104:25-30).
- Let sinners be consumed from the earth and let the wicked be no more. Bless the Lord, O my sol. Praise the Lord!" (Psalm 104:35)
- "The heavens are the Lord's heavens but the earth he has viven to human beings" (Psalm 115:16)

The Book of Proverbs:

- Whoever is righteous has regard for the life of his beast, but the mercy of the wicked is cruel (Proverbs 12:10).

The Book of Isaiah:

- "They will neither harm nor destroy on all my holy mountain, for the earth will be full of the knowledge of the LORD as the waters cover the sea" (Isaiah 11:9).
- Behold, the LORD will empty the earth and make it desolate, and he will twist its surface and scatter its inhabitants. And it shall be, as with the people, so with the priest; as with the slave, so with his master; as with the maid, so with her mistress; as with the buyer, so with the seller; as with the lender, so with the borrower; as with the creditor, so with the debtor. The earth shall be utterly empty and utterly plundered; for the LORD has spoken this word. The earth mourns and withers; the world languishes and withers; the highest people of the earth languish. The earth lies defiled under its inhabitants; for they have transgressed the laws, violated the statutes, broken the everlasting covenant. Therefore a curse devours the earth, and its inhabitants suffer for their guilt, therefore the inhabitants of the earth dwindled, and few people are left (Isaiah 24:1-6).

- "Terror, and the pit, and the snare are upon you, O inhabitant of the earth! Whoever flees at the sound of the terror shall fall into the pit, and whoever climbs out of the pit shall be caught in the snare. For the windows of heaven are opened, and foundations of the earth tremble. The earth is utterly broken, the earth is torn asunder, the earth is violently shaken. The earth staggers like a drunkard, it sways like a hut, its transgression lies heavy upon it, and it falls and will not rise again. (Isaiah 24-17-20)
- "The wild animals honour me, the jackals and the owls, because I provide water in the desert and streams in the wasteland, to give drink to my people, my chosen, the people I formed for myself that they may proclaim my praise" (Isaiah 43:20-21).
- Lift up your eyes to the heavens, and look at the earth beneath; for the heavens vanish like smoke, the earth will wear out like a garment, and they who dwell in it will die in like manner; but my salvation will be forever, and my righteousness will never be dismayed (Isaiah 51:6).
- "For behold, I create new heavens and a new earth, and the former things shall not be remembered or come into mind (Isaiah 65:17).

The Book of Jeremiah:

- And I brought you into a plentiful land to enjoy its fruits and its good things. But when you came in, you defiled my land and made my heritage an abomination (Jeremiah 2:7).
- How long will the land mourn and the grass of every field wither? For the evil of those who dwell in it the beasts and the birds are swept away, because they said, "He will not see our latter end" (Jeremiah 12:4).

The Book of Ezekiel:

- "Son of man, prophesy against the shepherds of Israel; prophesy and say to them: 'This is what the Sovereign LORD says: Woe to the shepherds of Israel who only take care of themselves! Should not shepherds take care of the flock? You eat the curds, clothe yourselves with the wool and slaughter the choice animals, but you do not take care of the flock. You have not strengthened the weak or healed the sick or bound up the injured. You have not brought back the strays or searched for the lost. You have ruled them harshly and brutally" (Ezekiel 34:2-4).
- "Is it not enough for you to feed on the good pasture, that you must tread down with your feet the rest of your pasture; and to drink of clear water, that you must muddy the rest of the water with your feet?" (Ezekiel 34:18).

The Gospel According to Mathew:

- "Look at the birds of the air: they neither sow nor reap nor gather into barns, and yet your heavenly Father feeds them. Are you not of more value than they?" (Mathew 6:26).

The Gospel According to Luke:

- "Consider the ravens: they neither sow nor reap, they have neither storehouse not barn, and yet God feeds them. Of how much more value are you that the birds! And can any of you by worrying add a single hour to your span of life? If then your are not able to do so small a thing as that why do you worry about the rest? Consider the lilies, how they grow: they neither toil nor spin, yet I tell you, even Solomon in all his glory was not clothed like one of these. But if God so clothes the grass of the field, which is alive today and tomorrow is thrown into the oven, how much more will he clote you-you of little faith" (Luke 12:24-28).

The Gospel According to John:

"Through him all things were made; without him nothing was made that has been made" (John 1:3).

The Epistle Paul to Romans:

- "Since what may be known about God is plain to them, because God has made it plain to them. For since the creation of the world God's invisible qualities—his eternal power and divine nature—have been clearly seen, being understood from what has been made, so that men are without excuse" (Romans 1:19-20).
- "For we know that the whole creation has been groaning together in the pains of childbirth until now" (Romans 8:22).

The Epistle of Paul to Colossians:

- "He is the image of the invisible God, the firstborn of all creation. For by him all things were created, in heaven and on earth, visible and invisible, whether thrones or dominions or rulers or authorities—all things were created through him and for him. He is before all things, and in him all things hold together" (Colossians 1:15-17).

The First Epistle of Paul to Timothy

- "For everything created by God is good, and nothing is to be rejected if it is received with thanksgiving' (I Timothy 4:4).

The Book of Revelation:

- "Worthy are you, our Lord and God, to receive glory and honor and power, for you created all things, and by your will they existed and were created" (Revelation 4:11).
- "The nations raged, but your wrath came, and the time for the dead to be judged, and for rewarding your servants, the prophets and saints, and those who fear your name, both small and great, and for destroying the destroyers of the earth" (Revelation 11:18).
- "Then I saw a new heaven and a new earth, for the first heaven and the first earth had passed away, and the sea was no more" (Revelation 21:1).
- "Then the angel showed me the river of the water of life, bright as crystal, flowing from the throne of God and of the Lamb through the middle of the street of the city; also, on either side of the river, the tree of life with its twelve kinds of fruit, yielding its fruit each month. The leaves of the tree were for the healing of the nations" (Revelation 22:1-2).

These and many other textual references of the Bible are very clearly emphasize the Biblical attitude towards special attention and care for the creation of God and environment around us.

2) Christian Perspective on Environment

Life expectancy in advanced economies has risen from about thirty years to nearly eighty in the 18th to 20th centuries. Cures have been found to once-fatal diseases, and some diseases have been eliminated entirely. Famine, which once occurred, on average, seven times per century in Western Europe and lasted a cumulative ten years per century, is now unheard of there. While the average Western European family in A.D. 1700 lived in a hovel with little or no furniture, no change of clothing, and barely enough food to sustain a few hours' agricultural labour per day[2] and, of course, they also lacked electricity, plumbing, water and sewage treatment, and all the appliances we often take for granted, but today the average family lives in a well-built home with all those amenities, along with enough food to make obesity, not hunger, the most common nutritional problem even among the "poor."[3] Such advances in the West have been the fruits of freedom, knowledge, and hard work–all resting substantially on the foundation of biblical

---

[2] Robert William Fogel, "The Contribution of Improved Nutrition to the Decline in Mortality Rates in Europe and America," in *The State of Humanity*, ed. Julian L. Simon (New York: Blackwell, 1995), 61-71.

[3] E. Calvin Beisner, "Sixpence None the Richer: Economics–A Millennium of Human Progress," *World* 14 (July 31, 1999): 20-25. For voluminous statistics and able discussions on these and dozens of other elements of material progress, see Julian L. Simon, ed., *The State of Humanity* (New York: Blackwell, 1995).

Christianity's worldview and ethic of service to God and neighbour.[4] These advances have also given rise to a laudable expansion in people's focus on the need for environmental stewardship. For as people come to feel more secure about their basic needs, they begin to allocate more of their scarce time, energy, and resources to attaining formerly less urgent ends. Consequently, the movement for environmental protection has grown as Western wealth has grown, giving rise to a strong environmental consciousness and to protective environmental legislation.[5]

The world's less developed countries, where material progress began much later, have been catching up in 20th century, as shown especially by rapidly rising life expectancy (from about 30 years in 1900 to about 63 years today).[6] Nonetheless, in many developing countries, the basics of sufficient and pure water and food, along with clothing, shelter, transportation, health care, communication, and so forth, still remain elusive for many people. For them, continued economic advance is crucial for health and even for life itself: It is small wonder that their attention focuses more on immediate consumption needs than on environmental protection. Tragically, however, people with a strong environmental consciousness who live predominantly in Western countries sometimes seek to impose their own environmental sensibilities on people still struggling to survive. In fact, further advances in human welfare for the poor are now often threatened by a belief in the West that human enterprise and development are fundamentally incompatible with environmental protection, which is seen by some as the quintessential value in evaluating progress. This false choice not only threatens to prolong widespread poverty, disease, and early death in the developing world, but also undermines the very conditions essential to achieving genuine environmental stewardship.

It is an attempt to review theological and ethical foundations we believe are essential to sound environmental stewardship; and discuss some of the more important environmental concerns that require attention from Christian perspective. We need to work out for a vision for environmental stewardship that is wiser and more biblical than that of mainstream environmentalism, one that puts faith and reason to work simultaneously for people and ecology, that attends to the demands of human well-being and the integrity of creation. Such an

---

[4] Cf. E. Calvin Beisner, *Prosperity and Poverty: The Compassionate Use of Resources in a World of Scarcity,* (Wheaton, Ill.: Crossway Books, 1988), and *Prospects for Growth: A Biblical View of Population, Resources, and the Future,* (Wheaton, Ill.: Crossway Books, 1990); and Nathan Rosenberg and L. E. Birdzell, Jr., *How the West Grew Rich: The Economic Transformation of the Industrial World,* (New York: Basic Books, 1986).

[5] Refer for details E. Calvin Beisner, et.al (eds), "A Biblical Perspective on Environmental Stewardship", *Public Policy: Environmental Stewardship in Judo-Christian Tradition: Jewish, Catholic and Protestant Wisdom on Environment,* https://acton.org/public-policy/environmental-stewardship/theology-e/biblical-perspective-environmental-stewardship accessed on 17-07-17

[6] Nicholas Eberstadt, "World Depopulation: Last One Out Turn Off the Lights," *Milken Institute Review* 2 (first quarter 2000): 38

approach to environmental stewardship will, we believe, promote human justice and shalom, as well as the well-being of the rest of God's creation, which his image-bearers have been entrusted to steward for his glory.

A) Christian Stewardship based on Biblical and Ethical Foundations

The Creator of all things, God the Almighty, rules over all and deserves our worship and adoration (Psalm. 103:19-22). The earth, and, with it, all the cosmos, reveals its Creator's wisdom and goodness (Psalm. 19:1-6) and is sustained and governed by his power and loving kindness (Psalm. 102:25-27; Psalm. 104; Colossians. 1:17; Hebrews. 1:3, 10-12). Human beings, both men and women, were created in the image of God, given a privileged place among creatures, and commanded to exercise stewardship over the earth (Genesis. 1:26-28; Psalm. 8:5). Fundamental to a properly Christian eco-theology and ethics, then, are the Creator/creature distinction and the doctrine of humankind's creation in the image of God. Some environmentalists, especially those in the "Deep Ecology" movement, divinize the earth and insist on "biological egalitarianism," the equal value and rights of all life forms, in the mistaken notion that this will raise human respect for the earth. Instead, this philosophy negates the biblical affirmation of the human person's unique role as steward and eliminates the very rationale for human care for creation. The quest for the humane treatment of beasts by lowering people to the level of animals leads only to the beastly treatment of humans.[7]

The image of God consists of knowledge and righteousness, and expresses itself in creative human stewardship and dominion over the earth (Genesis. 1:26-28; 2:8-20; 9:6; Ephesians. 4:24; Colossians. 3:10). Our stewardship under God implies that we are morally accountable to him for treating creation in a manner that best serves the objectives of the kingdom of God; but both moral accountability and dominion over the earth depend on the freedom to choose. The exercise of these virtues and this calling, therefore, require that we act in an arena of considerable freedom–not unrestricted license, but freedom exercised

---

[7] For more information on this kind of argument refer, for example, The classic work leading to biological egalitarianism is Peter Singer's *Animal Liberation: A New Ethics for Our Treatment of Animals* (New York: Random House/New York Review of Books, 1975). See also John Harris, Stanley Godlovitch, and Roslind Godlovitch, *Animals, Men, and Morals* (New York: Taplinger Publishing, 1972); and Arne Naess, *Ecology, Community, and Lifestyle: Outline of an Ecosophy,* trans. and rev. David Rothenberg (Cambridge and New York: Cambridge University Press, 1989). For critique, see E. Calvin Beisner, *Where Garden Meets Wilderness: Evangelical Entry into the Environmental Debate* (Grand Rapids, Mich.: Eerdmans Publishing/Acton Institute, 1997), appendix 2; Thomas Sieger Derr, *Environmental Ethics and Christian Humanism* (Nashville, Tenn.: Abingdon Press, 1996), chapter 1, and "Human Rights and the Rights of Nature," *Journal of Markets and Morality* (forthcoming); Robert Royal, *The Virgin and the Dynamo: Use and Abuse of Religion in Environmental Debates* (Grand Rapids, Mich.: Eerdmans Publishing, 1999), chapter 4; and Charles T. Rubin, *The Green Crusade: Rethinking the Roots of Environmentalism* (New York: Free Press, 1994), chapter 4.

within the boundaries of God's moral law revealed in Scripture and in the human conscience (Exodus. 20:1-17; Deuteronomy. 5:6-21; Romans. 2:14-15). These facts are not vitiated by the fact that humankind fell into sin (Genesis. 3). Rather, our sinfulness has brought God's responses, first in judgment, subjecting humankind to death and separation from God (Genesis. 2:17; 3:22-24; Romans. 5:12-14; 6:23) and subjecting creation to the curse of futility and corruption (Genesis. 3:17-19; Romans. 8:20-21); and then in restoration, through Christ's atoning, redeeming death for his people, reconciling them to God (Romans. 5:10-11, 15-21; 2 Corinthians. 5:17-21; Ephesians. 2:14-17; Colossians. 1:19-22), and through his wider work of delivering the earthly creation from its bondage to corruption (Romans. 8:19-23). Indeed, Christ even involves fallen humans in this work of restoring creation (Romans. 8:21). As Francis Bacon put it in *Novum Organum Scientiarum* (*New Method of Science*), "Man by the Fall fell at the same time from his state of innocence and from his dominion over creation. Both of these losses, however, can even in this life be in some parts repaired; the former by religion and faith, the latter by the arts and sciences."[8] Sin, then, makes it difficult for humans to exercise godly stewardship, but the work of Christ in, on, and through his people and the creation makes it possible nonetheless.

God set aside a unique place, when he created the world, the Garden of Eden, and placed in it the first man, Adam (Genesis. 2:8-15). God instructed Adam to cultivate and guard the Garden (Genesis. 2:15) to enhance its already great fruitfulness and to protect it against the encroachment of the surrounding wilderness that made up the rest of the earth. Having also created the first woman and having joined her to Adam (Genesis. 2:18-25), God commanded them and their descendants to multiply, to spread out beyond the boundaries of the Garden of Eden, and to fill, subdue, and rule the whole earth and everything in it (Genesis. 1:26, 28). Both by endowing them with his image and by placing them in authority over the earth, God gave men and women superiority and priority over all other earthly creatures. This implies that proper environmental stewardship, while it seeks to harmonize the fulfilment of the needs of all creatures, on the other hand puts human needs above non-human needs when the two are in conflict.

Some environmentalists reject this vision as "anthropocentric" or "speciesist," and instead promote a "biocentric" alternative. But the alternative, however attractively humble it might sound, is really untenable. People, alone among creatures on earth, have both the rationality and the moral capacity to exercise stewardship, to be accountable for their choices, to take responsibility for caring not only for themselves but also for other creatures. To reject human stewardship is to embrace, by default, no stewardship. The only proper alternative

[8] Quoted in Francis A. Schaeffer, "How Should We Then Live?" in *The Complete Works of Francis A. Schaeffer: A Christian Worldview* (Westchester, Ill.: Crossway Books, 1982), 5:159.

to selfish anthropocentrism is not biocentrism but theocentrism: a vision of earth care with God and his perfect moral law at the center and human beings acting as his accountable stewards.[9]

Two sets of interrelated conditions are necessary for responsible stewardship. One set of conditions is related to the freedom that allows people to use and exchange the fruits of their labour for mutual benefit (Matthew 20:13-15). These conditions–knowledge, righteousness, and dominion–provide an arena for the working out of the image of God in the human person. Another set of conditions is related to responsibility, especially to the existence of a legal framework that holds people accountable for harm they may cause to others (Romans 13:1-7; Exodus 21:28-36; 22:5-6). These two sets of conditions provide the safeguards necessitated by human sinfulness. Both sets are essential to responsible stewardship; neither may be permitted to crowd out the other, and each must be understood in light of both the image of God and the sinfulness of man.

B) Christian Concern on Eco-friendly Development

Materially, the world is a far, far better place today than it was not only one millennium ago, but even one century ago. Every raw material–mineral, plant, and vegetable–that plays a significant role in the human economy is more affordable (which economists recognize as meaning more abundant), in terms of labour costs, today than at any time in the past. Every manufactured product is more affordable than it has ever been.[10] And in producing all this great abundance, we have also reduced much health-threatening pollution, especially in the developed world.[11] Put simply, the world is both a wealthier and a healthier place today than ever before. This rosy picture, however, must not generate uncritical applause

[9] See Michael B. Barkey, "A Framework for Translating Environmental Ethics into Public Policy," *Journal of Markets and Morality*; E. Calvin Beisner, "Stewardship in a Free Market," in *The Christian Vision: Morality and the Marketplace,* ed. Michael Bauman et al. (Hillsdale, Mich.: Hillsdale College Press, 1994), and *Where Garden Meets Wilderness: Evangelical Entry into the Environmental Debate* (Grand Rapids, Mich.: Eerdmans Publishing/Acton Institute, 1997), appendix 2; Thomas Sieger Derr, *Environmental Ethics and Christian Humanism* (Nashville, Tenn.: Abingdon Press, 1996), chapter 1, and "Human Rights and the Rights of Nature," *Journal of Markets and Morality* (forthcoming); and Peter J. Hill, "Biblical Principles Applied to a Natural Resources/Environment Policy," in *Biblical Principles and Public Policy: The Practice,* ed. Richard Chewning (Colorado Springs: NavPress, 1991), 169-182.

[10] Cf. William J. Hausman, "Long-Term Trends in Energy Prices"; Morris A. Adelman, "Trends in the Price and Supply of Oil"; Bernard L. Cohen, "The Costs of Nuclear Power"; John G. Myers, Stephen Moore, and Julian L. Simon, "Trends in Availability of Non-Fuel Minerals"; H. E. Goeller, "Trends in Nonrenewable Resources"; and Roger A. Sedjo and Marion Clawson, "Global Forests Revisited," in *The State of Humanity,* ed. Julian L. Simon (New York: Blackwell, 1995).

[11] Refer, William J. Baumol and Wallace E. Oates, "Long-Run Trends in Environmental Quality"; Derek M. Elsom, "Atmospheric Pollution Trends in the United Kingdom"; and Hugh W. Ellsaesser, "Trends in Air Pollution in the United States," in *The State of Humanity,* ed. Julian L. Simon (New York: Blackwell, 1995).

for economic development. Development can be positive or negative. While the fact that life expectancy keeps rising suggests that the net effect of development on human life has been positive, this does not imply that every instance of development is unmixedly beneficial, either to people or to creation. A biblical worldview and an institutional framework for prudent decision making, which we shall set forth below, are essential to ensuring that positive, rather than negative, development takes place.

Christianity supports appropriate development not for its own sake but, for example, because it uplifts the human person through work and the fruits of that labour, empowering people to serve the poor better, to uphold human dignity more, and to promote values (environmental, aesthetic, etc.) that we otherwise could not afford to promote. The Christian tradition clearly affirms that the accumulation of material wealth should not be the central aim of life; yet people are to use wisely the gifts of creation to yield ample food, clothing, health, and other benefits. It is obvious that the great advance in wealth over the past century has taken place only in a small proportion of countries, namely, the liberal democracies and free economies of the West. Enough is now known about the administration of national economies to conclude safely that free-market systems minimize the waste of resources, and allow humans to be free and to flourish. All other systems that humans have tried lead to endless and unnecessary poverty, hunger, and oppression. For this reason, the religious communities of the Protestant tradition must take very seriously the claim that free markets and liberal democracy are essential to human welfare and therefore have a moral priority on our thinking about how society ought to be ordered.

But an ideological difficulty at present is that Western Protestant churches take too much of the present affluence for granted, misunderstand its origins, and overstate the value of the environmental amenities that have been given up to attain it. Today, this is leading many to embrace policy platforms that are explicitly against economic growth, and that give undue privilege to the preservation of the environmental status quo. This agenda threatens to deny those outside the West the very benefits that we ourselves have attained, and, ironically, it may burden the developing world with even worse environmental problems down the road. This essay challenges the arguments behind the anti-growth environmentalist agenda that is ubiquitous in today's mainstream churches, and argues that a biblical stance is entirely coherent with free-market democracy oriented toward sustainable economic growth as well as development should be eco-friendly.

C) Inter-relation between Economics and Environmental Trends

There is a direct and positive correlation between freedom and economic development and between economic development and environmental improvement. Necessarily, then, there is also a positive correlation between freedom and environmental quality. Economists find that free economies outperform planned and controlled economies not only in the production and distribution of wealth but also in environmental protection. Freer economies use fewer resources and emit less pollution while producing more goods per man-hour than less free economies. Economic demographer Mikhail Bernstam explains:

> Trends in pollution basically derive from trends in resource use and, more broadly, trends in production practices under different economic systems. In market economies, competition encourages minimization of production costs and thus reduces the use of resources per unit of output. Over time, resource use per capita and the total amounts of resource inputs also decline and this, in turn, reduces pollution....
>
> By contrast, regulated state monopolies in socialist economies maximize the use of resources and other production costs. This is because under a regulated monopoly setting, prices are cost-based, and profits are proportional to costs. Accordingly, the higher costs justify higher prices and higher profits. This high and ever-growing use of resources per unit of output explains the high extent of environmental disruption in socialist countries.[12]

It is not only competition in free economies that encourages better stewardship of natural resources, it is also the incentive people have to protect property in which they have a financial stake. On the one hand, people naturally want their own homes and workplaces, and, by extension, their neighbourhoods, to be clean and healthful, so they seek to minimize pollution. On the other hand, in a legal framework in which polluters are made liable for damage done to others' person or property, people also seek to minimize pollution that falls upon others. Moreover, a dynamic economy works to reduce pollution by finding the most efficient means of doing so. This contrasts with a command-and-control approach, in which regulators are likely to mandate particular technologies and methods for pollution control with little regard for overall social efficiency.

It can be notable that free economies improve human health, raise living standards and life expectancy, and positively affect environmental conditions, doing all these things better than less free economies do. Further, the wealthier those economies become, the better they foster environmental protection. "If pollution is the brother of affluence," it has been written, then "concern about pollution is affluence's child."[13] Even if some pollution emissions rise during early economic development, the beneficial effects to human life of increased production far outweigh the harmful effects of the resulting pollution, as demonstrated in declining disease and mortality rates and in rising health and life expectancy, even

---

[12] Mikhail Bernstam, "Comparative Trends in Resource Use and Pollution in Market and Socialist Economies," in *The State of Humanity*, ed. Julian L. Simon (New York: Blackwell, 1995), 520.

[13] Cf. Ronald Bailey, "Earth Day: Then and Now," *Reason* 31 (May 2000): 23.

during that early stage. But soon, increasing wealth enables citizens to invest more resources on environmental protection, and emission rates fall.

Understanding the environmental transition, we should not be surprised to find that air, water, and solid waste pollution emissions and concentrations have been falling across the board in advanced economies around the world for the last thirty to forty years. Thus, for example, in the United States, national ambient airborne particulate emissions fell by about 80 percent from 1940 to 1994, and total suspended particulates fell by about 84 percent from 1957 to 1996; sulfur dioxide (so^2) emissions fell by about 34 percent from 1973 to 1994, and so^2 concentrations fell by about 80 percent from 1962 to 1996; carbon monoxide emissions fell by about 24 percent from 1970 to 1994; nitrogen oxide emissions peaked around 1972 and have declined slightly since then, while concentrations have fallen by about a third since 1974; volatile organic compounds emissions peaked in the late 1960s and by 1994 had fallen by about 30 percent; ozone concentrations fell by about 30 percent from the early 1970s to 1996; lead emissions (probably the most hazardous air pollutant) fell over 98 percent from 1970 to 1994, and concentrations also fell by about 98 percent.[14]

The rapid decline in pollution in advanced economies over the last thirty to fifty years–a decline that is continuing today–is not matched in very poor countries in early stages of economic development. But there is reason to be confident that the environmental transition not only will occur in the latter countries as surely as it has in the former, but also that it can and will occur more rapidly, with lower pollution peaks and more rapid improvements following them. Why? Because today's developing countries can cheaply import ready-made environmental protection technologies and technical know-how developed by others elsewhere at a much higher cost. That is, pollution abatement will become affordable in developing countries at much lower levels of economic development than it did in countries that progressed earlier. This is one reason trade and open dialogue between peoples are so important; they allow for the diffusion of environmentally friendly technologies and methods. Just as some countries went through the demographic transition long ago and others more recently, while some are in the midst of it now and others have yet to begin it, so some countries are long past the peak in the pollution transition, while others are at or just approaching it, and still others are just beginning the uptrend in pollution.[15]

People, very often, have been misunderstood about the impact of growing human population and growing economies. Fundamentally, it is because they

[14] Calculated from statistics in *Earth Report 2000: Revisiting the True State of the Planet,* ed. Ronald Bailey (New York: McGraw-Hill, 2000), 291-310.

[15] I personally observed the decline in pollutants during my visits in the developed countries like Germany in May 2016 and in Canada in May to July 2017. In comparing to my native country India, these developed countries have taken certain eco-friendly activates in reducing pollution in atmosphere to protect environment. India is not yet freed from pollution.

have not understood the full potential of the human person. They have considered people basically as consumers and polluters. They have not seen them–as they are presented in Scripture–as made in God's image, to be creative and productive, as he is (Gen. 1:26—28; 2:15), and as given a role in the restoration of earth from the effects of God's curse because of human sin (Rom. 8:15—25). But that biblical understanding of human nature leads Christians to expect precisely what we have seen: that, particularly when accompanied by properly formed human institutions and scientific understanding built on a biblical worldview, people can produce more than they consume and can actually improve the natural world around them.

D) Environmental and Human Concerns for Present and Future

In spite of the encouraging picture painted by all these general observations in preceding discussion, many people continue to fear that we face serious threats to human well-being and to the environment as a whole. How realistic are these fears, and, to the extent that there are real dangers, what can we do about them? Let's look at three important concerns from Christian point of view: "population growth", "global warming", and rampant "species extinction".

i) Population Growth:

Riane Eisler, cultural historian and evolutionary theorist, writes:

> "The population crisis," lies at the heart of the seemingly insoluble complex of problems futurists call the world problematique. For behind soil erosion, desertification, air and water pollution, and all the other ecological, social, and political stresses of our time lies the pressure of more and more people on finite land and other resources, of increasing numbers of factories, cars, trucks, and other sources of pollution required to provide all these people with goods, and the worsening tensions that their needs and aspirations fuel.[16]

Eisler's words represent a common understanding of population growth among environmentalists: It threatens the earth with resource depletion and pollution. As we have seen, however, empirical observation, as well as biblical understanding of the implications of the image of God in the human person, suggests the opposite conclusion.

Nonetheless, many people still fear population growth because they believe it leads to overpopulation. When asked what they mean by *overpopulation,* they usually speak of crowding and poverty. Yet the assumption that high population density begets those things is mistaken. Some of the most desirable places to live in the world are also among the most densely populated. Manhattan, for instance, with its density of over 55,000 people per square mile, also has very high

[16] Riane Eisler, *The Chalice and the Blade: Our History, Our Future,* (Cambridge, Mass.: Harper and Row, 1987), 174-175.

rents–a sure sign that plenty of people really want to live there, despite its high density. Or maybe, instead, they want to live there precisely because of its high density. The teeming population of Manhattan brings together a magnificent mix of human talent that makes life there fascinating, challenging, and rewarding for its millions. Similar things are true of all the world's great cities. With all their problems, they clearly attract more people than they drive away. Why should we question people's judgments about where they choose to live?

Some people think high population density lies at the root of poverty in developing nations such as China, India and those in sub-Saharan Africa. Yet China's population density is less than one-fifth of Taiwan's, and, aside from their forms of government, the two countries have very similar cultures. Taiwan, however, produces about five times as much wealth per capita as China. And the Netherlands, with population density nearly four times China's, produces more than ten times as much wealth per capita. And sub-Saharan Africa? Despite the common belief that it is overpopulated, it actually suffers instead from such low population density (just over half that of the world as a whole and lower than the average densities of the high-, middle-, and low-income economies of the world) that it cannot afford to build the infrastructure needed to support a strong economy.[17]

The images evoked by the term overpopulation–hungry families; squalid, overcrowded living conditions; early death–are real enough in the modern world, but these are properly described as problems of poverty.[18] Despite all this, some people still fear population growth. Their fears, however, lack both biblical and empirical bases. First, the Bible presents human multiplication as a blessing, not a curse (Gen. 1:28; 8:17; 9:1, 6-7; 12:2; 15:5; 17:1-6; 26:4, 24; Deut. 7:13-14, cf. 30:5; 10:22, cf. 1:10; Ps. 127:3-5; 128:1, 3; Prov. 14:28); in contrast, a decline in population was one form of curse God might bring on a rebellious people (Lev. 26:22; Deut. 28:62-63). Second, although some people continue to believe projections made thirty and forty years ago of the world population topping twenty, thirty, or even forty billion in the next century or so, demographic trends indicate that the reality will be quite otherwise. Those projections were made based on the highest population growth rate the world has ever seen–about 2.2 percent per year in the 1960s, the peak of the global demographic transition. But by the year 2000, the worldwide population growth rate had dropped to about 1.3 percent per year, and it is expected to drop even further as the demographic transition plays itself out. Eberstadt explains:

---

[17] E. Calvin Beisner, "Anomalies, the Good News, and the Debate over Population and Development: A Review of Susan Power Bratton's Six Billion and More," *Stewardship Journal* - 3 (summer 1993): 44-53.

[18] Nicholas Eberstadt, "Population, Food, and Income: Global Trends in the Twentieth Century," in *The True State of the Planet,* ed. Ronald Bailey (New York: Free Press, 1995), 14-15.

> Today, almost one-half of the world's population lives in 79 countries where the total fertility rates [trfs] are below replacement (an average of 2.1 children per woman over her lifetime).... The trfs in countries with above-replacement rates are beginning to fall. For all Asia, trfs have dropped by over one-half from 5.7 children per woman in the 1960s to 2.8 today. Similarly, Latin America's average trfs fell from 5.6 in the 1960s to 2.7 today. If U.N. median-variant projections of world population turn out to be correct, world population will be 7.5 billion in 2025 and 8.9 billion in 2050.
>
> But even that might be overstating likely future population. "If present global demographic trends continue, the U.N. low-variant projections are likely. That would mean that world population would top out at 7.5 billion in 2040 and begin to decline."[19]

There is no good reason to believe that overpopulation will become a serious problem for the world. On the contrary, the more likely problem is that an aging world population will put greater stress on younger workers to provide for older, disabled persons.[20] Such a prospect, coupled with the sanctity of human life, makes all the more tragic the support in many quarters for morally illicit means of population control. Only genuine barriers to human flourishing create the problems associated with "overpopulation"; attacking problems such as poverty head-on is a far better way of improving human welfare and upholding human dignity than simply deeming certain lives unworthy of living and so, in the name of fighting "overpopulation," embracing abortion, euthanasia, and other actions that undermine the sanctity and dignity of human life.

ii) Global Warming:

Many environmentalists maintain that "global warming" is the biggest of all environmental problems today our contemporary world facing. Ironically, the great fear thirty years ago was of global cooling, for scientists recognized then

---

[19] Nicholas Eberstadt, "World Population Prospects for the Twenty-First Century: The Specter of 'Depopulation'?" in *Earth Report 2000: Revisiting the True State of the Planet,* ed. Ronald Bailey (New York: McGraw-Hill, 2000), 64. See also Nicholas Eberstadt, "World Depopulation: Last One Out Turn Off the Lights," *Milken Institute Review* 2 (first quarter 2000): 37—48.

[20] On population in general, see E. Calvin Beisner, *Prospects for Growth: A Biblical View of Population, Resources, and the Future* (Wheaton, Ill.: Crossway Books, 1990), and "*Imago Dei* and the Population Debate," in *Where Garden Meets Wilderness: Evangelical Entry into the Environmental Debate* (Grand Rapids, Mich.: Eerdmans Publishing/Acton Institute, 1997); Julian L. Simon, *The Economics of Population Growth* (Princeton: Princeton University Press, 1977), *Population Matters: People, Resources, Environment, and Immigration* (New Brunswick, N.J.: Transaction, 1990), and *The Ultimate Resource 2,* rev. ed. (Princeton: Princeton University Press, 1996); Max Singer, *Passage to a Human World: The Dynamics of Creating Global Wealth* (Indianapolis: Hudson Institute, 1987); Michael Cromartie, ed., *The Nine Lives of Population Control* (Washington, D.C., and Grand Rapids, Mich.: Ethics and Public Policy Center/Eerdmans Publishing, 1995); and Michael B. Barkey, Paul Cleveland, and Gregory M. A. Gronbacher, "Population, the Environment, and Human Capital".

that the earth is nearing a downward turn in its millennia-long cycle of rising and falling temperatures, correlated with cycles in solar energy output. But no more. Now people fear that rising atmospheric carbon dioxide, called a "greenhouse gas" because it traps solar heat in the atmosphere rather than allowing it to radiate back into space, will cause global average temperatures to rise. The rising temperatures, they fear, will melt polar ice caps, raise sea levels, cause deserts to expand, and generate more and stronger hurricanes and other storms. Are there good reasons for these fears?

While atmospheric carbon dioxide (co^2) is certainly on the rise, and global average temperature has almost certainly risen slightly in the last 120 years or so, it is by no means certain that the rising temperature stems from the rising co^2. The most important contrary indicator is that the sequence is the reverse of what the theory would predict. Almost all of the approximately 0.45°C increase in global average temperature from 1880 to 1990 occurred before 1940, but about 70 percent of the increase in co^2 occurred after 1940. If the rising co^2 was responsible for the rising average temperature, the reverse should have been the case. In addition, roughly two-thirds of the overall increase is attributable to natural, not manmade, causes (primarily changes in solar energy output).[21]

iii) Species Extinction:

The Bible clearly indicates that God takes delight in his many creatures (Job 38:39-39:30; 40:15-41:34; Ps. 104:14-23). This entails the importance of stewardship of life itself. Confronted with claims that anywhere from 1,000 to 100,000 species are going extinct per year and that many or most of the extinction is caused by human action,[22] Christians must wonder whether they have failed in their stewardship obligation. However, in the spirit of 1 Thessalonians 5:21 ("Test all things; hold fast to what is good"), we can insist that claims of species extinction rates be tested empirically and that the significance of these numbers be carefully evaluated in the proper context. When the claims are tested, they are found to be highly dubious. When two eminent statisticians challenged the claims, asserting that no empirical field data existed to support them,[23] the International

---

[21] Robert C. Balling, *The Heated Debate: Greenhouse Predictions Versus Climate Reality* (San Francisco: Pacific Research Institute, 1992), 65-69.

[22] Cf. Robert M. May, "Conceptual Aspects of the Quantification of the Extent of Biological Diversity," in *Biodiversity: Measurement and Estimation,* ed. D. L. Hawksworth (London: Royal Society/Chapman and Hall, 1995), 13-20; Paul R. Ehrlich and Anne Ehrlich, *Extinction: The Causes and Consequences of the Disappearance of Species* (New York: Random House, 1981); John Tuxill and Chris Bright, "Losing Strands in the Web of Life," in *The State of the World 1998,* ed. Lester R. Brown, Christopher Flavin, and Hilary French (New York: W. W. Norton, 1998); Jessica Hellman et al., *Ecofables/Ecoscience* (Stanford, Calif.: Stanford University/Center for Conservation Biology, 1998); and Mark H. Williamson, *Island Populations* (Oxford: Oxford University Press, 1981).

[23] Julian L. Simon and Aaron Wildavsky, "On Species Loss, the Absence of Data, and Risks to Humanity," in *The Resourceful Earth,* ed. Julian L. Simon and Herman Kahn (Oxford and New

Union for the Conservation of Nature (IUCN) responded by commissioning a major worldwide field study. The result was a book[24] in which author after author admits that, despite expectations to the contrary based on theoretical models, field research yields little or no evidence of species extinction, even in locales–such as heavily depleted rain forests–in which the highest rates were anticipated. In that volume, V. H. Heywood, former director of the scientific team that produced the Flora Europea, the definitive taxonomic compilation of European plants, and S. N. Stuart, executive officer of the Species Survival Commission at the IUCN, wrote, "IUCN, together with the World Conservation Monitoring Centre, has amassed large volumes of data from specialists around the world relating to species decline [worldwide], and it would seem sensible to compare these more empirical data with the global extinction estimates. In fact, these and other data indicate that the number of recorded extinctions for both plants and animals is very small." They add,

> Known extinction rates [worldwide] are very low. Reasonably good data exist only for mammals and birds, and the current rate of extinction is about one species per year.... If other taxa were to exhibit the same liability to extinction as mammals and birds (as some authors suggest, although others would dispute this), then, if the total number of species in the world is, say, 30 million, the annual rate of extinction would be some 2,300 species per year. This is a very significant and disturbing number, but it is much less than most estimates given over the last decade.[25]

None of this means that there are not particular species that are, in fact, endangered and that can benefit from careful conservation efforts. But as field ecologist Rowan B. Martin points out, when monetary values are more fully aligned with other human values, the institutional arrangement allows for the maximization of both values:

> Western scientists, activists, and agencies favour the creation of reserves in developing nations to preserve biological diversity. However, this strategy is often an unworkable form of "eco-imperialism." Recent studies show that the majority of reserves are failing to conserve biodiversity, are financially unsustainable, and were irrelevant to 95 percent of the people in the countries where they were located. An alternative strategy, which has had considerable success, is empowering local people to control the wildlife resources in their area. In many parts of Southern Africa, where full rights of access and control over wildlife have been granted to landholders (of both private and communal land), biodiversity is better conserved in the areas

York: Blackwell, 1984), 171-183.

[24] Timothy C. Whitmore and Jeffrey A. Sayer, ed., *Tropical Deforestation and Species Extinction* (London and New York: Chapman and Hall, 1992).

[25] *Ibid,* 93-94

surrounding national parks than in the parks themselves. Additionally, the areas surrounding the parks are economically more productive than the state-protected areas. In Southern Africa and other parts of the world, conservation of biological resources would be a profitable activity and not a cost if the correct institutional arrangements were developed, including a stronger reliance on private property and communal tenure systems.[26]

E) Market Morals and Environmental Concerns

It is discussed to some extent that economic growth itself is an important step toward environmental protection. It makes good stewardship affordable and technically possible. Nonetheless, economic growth by itself is not enough. Human initiative needs to take place within an institutional framework that promotes environmental stewardship. Therefore, we need to examine more closely what is institutionally necessary to help further the goal of environmental protection.[27] While some concerns about the environment are overstated, others are quite real and need our attention. The fact that the world is not experiencing overpopulation or destructive, manmade global warming or rampant species loss does not mean that a change in policies or practices is not needed to address other issues.

Christians have every reason to embrace an appropriate environmental ethic, one that honours creation but distinguishes it from the Creator. However, simply recommending reformation of our worldview is not sufficient. Our ability to act responsibly toward nature has been hindered by our alienation from God. The original Fall and our continued rebellion mean that we act selfishly, that

---

[26] Rowan B. Martin, "Biological Diversity: Divergent Views on Its Status and Diverging Approaches to Its Conservation," in *Earth Report 2000: Revisiting the True State of the Planet,* ed. Ronald Bailey (New York: McGraw-Hill, 2000), 205.

[27] For more information on "Environmental and Market Virtues" refer - Peter J. Hill, "Biblical Principles Applied to a Natural Resources/Environment Policy," in *Biblical Principles and Public Policy: The Practice,* ed. Richard Chewning (Colorado Springs: NavPress, 1991), 169-182; "Can Markets or Government Do More for the Environment?" in *Creation at Risk? Religion, Science, and Environmentalism,* ed. Michael Cromartie (Washington, D.C.: Ethics and Public Policy Center/Eerdmans Publishing, 1995); and "Takings and the Judeo-Christian Land Ethic: A Response," *Religion and Liberty* 9 (March/April 1999): 5-7. Other studies indicating the importance of private property and free markets to environmental protection include Bernard J. Frieden, *The Environmental Protection Hustle,* (Cambridge, Mass.: MIT Press, 1979); Terry L. Anderson and Donald R. Leal, *Free Market Environmentalism* (San Francisco: Pacific Research Institute, 1991); Terry L. Anderson, ed., *Multiple Conflicts over Multiple Uses* (Bozeman, Mont.: Political Economy Research Center, 1994); Elizabeth Brubaker, *Property Rights in the Defense of Nature* (London and Toronto: Earthscan/Environment Probe, 1995); John A. Baden and Douglas S. Noonan, ed., *Managing the Commons,* 2nd ed. (Bloomington: Indiana University Press, 1998); Timothy D. Terrell, "Property Rights and Externality: The Ethics of the Austrian School," *Journal of Markets and Morality* 2 (fall 1999): 197—207; and Michael B. Barkey, "Translating Environmental Ethics into Public Policy," *Journal of Markets and Morality.*

we have limited knowledge, and that we often fail to recognize the full potential in the created order. In view of these failings, we must not rely on worldview alone to lead us to good decisions about creation but must also examine the other influences of decision making, namely, information and incentives.

Environmental problems are traditionally seen as a result of market failure and as ample justification for the government to involve itself in the economy much more directly and forcefully to solve these problems. But it is an error to assume that, just because the market does not presently solve certain problems, government can effectively intercede to do so. Information and incentives are very much affected by the institutional order of a society. The social institutions pertinent to environmental and resource issues are the rules that assign responsibility–that is, property rights that determine who can take what actions and who gets a hearing with regard to those actions. These rules are crucial determinants of what information is generated and what incentives the decision makers face.

Property rights generate appropriate information and incentives to the extent that they embody three characteristics: exclusivity, liability, and transferability. Exclusivity means that the owner of a resource is able to capture a return from using the property in a way that is advantageous to other people, and it also means that an owner can exclude others from benefiting from the use of the property unless they have secured the owner's permission. If exclusivity does not exist, a resource will be overused.

Liability forces a resource owner to bear the costs of actions that harm others. If property rights fully embody liability, costs are not imposed on others without their willing consent. For instance, if a person allows another person to impose harm on him–that is, to use up some of the grass on his cattle ranch to feed his livestock–that person must receive what he believes to be adequate compensation for the harm. If liability were not fully attached to one's property–that is, one's cattle–a person could drive cattle across someone else's land, allowing them to remove some of the grass without providing compensation. Pollution is a notable example of an incomplete property right, of liability not being present. It is exactly analogous to the cattle example; individuals can use up some of another's resource–clean air–without appropriate compensation.

Transferability encourages owners to look for ways of using property that benefit others, a central obligation of the Christian faith. The fact that a piece of property can be bought or sold means that a resource owner who ignores the wishes of other people does so at a cost to himself, a reduction of wealth. If rights are not transferable, no such wealth loss is associated with ignoring the wishes of others. In other words, transferability encourages people to seek out and engage in the most mutually beneficial property arrangements possible.

Therefore, the attributes of exclusivity, liability, and transferability are essential for a well-functioning property rights system, one that fulfils the biblical mandate of holding individuals accountable for their decisions. If any one of those attributes is missing, people can act irresponsibly with regard to creation, at least in part because they do not have adequate information or appropriate incentives to make sound decisions.[72]

Each of these proposals involves government action of some sort. Because the definition and the enforcement of property rights are at least, in part, a function of government, an alteration of those rights will probably involve government. However, one must carefully specify the type of action appropriate when suggesting that government is the answer to environmental problems. Seeing the problem as one of inadequate property rights gives positive guidance about how government can be most effective–through the clear specification of rights and the fuller defense of them. Unfortunately, too often, government's involvement in resource issues has not been framed in a property rights context and hence has not been as effective as possible.

All of this reaffirms the need for a biblically based view of nature and of man so that the desires represented in the marketplace will come closer to God's desires. At the same time, however, it is not clear that any alternative democratic institutional structure would lead to a more godly environmental policy. The biblical mandate of valuing nature but making use of it does not offer much guidance as to the particulars of resource use. Evidently, God has allowed man to work out those details on the basis of his own perceptions of needs–with those needs appropriately informed by an awareness of God and his principles.

We are limited by human desires, as imperfect as they might be, as our standard to measure how resources should be used. God has given us the opportunity and responsibility to manage his creation, and it therefore seems appropriate to have an institutional structure that reflects human desires and holds individuals accountable as to whether they use their resources according to those desires. Such a structure is the system of property rights described earlier. If this seems a weak defence of property rights, that may be because it is. One can conceive of many cases where a system of well-defined and enforced property rights results in resource use that seems to violate God's standards. However, it is difficult to conceive of another property rights structure that does better at making sure God's standards are not violated. The two most obvious alternatives–common property and government ownership–both suffer from such obvious faults, such as the tragedy of the commons, that they are clearly inferior choices.

First, a private-property system will not produce zero pollution in the sense of stopping all alteration of the environment; but neither will it allow economic growth at all costs with material desires superseding all others. If property rights are fully defined and enforced, some emissions will still foul our air, not all water will be of pristine quality, and the use of nonrenewable resources will not drop to zero. However, the significant difference between this potential system of private-property rights and the one that currently exists is that actions altering the environment would take place only if all users of the environment were convinced that those actions were to everybody's mutual advantage. In other words, there would be no uncompensated losers. A person who valued an unspoiled view more than someone else valued a factory smokestack in the middle of that view would win out. The factory smokestack would not exist, at least not at that location. Such a property rights system would not stop economic growth but would allow it to occur only if the benefits were valued more highly than what was given up to get that growth. Such an approach to resource use seems appropriate, as we are to appreciate and value God's creation, but also see it as usable for human purposes.

Another component of a private-property rights system is that it does not depend on complete social agreement for action to take place. Diversity is permitted by virtue of the fact that a person who has strong feelings about resource use that differ from the group consensus can, under such a system, express those feelings through prices and markets. This can be of particular importance to Christians or environmentalists who find themselves at odds with prevailing wisdom about the environment. If such beliefs represent a minority position, they are much more likely to find expression in a system of private-property rights than under alternative rights arrangements.

Finally, a private-property rights system permits the fullest realization of the image of God in the human person. Genuine problems require genuinely creative solutions, and property harnesses human creativity to the realization of human needs. As history has repeatedly shown, it is the creative spirit of the human person that permits wise stewardship, and institutions that encourage this spirit are more likely to also facilitate environmentally sound ends.

But can we be assured that future generations will have a place in a free economy? What of God's concern for all people of all times? Is there not a chance that a system based on private-property rights will cater exclusively to the desires of the present generation compared to the needs of future ones? Again, the appropriate question to ask is, Compared to what? What alternative institutional arrangement will do a better job than one that embodies transferable property rights? It would be nice to posit a theocracy headed by an omniscient saint, and if that were a realistic alternative, markets would come out second-best. However, if we stick to real-world possibilities, well-defined rights that can be bought and sold look quite good indeed.

Contrast, for a moment, a resource being managed under two alternative regimes. Let us say that a resource is exhaustible; hence, it is important to give future generations some voice in the choice about the appropriate rate of use. Under the first regime, a pure democracy controls the use of the resource. With different expectations by members of the population about the resource's future value, the average perception will dominate. In other words, if the present generation thinks that, on average, the resource has a future value (discounted to the present) greater than its value in present consumption, it will be preserved. On the other hand, if the average expectation of the resource's future value is less than its value in present consumption, it will be consumed.

Now take the same resource, and the same population with the same set of preferences and expectations, but make the present/future allocation on the basis of transferable property rights. In this case, the resource is more likely to be preserved for the future because it is not the average perception about the future value of the resource that counts, but instead the perception of those most optimistic about its future value who express themselves in the marketplace. These individuals will purchase the resource in the expectation of a high future value, hold it out of consumption, and, in the process, preserve it for future generations. In fact, for any resource to be used in the present, all who believe it has some value in the future must be outbid.

All of this is not to say that altruistic feelings for future generations are unimportant. Under either system, such sentiments can result in greater preservation for future generations. Notice, however, that the political approach depends entirely on altruism, or people caring for future generations, while the market order allows those preferences to be expressed but also rewards individuals who, for selfish reasons, decide to withhold resources from present consumption.

Giving future generations a voice is a bit awkward. Their preferences will be expressed only in people who exist presently, so it is useful to have someone stand in for them today; they need agents to represent them. These agents cannot know perfectly the desires of people not yet born, but they can make educated guesses about these desires. In the market arena, these agents are either unselfish contributors to the future or speculators acting on their perception of future demands for resources. If their perceptions are correct, their wealth increases; if they guess incorrectly, they suffer a wealth loss. Thus, these agents have strong incentives to be well informed and to predict correctly the needs of future generations.

In a world where Christian charity and concern for others are sometimes in short supply, it is useful to have a mechanism that allows for future needs to be met, by those acting charitably and those pursuing profit. Again, institutional design is a fundamental component of a system that satisfies God's desire that we think not only of this generation.

Thus, freedom, property rights, and a legal framework that ensures that accountability attaches to freedom and property, work together to minimize pollution and improve human welfare. The more fully, then, a society embodies a Christian worldview, and the more its decision makers–private and public–embrace that value framework and operate with the information and incentives provided by a private-property legal regime with exclusivity, liability, and transferability, the more decisions with environmental impact are likely to be responsible and to minimize harm to people and the larger environment. The Christian worldview can be promoted by preaching, teaching, writing, and the like. But the information and incentives essential to proper decision making, even assuming a Christian worldview, are best generated by the price system of the free economy.

On the basis of a biblical worldview and ethics, as well as of sound science, economics, and public policy principles, we believe sound environmental stewardship celebrates and promotes human life, freedom, and economic development as compatible with, even essential for, the good of the whole environment. While we do not rule out all collective action, we believe market mechanisms are frequently better means, in both principle and practice, to environmental protection. They are less likely to erode important human freedoms and more likely to be cost-effective and successful in achieving their aims. While we understand that passions may energize in the pursuit of sound environmental policy, we also believe that reason, coupled with a commitment to "do justly, to love mercy, and to walk humbly with ... God" (Mic. 6:8), must ultimately guide environmental policy.

3) Christian Theological World View

There has been given considerable place for "eco-theology" in Christian theological world view.

A) Anthropocentric Theology

Western Christianity places human beings at the centre of the universe. American historian, Lynn White Jr, in one of his articles, "The historical root of our ecological crises" published in 1967 argued that the Judeo-Christian theology which the western Christianity inherited is fundamentally exploitative of the earth. It is anthropocentric theology,[28] placing humanity in the centre of all creations. This is to imply that all other creatures are inferior to Human beings. This is to suggest that all created things are to be serving the wants of humankind because under this worldview, human is the centre of all. This is precisely the reason why human took for granted or finds basis for the exploitation of creation.

B) The "Dominion" Worldview

Human over nature[29] theology has been responsible for exploitation of creations as a means to satisfy humans' wants. Supposedly human centred reading of the text such as that of Genesis 1: 26 "rule over," Genesis 1:28, "subdue it" has been

[28] Huang Po Ho, *Embracing The Household of God – A Paradigm Shift from Anthropocentric Tradition to Creation Responsibility in Doing Theology* (Kolkata: SCEPTRE, 2014), 4.

[29] K. C. Abraham, *Eco-Justice- A New Agenda for Church Mission* (Bombay: BUILD Publication, n.d), 12.

interpreted to serve human's unlimited wants. Precisely such dominion theology has given the impetus or moral support to exploit the natural resources after all everything under the sky is in the hand of human being according to this worldview. Such kind of a worldview is not uncommon. This is the reason why masses of lands and forest have made way for construction of industry or Special Economic Zones which serves but a few handfuls.

C) Transcendental Theology

Most of our Christian Theology views God as a transcendent Reality. God is understood as other worldly, far away having no close affinity/relation with the rest of the creation.[30] This theological assertion asserts that God is not interested with the creation or is not actively involved with the creation. It dichotomises God and creation. Once a theological dichotomy of such is maintain, the world is considered as a less important because this world is not our home! The mindset of negligence or carelessness as far as the ecology is concern came out from such a worldview. Such theology presents God as not interested with the creation.

D) Patriarchal/ Hierarchical/Pyramidal Power Structure

Christian theological articulation presents a patriarchal or hierarchical understanding of God and the rest of the creation there of. Rosemary Radford Ruether in *Gaia and God* argues that traditional images of God as male set God apart from creation. There is this pyramidal power structure of God- Jesus Christ- Holy Spirit- Man- Women- Children- Creation. This power structure is pyramidal; the power which flows from the top to the bottom. A hierarchy of being puts God indefinitely above others: God as king, creator, master, etc. The worth of an individual or a natural object thus depends on its position in the hierarchy, instead of its intrinsic value and dignity.[31] This is exactly the reason why the creation fall into the lowest of the hierarchical pyramid thereby prompting subjugation of the creation.

E) Dualistic Theology

A dualistic worldview separates the mind from the body, the male from the female and humans from the non-human world. This theology fails to see human beings as a physical being. It advocates dichotomy between secular and sacred, earthly and heavenly, mundane life and spiritual life.[32] The western Christian worldview

---

[30] Leonardo Boff, *Ecology and Liberation*, translated by John Cumming (New York: Orbis Book, 1995), 45.

[31] Kwok Pui- Lan, "Ecology and the Recycling of Christianity," in *Ecotheology- Voices from South and North,* edited by David G. Hallman (New York: Orbis Books), 109.

[32] Yangkahao Vashum, "Tribal Theology: A Search for Relevant Theology and Ministry in Tribal Context," in *Tribal Theology – A Search for Quality Theological Education and Relevant Ministry,* edited by Yangkahao Vashum (Jorhat: Tribal Study Centre, 2009), 24.

maintaining a sharp distinction between secular and sacred, earthly and spiritual life compartmentalise every aspects of human's life. This theology therefore advocates distinction between human and creation as subject and the object. It is for this reason that the created world is understood as less important. According to dualistic worldview, the spirit is against the body.[33]

F) Individualised Salvation

Personal salvation was part of the gospel preached upon by the missionaries in the 19th and the 20th centuries. Woba James quoting Udayan Mishra asserts, "Christianity and western education brought in new values based on individualism which poses direct challenge to the collective life-pattern of the people."[34] Personal salvation as Woba James opines was responsible in ushering individualism.[35] Reflecting this statement upon the theological framework which were handed down to us theology becomes a matter of one's exclusive search for communion with God. The place of the individual replaced the communitarian values as such the creation outside of the self is of no business as long as one is saved. Thus, salvation is viewed in all exclusivity for human sans creation.

4) Christian Theological Response – Eco-Theology

Eco-theology is a form of constructive Christian theology that focuses on the interrelationships of religion and nature, particularly in the light of contemporary environmental concerns. Eco-theology generally starts from the premise that a relationship exists between human religious/spiritual world-views and the degradation of nature. It explores the interaction between ecological values, such as sustainability, care, protection, and the human domination of nature. It was developed as a movement which has produced numerous religious-environmental projects around the world. The burgeoning awareness of environmental crisis has led to widespread religious reflection on the human relationship with the earth. Such reflection has strong precedents in most religious traditions in the realms of ethics and cosmology, and can be seen as a subset or corollary to the theology of nature.[36]

It is important to keep in mind that eco-theology explores not only the relationship between religion and nature in terms of degradation of nature, but also in terms of ecosystem management in general. Specifically, eco-theology seeks not only to identify prominent issues within the relationship between nature and

---

[33] Kwok Pui Lan, "Ecology and the Recycling of Christianity," In *Ecotheology- Voices from South and North*, edited by David G. Hallman (New York: Orbis Books), 110.

[34] Woba James, *Major Issues in the History of Christianity in India: A Post Colonial Reading* (Mokokchung: TDCC Publications, 2013), 312.

[35] James, *Major Issues in the History of Christianity in India ...*, 312.

[36] *Brown, Valerie, "The Rise of Ecotheology"*, Retrieved 4 April 2012.

religion, but also to outline potential solutions. This is of particular importance because many supporters and contributors of eco-theology argue that science and education are simply not enough to inspire the change necessary in our current contemporary environmental crisis.

The relationship of theology to the modern ecological crisis became an intense issue of debate in Western academia in 1967, following the publication of the article, "The Historical Roots of Our Ecological Crisis," by Lynn White, Jr., Professor of History at the University of California at Los Angeles. In this work, White puts forward a theory that the Christian model of human dominion over nature has led to environmental devastation, providing a voice for "The Ecological Complaint."[37] In 1973, theologian Jack Rogers published an article in which he surveyed the published studies of approximately twelve theologians which had appeared since White's article. They reflect the search for "an appropriate theological model" which adequately assesses the biblical data regarding the relationship between God, humans, and nature. The following are, perhaps, some of the major concerns of Christian "eco-theology".

A) Redemption of Creation

Mark 16:15 presents the command to go into the entire world and proclaim the good news to the whole creation. The good news here is none other than liberation of the creation.[38] Roman 8th chapter presents the groaning of the environment and the subsequent search for redemption of all creation. Paul writes, "We know that the whole creation has been groaning in labour pains until now" (Romans 8:22). The understanding of the groaning in labour pain of the creation can be interpreted as the state of ecological crisis today.[39] It is of primary importance to understand that the search towards the final fulfilment and restoration of the creation in its pristine image does not speak exclusively of Human kind but inclusive of the whole creation. Paul therefore asserts in Romans 8:21-23, "that the creation itself will be set free from its bondage to decay and will obtain the freedom of the glory of the children of God. We know that the whole creation has been groaning in labour pains until now; and not only the creation, but we ourselves, who have the first fruits of the Spirit, groan inwardly while we wait for adoption, the redemption of our bodies." Such internalizing of the holistic approach of liberation that encompasses the whole creation certainly underlines the significance of all creation and redemption whole creation.

---

[37] White, Lynn. "The Historical Roots of Our Ecological Crisis", Retrieved 4 April 2012;. Cengage, Gale. "Ecotheology", in *Encyclopedia of Science and Religion,*. Retrieved 4 April 20.

[38] Paulachan Kochappilly, "Ecological Crisis and Christian Response," in *Theology for Our Times*, edited by Reji Samuel (Bangalore: Ecumenical Christian Centre, 2015), 17.

[39] Zunecho Thingo, "Deriving Ecological Values from the Chakhesang Naga Tribal Perspective," in *Tribal Ecology*, edited by Razouselie Lasetso, Marlene Ch. Marak and Yangkahao Vashum (Jorhat: ETC Programme Coordination, 2012), 155-156.

B) Goodness in all God's Creation

The account of creation from the book of Genesis presents God pronouncement of goodness in all God's creation at the end of each creation (Genesis 1:4; 1:31). One can draw out the divine recognition of the goodness of things in creation.[40] In the Noah's ark during the flood we find humans and creatures shared the same home. The intrinsic well being and goodness with which God created the creation is lost. There is this spirituality involved in the creation at the creation. This goodness in God's creation demands an Eco-spirituality, a radical change in our attitude and concepts towards the fellow-creatures which was at one point of time pure. It demands a renewal of the reciprocal relationship that was there in the past. It calls for an Eco-spirituality in which the Christian faith and hope for "a new heaven and new earth" shall restore, renew and redeem creation in its prime and pure goodness.[41]

C) Jesus' Affirmation of Created Things

In Jesus we see an affirmation of the "small things" of life. He drew inspiration from them in his teachings and his ministry- a lily in the field, a stone, a child, a mustard seed, grains of wheat, fish and loaves of bread, pigs, spit and mud, the sparrow and birds in the air.[42] The implication of Jesus' employment of environmental terms certainly depicts Jesus embracing of the creation. It shed light on the importance of creation. This provides a theology of creation in which one has to look, watch and learnt from the created things. It depicts the closeness of humanity with creation.

D) Stewardship of God's Creation

"Let us make humankind in our image, according to our likeness; and let them have dominion (Gen 1:26) and "Be fruitful and multiply, and fill the earth and subdue it; and have dominion" (Gen 1:28) are to be understood as human beings in a representation of God in creation helping to carry out God's creative work. Here, the power to subdue and dominion is to be exercised for stewardship, to act with justice and benevolence and not for destruction.[43] This is how the dominion and subdue have to be understood. It is again not mere representation but that which culminates in rest on Sabbath, a celebration in the perfectness and goodness of all creation (Gen 2:2-3). This interpretation has been aptly supported by the second account of creation in Genesis 2:15 where God said, "Till it and keep it."

---

[40] Kochappilly, "Ecological Crisis and Christian Response ...," 6.

[41] Thingo, "Deriving Ecological Values ...," 213-214.

[42] Aruna Gnanadason, "Women, Economy and Ecology," in *Green Theology*, edited by Wati Longchar (Kolkatta: PTCA, 2012), 184.

[43] Jacinta Prakashappa, "Re-reading the Creation Story," in *Envisioning a New Heaven and a New Earth*, edited by Lalrinawmi Ralte (Nagpur: NCCI/ISPCK, 1998), 122.

The meaning is clear, human are to be a friend of nature, work with nature.[44] This is to say that human beings can be human only by way of labouring and caring for the manifestation of God. It is an ethical call from anthropocentrism to bio-centrism.[45]

E) Eco-Trinitarian Communion

God in three persons co-exist eternally, distinctly and unitedly. There is no subordination but a common bond of correlations and communion. Likewise the universe is the reproduction of this diversity and of this union.[46] God sacramentalizes every bit of creations; distinct yet in harmony because the "Breathe of God" blows over every creation. Creation-God-Human like the Trinitarian concept of God is a relationship that can never be separated. All creation exists so that we may accept the invitation to share in God's abundance and accompany God in the divine venture undertaken within our humanity and createdness.[47] God the Creator designed creations, God the Son is Immanuel and God the Spirit creates and re-creates the whole cosmos. It is the Spirit that moves and acts in all creations, that fill the earth and who constantly renews the structure of the cosmos.

F) Passionate Spirituality

In the past, spirituality has been seen as synonymous with asceticism, spiritual discipline, meditation, prayer and other worldly pursuits. According to dualistic worldview, the spirit is against the body, the emotion and the appetite. We now need to speak of a holistic and embodied spirituality. Instead of being passive and emotionless, this spirituality must be passionate, erotic and full of fire. This passionate spirituality must enable us to work for peace. Peace is not the absence of war or conflict, but harmony, well being and blissfulness because of just relationships.[48] This passionate spirituality is no longer other worldly but this worldly, one that embrace the whole of the creation, one that helps us being mindful and present amidst the creation. Such passionate spirituality provides room for engagement with the world around us; therefore we become part of this world, God immanent here and now.

G) The Earth as God's Image

We do find multi-dimensional and complex metaphors for God in the Bible: some relevant metaphors for us here are those which image of God as a compassionate,

---

[44] Boff, *Ecology and Liberation* ..., 45.

[45] Lan, "Ecology and the Recycling of Christianity ...," 108-109.

[46] Boff, *Ecology and Liberation* ..., 48.

[47] Boff, *Ecology and Liberation* ..., 51.

[48] David G. Hallman, *Ecotheology: Voices from South and North* (New York: Orbis Books), 110.

feminine, mothering God who fills the earth with grace and creative power. God is imaged as shepherd (ps. 23:1, Matt. 18:10-14); as potter (Jer. 18:1-6); as mother (Isa. 42:14, Luke 15:8-10). From an implicitly dualistic, hierarchical, individualistic and utilitarian subject-object relationship with God and the earth we need to move intentionally to a subject-subject relationship which affirms the intrinsic value, the integrity and goodness of all of creation.[49] If the Earth is God's image certainly the creation is holy and therefore should also reflect the unbroken image of God. God is in everything, God flows through all things; God is present in everything and makes of all reality a temple and vice versa. It is said therefore, "it is in him that we live and move and have our being" (Acts 17:28).

H) The Earth as God's Body

Employing a metaphorical study of Revelation 12:1-6 "The Woman and the Dragon" Gabriele Dietrich, writing from the perspective of fisher folk woman and urban poor women in India, reflects on earth as the body of God. For her what is of crucial importance in ecological theology is the "sustaining power of women who keep life going by the labour of their wombs and of their hands." Like the birth pang of a mother, it is the creation that bears the pangs of human destruction, like the womb of woman who sustains and give birth to a child it is also the creation that sustain and give birth to humanity. She reads the vision in Revelation 12th chapter as a symbolic of this interconnection between the power of women and of the earth. To her the dragon in the revelation's vision represents, "the destructive power, which inspires the tyrannical empires, which tries to devour the child and kill the woman." She therefore believes that the labour of women and the Earth will be redeemed, "by breaking down the patriarchal conditions of the production of life in the new community of the people of God, which will be rescued by the alliance with the earth."[50]

Creation finds its completeness and fulfilment in God, the creator and sustainer of all living being. Both the spiritual and materials worlds cannot be separated from each other. We have a common origin, a common God. This idea helps us to reflect on human's ecological responsibility. The relationship between humanity and environment cannot be reduced to mere need and use alone. It demands a harmonious relationship. It includes the responsibility of care, love and respect. This theological affirmation needs to be integrated in our faith practices, if we want to make our cosmos sustainable. Our spirituality and theology therefore should be ecological oriented rather than anthropocentric, hierarchical and patriarchal.

---

[49] Aruna Gnanadason, "Woman, Patriarchy and Creation: Insights from Eco-Feminist Theology," in *Green Theology*, edited by Wati Longchar (Kolkata; Shrach, 2014). 94.

[50] Aruna Gnanadason, "Woman, Patriarchy and Creation ...," 95-96.

The challenge to all of us is to understand what it means to be human in this more than human world. One has to assume the responsibility as steward of God. There is a need in shift, from anthropocentrism to bio-centrism, from transcendental worldview to immanence as the basis of our theological reconstruction. God exist in close affinity with creation. What is a creation without the breath of the creator? The character study of God, Jonah and the animal portrays an unmistakable relation between God and creation. God therefore said, "And should I not be concerned about Nineveh, that great city, in which there are more than a hundred and twenty thousand persons who do not know their right hand from their left, and also many animals?" (Jonah 4:11). Therefore, Human are not alone but the identity of Humanity is defined and understood in close affinity to God and Creation. The Bible, Christian theology upholds care for creation, and therefore Christian's objective is to protect goodness of God's creation, which sum up in the inclusive and positive attitude that a Christian individually, as well as, Church collectively should have towards the environment and ecological resources of this world.

Chapter 9

Islam and Eco-Concerns

The reality of climate change calls for a re-evaluation of our actions and a redirection of our energies towards the reduction or possible reversal of the looming environmental crisis. The rapid deterioration of human environment is one the striking manifestations of not only the crisis of Western science and technology, but also crisis of values. The nature is at the brink of destruction without proper implementation of ideals to save it. Religions have a great role to play in the preservation of environment as most religions places high value for environment and its constituents. Islam is one of such religions that gives importance to the environment.

Religious leaders are challenged to look into their traditions for any inspiration that could guide us towards averting this global disaster. This new demand on old traditions forces us to look creatively at the world's religious heritage and reinterpret or reapply sacred texts and principles to our present problem. It is surprising, however, that the texts of the Islamic religious tradition speak directly on many issues that are pertinent to our problem. Hence, the task for the Muslim expositor here is not so much a reinterpretation of the traditions, but mainly a reapplication of old texts to new problems.

1) Islamic View on Environmentalism:

Islam is one of the major religions of the world and it's religious scripture Quran contains many resources on ecology and environment. Islam as one of the major "universal" faiths, it is practiced in virtually every country on earth. Although, the overwhelming majority of Muslims today are not Arabs and do not live in the Middle East, the influence of Arab culture on the cosmopolitan tradition of Islam is undeniable. As a desert dweller the Prophet Muhammad must have been sensitive to the delicate natural balance within which his people were able to survive. The Quran is stuffed with references to the precious resources of water, air, and land, and proscribes wastefulness. The Hadith likewise report the Prophet's concern for the protection of natural resources and its equitable availability to all. Clearly, from its very origins fourteen centuries ago Islam offers a basis for ecological understanding and stewardship.[1]

2) Qur'an and Ecological Concerns:

The act of creation, according to the Qur'an, is a process and not a momentary activity. God is always active and continue the act of creation by developing all beings from one stage to another.[2] The Islamic view of the natural order and the environment has its roots in the Quran. The Quran does not draw a clear line of demarcation between the natural and the supernatural or between the world of humans and that of nature. The Quran does not regard the world of nature as its natural enemy to be conquered and subdued but as an integral part of human's religious universe sharing in his earthly life and in a sense even ultimate destiny.

2.1) Eco-Islam: Relevant References from Quran:

For Muslims the Qur'an is the ultimate green-guide. Believed to be a sublime revelation with remarkable ideas, this divine scripture is scrupulously read by Muslims for spirituality. But it doesn't limit to only spirituality. Faith in environment is also an important aspect of Islamic faith, since Muslims believed that God created this universe, hence, we need to be careful towards His creation. The Qur'an therefore, doesn't just link belief in One God (*Tawheed*) to being nice to plants and keeping a pet. The Qur'an glorifies nature and wildlife as an earthly heaven, a mirror to the lush forests of Paradise above. Ethics and equilibrium are key ingredients to peace (*salaam*) and even vegetarian living. Here are some key quotes from the Qur'an that show what Eco-Islam is really about.[3]

2.1.1) Anti-Corruption

Living a balanced, moderate life is easy to say, harder to follow through. Even Muslims-the wealthier, western Muslims-have a difficult time living purely 'off the land'. Yet this doesn't detract from the verses: "...And do not desire corruption in the land. Indeed, God does not like corruptors." (Qur'an 28:77). "...And do not commit abuse on the earth, spreading corruption." (Qur'an, 2:60)

[1] Seyyed H. Nasr, "Islam and the Environmental Crisis," *Islam and the Environment,* edited by A. R. Agwan (New Delhi: Institute of Objective Studies, 1997), 16. Hereafter referred to as Nasr, *Islam...,*

[2] Jose Abraham, "An Ecological Reading of the Qur'anic Understanding of Creation," *Bangalore Theological Forum,* 33/1 (June, 2001), 167.

[3] http://www.theecomuslim.com/2013/03/10-environment-quran-verses.html 17-07-17.

How many forms of corruption are there? Crime, political fraud, illegal banking systems, theft, rape and so on. Now add to that list littering, deforestation, toxic waste and pesticides. Sure, these are hardly equivalent to murdering but in the long run, these things take human lives too, a fact. That is what the Qur'an is alarming readers about.

Corruption we may find in many fields nowadays like political parties, government administrations, education institutions, medical organizations, business firms, religious centres, spots competitions and even we are hearing about corruption in judicial systems and also in environmental managements. In the end, when we don't restore these things to harmony we only end up polluting our own little bubble of survival. That is why God says our catastrophes are self-inflicted; "corruption has appeared throughout the land and sea by what the hands of people have earned". As if to give a wake-up call, people are told these catastrophic processes can heal and eliminate social and natural disorders, but through belief in God and respect for nature. "...So... let them taste part of (the consequences of) what they have done that perhaps they will return (to righteousness)." (Qur'an 30:41)

2.1.2) Human Beings:

"Indeed, We offered the Trust to the heavens and the earth and the mountains, and they declined to bear it and feared it; but man [undertook to] bear it. Indeed, he was unjust and ignorant. (Qur'an 33:72) In Arabic the word for earthling is *Khalifa* (خليفة) pronounced kha-leaf-ah. This is a magnificent word with multiple meanings like deputy, guardian, 'friend of Earth' and viceroy, although it all boils down to "stewardship". Human beings are the most intelligent beings on earth so it makes sense that we have the responsibility to care for our planet, to give it a hug and a health check now and again.

"And it is He (God) who has made you successors (*khala'ifa*) upon the earth and has raised some of you above others in degrees [of rank] that He may try you through what He has given you. Indeed, your Lord is swift in penalty; but indeed, He is Forgiving and Merciful." (Qur'an 6:165).

Interestingly, this idea of humans being 'successors' or stewards resonates in the Bible, particularly in Exodus and Corinthians. In the well-known Genesis verses the earliest humans alive are taught to sow and reap from the fields, in order to understand the functionality of earth and be in awe of its beauty. The Torah too instructs its followers with a job description similar to a noble janitor. Muslims are supposed to hold this responsibility deeply. We are not the masters but we have been given a short-term trust. Anyone who creates corruption and pollution abuses their power and has violated this trust. Such a person fails as a Human and needs to earn the title back.

2.1.3) Water Preservation:

One of the major ecological problems of our contemporary times is "water pollution". It is human responsibility to preserve clean water and provide clean water where it's needed. Water is polluting rapidly due to industrialization, deforestation, urbanization and use of chemicals and pesticides in agriculture sectors. Misuse of water is another factor led to ecological crisis. Water is a huge life-providing theme in the Qur'an. God talks about how He creates life through water then sustain it by streams, the rains, rivers and oceans that are homes for so many creatures. "And Allah has sent down rain from the sky and given life thereby to the earth after its lifelessness. Indeed in that is a sign for a people who listen." (Qur'an, 16:65)

In the Qur'an, God uses the analogy of life and death for Muslims to recognise the value of water. Prophet Muhammad, peace be upon him, said that one day people will wage war over rivers of gold. He was talking about water. We have taps that fill our basins with gold, but we cannot afford overflows while people wait for the rains. Third-world countries in desert climates are counting on us to give the cost of our water to them. "And We have sent down blessed rain from the sky and made grow thereby gardens and grain from the harvest." (Qur'an, 50:9) As water is another natural creation, Muslims believe it belongs to God and nobody can monopolise it. Water is for sharing and there is enough water for all.

2.1.4) Plantation:

The Qur'an contains lots of horticultural information which science has reaffirmed by more than 90%. Like previous revelations in the Gospels and Torah, Quranic plants are mentioned in detail with the medicinal properties of herbs being highlighted. God speaks about His creative design and the nutrition available from natural produce as an encouragement to eat healthily: "And it is He who sends down rain from the sky, and We produce thereby the growth of all things. We produce from it greenery from which We produce grains arranged in layers. And from the palm trees - of its emerging fruit are clusters hanging low. And [We produce] gardens of grapevines and olives and pomegranates, similar yet varied. Look at [each of] its fruit when it yields and [at] its ripening. Indeed in that are signs for a people who believe." (Qur'an, 6:99)

Among the plants mentioned in the Qur'an there is garlic, grapes, pomegranate, herbs, dates, ginger, olives, lentils, onion, cucumber, figs, mustard, a variety of trees including the cedar and the acacia flower. What do we learn from this? Plants are already part of our diet so there's not much impetus to start talking to trees but we could always take it a step further. Today, we are facing another important ecological danger is decline in bio-diversity and particularly species extinction from plant kingdom of God.

Plants have been playing major role in purifying air pollution, producing living oxygen, giving food and shelter to living beings, and above all protecting eco-system on the earth. An Eco-Muslim has obligation to protect God's plant kingdom as a pro-gardener and will always encourage people to grow something. Cut a tree, plant a tree should be in practice. For every bouquet of flowers we use, plant flower seeds; grow fruit trees that makes our environment healthy.

2:1:5) Treating Animals with Dignity:

"And there is no creature on [or within] the earth or bird that flies with its wings except [that they are] communities like you. We have not neglected in the Register a thing. Then unto their Lord they will be gathered." (Qur'an 6:38). God uses the word 'community' (*umma*) to describe the similarity between people and animals. We have our social groups, animals have theirs. There is a beauty and majesty in the innate construct of swimming shoals of fish or flocks of birds dancing in the skies. Muslims reflect, where do penguins learn parenting skills? How do baby turtles know to head to water? For Muslims, this answer is divinely inspired.

It's a sad reality that animal rights are grossly violated throughout the Muslim world. Violence like hunting for skins or tusks means that several animal species are extinct. Imagine those animals were ethnicity groups, could you really accept all of Europe or south-east Asia being wiped out? I don't think so. In many countries animals are needlessly killed or eaten without health considerations. For Islam, both actions are illegal. This is why pork is unlawful (*haram*); it's very unhealthy. A few animals cannot be consumed under Islamic law and all animals have to be raised with dignity, with the exception of an attack (think poisonous snakes!)

A whole chapter in the Qur'an is dedicated to bees (*An-Nahl* 16:68-69), elevating the magic involved for turning nectar into honey. People are not supposed to disrupt honeycombs or knock down 'live' hives. In this instance, giving back would involve planting yellow coloured flowers to help bees collect nectar or supporting a bee farm. In Islamic law animals like cattle and poultry are lawful to eat because they are healthy and they have been made by God to be consumed (see *Mai'dah*, 5:4). For an Islamic slaughtered the animals needs healthy grazing without hormones, given tenderness with freedom to roam and then prepared for slaughtering (*zabiha*). The *Zabiha* method involves covering the animal's eyes and reading God's name (*takbir*) to help the animal submit. Without good health, the animal may be *Zabiha* but it will not be lawful (halal) to eat.

2:1:6) Protection of Ozone Layer:

The ozone "hole" over the Antarctica is a phenomenon whereby the stratosphere is thinned out (it's not really a hole). It's caused by refrigerants: CFC's, halons and freons. These have been banned since the 1970s but we still lose a few percentile of ozone each year, and the increased thinning means the earth is losing its protective layer. The Qur'an mentions the atmosphere in embracing language:

> "And We made the sky a protected ceiling (canopy), but they, from its signs, are turning away." (Qur'an, 21:32)

> "It is Allah who made for you the earth a place of settlement and the sky a ceiling and formed you and perfected your forms and provided you with good things. That is Allah, your Lord; then blessed is Allah, Lord of the worlds." (Qur'an, 40:64)

God has wrapped the earth with atmosphere and humans have burned it away. Restoring it requires global diligence and commitment to neutralising toxic gases/radiation. It is asking a lot from billions of people yet I believe it is the only way to go about it. Fight existing organisations that pollute the most and get politically involved to shake up government awareness. Environmental action is always on the agenda but not many have the courage to follow-through. Nuclear plants and factories have protected by legal rights to emit certain amounts of pollution and waste, we may not always defeat those. But doing our individual part can collectively heal the "hole" in the sky over the years.

2:1:7) Awareness of Creation:

After reading such a variety of information from the Qur'an, it's better to look at Eco-Islam ideas as a whole. The Qur'an is a book for thinkers and is open to anyone not afraid to read. This is what the Qur'an also says about rain, mountains, rivers, seas, weather and so on as follows:

> "Do you not see that Allah sends down rain from the sky and makes it flow as springs [and rivers] in the earth; then He produces thereby crops of varying colours; then they dry and you see them turned yellow; then He makes them [scattered] debris. Indeed in that is a reminder for those of understanding." (Qur'an, 39:21)

> "And He has cast into the earth firmly set mountains, lest it shift with you, and [made] rivers and roads, that you may be guided," (Qur'an, 16:15)

> "He released the two seas, meeting [side by side]; Between them is a barrier [so] neither of them transgresses." (55:19-20)

> "And it is He who sends the winds as good tidings before His mercy until, when they have carried heavy rainclouds, We drive them to a dead land and We send down rain therein and bring forth thereby [some] of all the fruits. Thus will We bring forth the dead; perhaps you may be reminded." (7:57)
> "It is Allah who sends the winds, and they stir the clouds and spread them in the sky however He wills, and He makes them fragments so you see the rain emerge from within them. And when He causes it to fall upon whom He wills of His servants, immediately they rejoice." (30:48)

"It is He who shows you lightening, [causing] fear and aspiration, and generates the heavy clouds." (13:12)

All these verses are amazing starting points for activism. Environmental welfare is described as something sacrilegious, beneficial for us. By reading these verses it should at the very least make you aware of Islam's harmonious core. Living as socially responsible and exemplary human beings is one of the Islamic commands of God.

2.2) God's Creation and Environment:

A number of words used in the Qur'an for 'creation' such as *khalq, bara, sawwara, ja'ala, bada'a* and *farara. Khalq* is the noun from of the verb *khalaqa* and it is used 249 times in the Qur'an. This word is used in the Qur'an to denote the act of creation and creation in its entirety. In the classcal language of Arabs, *khalq* is considered as an act of God and *Al-khaliq,* the Creator, is one of the names of God in the Qur'an. *Bara* is another term used for creation in the Qur'an, which means, "to form, to fashion or to shape." Arabs generally use this word to denote the act of "shaping of a reed" for writing, or "an arrow", or "a stick" or of a "piece of wood". *Al-ban,* one who shapes, is one of the names of God in the Qur'an (2:52; 59:24). This word has similar meanings as that of *khalaqa,* such as fashioning and shaping.

Another term, *sawwara* is used in the Qur'an (40:64; 64:3; 7:11; 3:6; 82:8; 59:24) indicating creation and it means "to from, to shape, to fashion, to sculpture, to picture" and so on. *Al-musawwir*, 'the Fashioner' is one the names of God in the Qur'an (59:24). *Sawwara* is an Arabic term implies giving definite form of colour, so as to make a thing exactly suited to a given end or object; hence the title *musawwir* means bestower of forms of colours; for this shows the completion of the visible stage of creation.[4] God fashions the creation by giving it form and colour and bestows each creature with "every details of its complicated spiritual and physical existence." Everything is being fashioned uniquely therefore each fits perfectly into the rest of creation.[5]

The word, *Ja'ala,* is also used 345 times in the Qur'an in relation to creation. This means "to make, to render, to form, to create, to prepare" and so on. It is used in the Qur'an with the sense of giving new shapes, forms, and dispositions. According to the Qur'an the act of creation also includes the process of giving colours, form, physical stature, assigning specific roles and conditions to fulfil these roles. The word *Bada'a* occurs fourteen times in the Qur'an and it means "to originate a thing, or to bring in to being or existence, or to make or to produce for

[4] Cf. Abdulla Yusuf'Ali, *The Meaning of the Holy Qur'an: Text, Translation and Commentary,* (New Delhi; Al Hasanat Books Pvt.Ltd, 1973), 1215.

[5] Yunus Negus, "Science Within Islam: Learning How to Care for Our World," in *Islam and Ecology*, ed. Fazlun M. Khalid and Joanne O'Brien (London: Cassell Publishers Limited, 1992), 40.

the first time."[6] *Al-badi*, which means the "Originator" is another name of God used in the Qur'an.

The Islamic perspective on the environment rests on the belief that Allah is the creator and sustainer of the universe. According to the Quran, all things have their origin by the command of God, "Be" (*kun*).[7] Accordingly, whole universe along with all of its factors has been created with perfect wisdom (*hikmah*). Everything created by Allah has a just purpose which must be fulfilled (Qur'an 16:3; 15:85). Nothing in creation is for sport or accidental and without design but with a serious purpose (*haqq*).[8] It brings value and importance to creation.[9] Moreover, nothing is permanent here; everything exists for a fixed period (Qur'an 46:3). As a work of God, creation then is a part of the *essence* of God and it manifests him. Quran affirms that all things are signs of God (Surah 2:164), which is to say that everything gives indication of God's nature and reality.[10] The Qur'an acknowledges an inseparable relation between God and the universe that is created, so that neither can be defined without referring to each other. God enters into the definition of the cosmos and cosmos enters the definition of God.[11]

The Qur'an says that *al-muhit* (who encompasses all things) is one of the 99 names of Allah. Allah says in the Qur'an 4:126): "But to God belong all things in the heavens and earth: and it is He who encompassed (*muhit*) all things. This term *Muhit* is also used in Arabic to denote 'environment'. In a deeper sense, it is always true to say that God Himself is the Ultimate Environment which surrounds and encompasses all things.[12] Seyyed Hossein Nasr is of opinion:

> To remember God is to see Him everywhere and to experience His reality as *al-Muhit*. Since the environment is not an ontologically independent order of reality, which is divorced from the Divine Environment, the environmental

---

[6] Jose Abraham, "An Ecological Reading of the Qur'anic Understanding of Creation"... 167.

[7] The creative command of God is explained in eight places in the Quran. See Qur'an 36:82; 2:117; 16:40; 6:37; 19:35; 3:47, 59; 40:68.

[8] Gordon D. Newby, *The Concise Encyclopedia of Islam* (England: One World Publication, 2002), 75. Hereafter referred to as Newby, *The Concise Encyclopedia...*,

In Arabic the word "*haqq*" is used primarily to explain the idea of permanence or fixity or the correctness or certainty, which is to mean the Divine Truth.

[9] Augustine Perumalil, *Religious Cosmologies* (Delhi: ISPCK, 2007), 168. Hereafter referred to as Perumalil, *Religious Cosmologies...*,

[10] Perumalil, *Religious Cosmologies...*, 166.

The Qur'an acknowledges an inseparable relation between God and the universe that is created, so that neither can be defined without referring to each other. Thus, the Qur'an defines God as "the First and the Last, the Outward and the Inward." (Surah 57:3).

[11] Augustine Perumallil, *Religious Cosmologies...* 158.

[12] Nurdeng Deurashe, "Maintaining a Healthy Environment: An Isslamic Ethical Approach," in *European Journal of Social Sciences*, 8/4 (2009), 527.

> crisis has been caused by human is refusal to see God as the real Environment which surrounds human and nourishes his/her life.[13]

As per Islamic theology, God made provisions for the sustenance and growth of countless varieties of creatures from microorganisms to the largest animals. These provisions are made available to meet their needs in every situation and stages of life. Existence of each and every thing, whether it is small or big, is important for the continuation of life. So each species is unique and makes its own specific contribution to the totality of life. This negates the superiority or importance of one species over against the other. Thus in the holistic perspective human being is not a supreme being but a part of the web of nature coexisting with other denizens of the cosmos.[14]

2.3) Environmental Balance

For the sustenance of his creation, God has placed a measured quantity of the environmental resources which matches the total demand of the resources in the universe. This implies the existence of environmental balance in the natural ecosystem. The Quran describes the notion of environmental balance in various terms like '*adl*', '*qadar*' and '*mouzoon*'.

(1) The term *adl* literally means acting justly, rightly, or equitably. While explaining the meaning of *adl*, one interpreter of the Quran has observed that the universe has been created in balanced form.[15]

(2) The Quranic term *qadar* gives even more direct meaning of the environmental balance. The literal meaning of *qadar* is a specified measure or amount either of quantities or qualities. This term corroborates the notion of balance in the following ayah: "Verily all things we have created in proportion and measure (Qur'an 54:59). This ayah makes a general statement about the existence of equilibrium in everything. The process of creation and growth of all things follows the principle of balance which, in the above ayah, has been referred to as 'proportion and measure.'

(3) The notion of environmental balance is further supported by another term *mouzoon,* which occurs in the first of the following ayahs:

> "And the earth we have spread out, set therein mountains firm and immovable and produced therein all kinds of things in due balance. And we have provided therein means of sustenance for you and for those whose sustenance you are not responsible (Qur'an 15:19-20).

---

13 Seyyed Hossein Nasr, "Islam and the Environmental Crisis," in *The Islamic Quarterly,* 34/4, (1990), 219.

14 A.R. Agwan,, "Introduction," in *Islam and the Environment,* ed. Ar. Agwan (New Delhi: Institute of Objective Studies, 1997), xii.

15 Maududi, Abu Al Ala, Tafheem-ul-Quran, vol. 5, p. 251.

According to above ayahs, all kinds of provisions have been made for the sustenance of human and the non-human beings in a way that the quantity demanded of these provisions equals their supply.[16]

2.4) Islamic Theology on God and Environment

The Quran depicts nature as being ultimately a theophany which both veils and reveals God. In a deeper sense, it can be claimed that according to the Islamic perspective, apart from being the creator, God himself is the ultimate environment which surrounds and encompasses human. It is of most significance that in the Quran God is said to be the All-Encompassing (*muhit*), as in the verse: "But to God belong all things in the heavens and on the earth: And he it is who encompasses (*muhit*) all things (Qur'an 4:126).

The term *muhit* also means environment. In reality, according to Quran, humans are immersed in the Divine *muhit* and are only unaware of it because of their own forgetfulness and negligence (*ghaflah*), which is the underlying sin of the soul to be overcome by remembrance (*dhikr*). To remember God is to see him everywhere and to experience his reality as *al-Muhit.*

The environmental crisis may in fact be said to have been caused by human's refusal to see God as the real "environment" which surrounds humans and nourishes his life.[17] The destruction of the environment is the result of modern human's attempt to view the natural environment as an ontologically independent order of reality, divorced from the Divine Environment without whose liberating grace it stifles and dies. To remember God as *al-muhit* is to remain aware of the sacred quality of nature, the reality of natural phenomena as signs (*ayat*) of God and the presence of natural environment as an ambience permeated by the Divine Presence of that Reality.[18]

2.5) The Nature in Islamic Spirituality: (Non-Human Beings)

Nature in Islamic spirituality is, consequently, not the adversary but the friend of the traveler upon the spiritual path and an aid to the person of spiritual vision in his/her journey. The Quranic revelation created not only a community of

---

[16] Abdullah Yusuf Ali, *The Meaning of the Holy Qur'an: Text, Translation and Commentary,* 640.

His commentary of the above-mentioned ayahs of Quran is worth noting. He writes: *"And every kind of thing is produced on the earth in due balance and measure. The mineral kingdom supports the vegetable and they are in their turn support the animal, and there is a link of mutual dependence between them. Excess is eliminated. The waste of one is made the food of another and vice versa. This is an infinite chain of gradation and interdependence..."*

[17] Nurdeng Deuraseh, "Maintaining a Healthy Environment: An Islamic Ethical Approach," *European Journal of Social Sciences* 8/4 (2009): 527.

[18] Seyyed Hossein Nasr, "Islam and the Environmental Crisis," *The Islamic Quarterly* 34/4 (1990): 219.

Muslims but also an Islamic cosmic ambience in which the signs of God (*Ayat Allah*) beautify at once the souls of human and the expanses of the skies and seas, the birds and the fish, the stars and the creature living in the bosom of the earth.[19] As nature provides both material and spiritual sustenance for humanity, humanity should appreciate the forces of nature that make its life possible in the planetary ecosystem.[20]

According to the Qur'an, God made provisions for the sustenance and growth of countless varieties of creatures from microorganisms to the largest animals. These provisions are made available to meet their needs in every situation and stages of life. It emphasizes that everything has its value to life.[21] This negates the superiority or importance of one species over against the other. Thus, in the holistic perspective human being is not a supreme being but a part of the web of nature coexisting with other denizens of the cosmos.[22]

The spiritual life of a Muslim is in tune with nature. To perform ritual worship *salat*,[23] a Muslim must have a special relationship with his/her outer environment since the specific times of the ritual prayers are based on the position of the sun. Also, Islamic calendar follows the moon and it is utilized to determine the proper time for fasting and performing the pilgrimage to Makkah (*Hajj*). Thus, a Muslim is forced to follow the movements of the sun and the moon as part of his/her religious practice. Thus, nature is an ally of human beings in their quest for God, not an adversary.[24] Quran says, "There is not an animal that lives on the earth, nor a being that flies on its wings, but forms part of communities like you. Nothing have we omitted from the book, and they all shall be gathered to their Lord in the end (Sura 6:38)".

Therefore, according to Islam, creation is a self-manifestation of God, so that by looking at the universe one can gain knowledge of God. Through the universe God comes to be known, it is the created things themselves which reveal

---

[19] Seyyed Hossein Nasr, "The Cosmos and the Natural Order", in *Islamic Spirituality: Foundations,* ed. Seyyed Hossein Nasr, (London: SCM Press Ltd., 1989), 346.

[20] A.R. Agwan, "Towards an Ecological Consciousness", in *Islam and the Environment,* ed. A.R. Agwan, (New Delhi, Institute of Objective Studies, 1997), 3.

[21] Jose Abraham, "An Ecological Reading of the Quranic Understanding of Creation," *Bangalore Theological Forum,* 33/1 (June, 2001): 168. Hereafter referred to as Abraham, *An Ecological Reading...*,

[22] A.R. Agwan, "Introduction," in *Islam and the Environment*, edited by A.R. Agwan (New Delhi: Institute of Objective Studies, 1997), xii.

[23] Newby, *The Concise Encyclopedia...,* 190.

Salat is a ritual prayer. Participation in *salat* is generally regarded as the second of the five major duties or Pillars of Islam, ranking immediately after the declaration of faith.

[24] Abraham, *An Ecological Reading...*, 169.

the hidden treasure. Through the universe, God disclosed himself to his creatures. The creatures themselves are God's self manifestation.[25]

2.6) Humans Responsibility:

Qur'an declares that human beings should have responsibility of the creatures. The Islamic teachings concerning nature and the environment cannot be fully understood without dealing with the Islamic conception of humans. Human beings are the only creatures with the special qualities that enable them to serve the earth. One of these qualities is the ethical notion which leads them to care about their environment. Other qualities include the knowledge given to them in order that they might perfect their duties.[26] Quran says, "And He taught Adam the nature of all things;[27] then He placed them before the angels, and said: tell me the nature of these if ye are right (Surah 2:31)". The ability of Humankind which is unique to other creatures puts the surrounding creation in a very different position if humans do not do what is right for them. Humans were placed on earth and given the duty of operating the life-support system. Allah decided that this fantastic creature needed a manual to operate the magnificent system properly, or at least to operate that part of the complex cosmic system relevant to it.[28]

There are three words in the Qur'an: *Adam*, *bashar* and *insan* which are used to denote the human beings. According to Muhammad Iqbal, the Qur'an uses the word *bashar* or *insan* to denote the origin of human beings as living beings or social animals. The word *Adam* is used more as a concept than as the name of a concrete human individual and is reserved for the human beings in their capacity of God's vicegerent on earth.[29] Thus, the earth has been placed under human responsibility, to be cared for and not to be misused. This is evidenced in Qur'an 2:22, where the word *lakum* (for you) contains the message that the earth is not for one generation but for every generation, past, present and future.[30]

As per the instructions of Qur'an, after fashioning Adam in the proper proportions God blew breath (*nafakha*) of His Spirit (*ruh*) into the human being.[31] The breathing of Allah's Spirit into human is the faculty of God-like

---

[25] Abraham, *An Ecological Reading...*, 166.

[26] Mawil Y. Izzi Dien, "Islamic Ethics and the Enviornment," in *Islam and Ecology*, edited by Fazlun M Khalid and Joanne O'Brien (London: Cassell Publishers Limited, 1992), 27.

[27] The phrase, "the nature of all things" according to the commentator means the inner nature and qualities of things, and things here would include feelings. The particular qualities or feelings which were outside the nature of angels were put by Allah into the nature of human. Cf. Abdullah Yusuf Ali, *The Meaning of the Holy Qur'an: Text, Translation and Commentary*, 24.

[28] Mawil Y. Lzi Dien, "Islamic Ethics and the Environment", 28.

[29] Abraham, *An Ecological Reading...*, 170.

[30] Al Mawil Samarai, "The Human Appointment and Creation"," in *Islam and the Environment*, edited by A.R. Agwan (New Delhi: Institute of Objective Studies, 1997), 160.

[31] Cf. Abdulla Yusuf'Ali, *The Meaning of the Holy Qur'an...*, 513.

knowledge and will, which, is rightly used, would give human superiority over other creatures. The breathing of the spirit made them so unique in nature among other creatures, with their faculty of knowledge and freedom of choice, that even angels are ordered to prostrate before them (Surah 15:29-30; 32:9; 38:72). It is breathing of the spirit, which differentiates human beings from other creatures, which act provide them their ability of distinguishing right from wrong, their power of reasoning and their faculty of speech. Therefore, the gift of knowledge made human beings more responsible towards nature and other creatures.

In relation to the role of human beings, the Arabic term *khalifah* has been used uniquely. This word is translated into English as "successor, heir, or inheritor, deputy, vicegerent and trustee", that is one who has the ultimate ownership after the present possessor.[32] Hence, a *khalifah* is the one who inherits a position, a power, a trust, and who holds it responsibly and in harmony with its bestower.[33] Islam considers human as God's vice-regent (*al-khalifah*) on the earth and the Quran asserts explicitly, "*I am setting on the earth a vice-regent (khalifah)*" (Quran 2:30). The quality of vice-regency is, complemented by that of servant-ship (*al ubudiyyah*) towards God. Human is God's servant (*abd Allah*) and must obey him accordingly. As *abd Allah* he/she must be passive towards God and recipient of the grace that flows from the world above. As *Khalifat Allah* he/she must be active in the world, sustaining cosmic harmony and disseminating the grace for which he/she is the channel as a result of being the central creature in the terrestrial order.[34] Thus, "nothing is more dangerous for the natural environment than the practice of the power of vicegerency by a humanity which no longer accepts to be God's servant, obedient to his commands and laws."[35]

2.7) *Sakhkhara*: Relationship between Human and Non-Human

The Arabic word *Sakhkhara* (to subject) is used in the Qur'an to define the relationship between human and non-human. The Qur'an considers *Sakhkhara* as an activity of God (Surah 14:33). Non-human beings have value in itself and there is no evidence in the Qur'an to prove that it is created only to serve human beings. Qur'an declares:

> "It is Allah who hath created the heavens and the earth and sends down rain from the skies, and with it brings out fruits wherewith to feed you; it is He who hath made the ships subject to you, that they may sail through the sea by His command; and the rivers hath He made subject to you (Surah 14:32)."

---

[32] Abdulla Yusuf'Ali, The Meaning of the Holy Qur'an..., 279.

[33] Abd-al-Hamid, "Exploring the Islamic Environmental Ethics," in *Islam and the Environment*, edited by A.R. Agwan (New Delhi: Institute of Objective Studies, 1997), 41.

[34] Nasr, *Islam...*, 21; Abd-al-Hamid, *Exploring the Islamic...*, 43.

[35] Nasr, *Islam...*, 22.

It is realized that behind all our strength, skill and intelligence here is the power and goodness of Allah, who gave us all these things. Human can understand and control the forces of nature so as to bring them to his/her own service; we can only do so, because (1) humans have got these gifts from Allah, and (2) Allah has fixed definite laws in nature, of which he can take advantage by Allah's command and permission. He/she has been made Vicegerent on earth (Surah 2:30). Allah commanded the highest creatures to bow down to Adam (Surah 2:34). Human, by Allah's command, can use rain to produce food for them; make ships to sail the seas; use rivers as highways and cut canals for traffic and irrigation.[36]

So, Scholars reinterpreted the word *Sakhkhara* differently from its literal meaning, i.e., "subservience."[37] According to Seyyed Hossein Nasr, when the Qur'an states that God has "subjected (*sakhkhara*)" nature to human does not mean the ordinary conquest of nature as claimed by so many modern Muslims thirsty for the power which modern science bestows upon human. Rather, by it is meant the dominion over things which human is allowed to exercise only on the condition that it be according to God's law and precisely because he/she is God's vicegerent on earth, being therefore given a power which ultimately belongs to God alone and not to him/her as merely a creature born to journey through this earthly life and to return to God at the moment of death. Since God is the Creator, as one of the creatures, human beings do not have authority over creation except through God. But, as vicegerents of God human's responsibility is to protect creation and be a part of God's recreation process.[38]

"Subservience" of everything to human in the heavens and the earth, according to Abd-al-Hamid, should not be taken as a right to dominate or exploit as that would make a mockery of Allah's statement that: "He has made subservient to you the sun and the moon pursuing their courses, and He has made subservient to you the night and the day (Surah 14:33)." The term 'subservient' would be more accurately translated as 'of service, of benefit', and Allah has thus made human to derive benefits from the whole of creation by virtue of the trust "*amanah*" placed with human by Allah. Nor should these benefits be seen in utilitarian terms only, the natural world is also a means by which human may reflect and contemplate, and is a source of beauty and contentment to him/her, in other words, it has a deep meaning for spiritual value. Thus, the love of Allah is shown by the recognition of, and reverence for, and preservation of the beauty created by Him.[39]

---

[36] Abdulla Yusuf'Ali, The Meaning of the Holy Qur'an..., 513.

[37] Jose Abraham, "An Ecological Reading of the Qur'anic Understanding of Creation", 169.

[38] Nasr, *Islam...*, 22.

[39] Abd-al-Hamid, "Exploring the Islamic Environmental Ethics," in *Islam and the Environment,* ed., A.R. Agwan, (New Delhi: Institute of Objective Studies, 1997), 47-48.

3) *Hadith* and Environmental Concerns:

Hadith, in religious usage, is often translated as "tradition" meaning a report of the deeds and saying of Muhammad and his companions. Out of the scores of books written on the subject of the traditions, six are considered to be of extraordinary importance by Muslim scholars. They are known as the *Sahih Sittah* (the six authentic ones). They are, 1) *Sahih Bukhari,* 2) *Sahih Muslim;* 3) *Jaml Al-Tirmidhi;* 4) *Suman Abu Daud;* 5) *Sunan Ibn Majah* and 6) *Suman Nisai.*[40] Next to revelation, the *Hadith* of Prophet Muhammad acquires a very important position in Islam. The traditions not provide a commentary on the Quranic verses but also touch and demonstrate the methods to put them into practice. Muslims believed that the Prophet Muhammad was sent by God as "a mercy to all beings", he has shown us, through his commandments and teachings, how to tend and care for the creatures.[41] As in the Qur'an there are many *Hadith* related to nature but here we will confine to only few areas.

The traditions of Prophet which occupies second in command in Islamic theology, alludes to several instances when the Prophet gave preference to ecological balance: Ablution (with water) is a must before every prayer and the Prophet has given it a top position among the obligatory duties taught by Islam. Prodigality was condemned by him. Wastage of energy, water and other natural resources were denounced by the teachings even in acts like eating. He commanded, "Kill not your heart with excess of eating and drinking." In the light of the above traditions the environmental hygiene was given special importance during the peak of Islamic civilization.[42] The Prophet said, "the merciful are shown mercy by the All-Merciful. Show mercy to those on the earth, and He who is in the heaven will show mercy unto you."[43]

God commanded human to provide for the needs of any animal under their care, and he warned that a person who causes an animal to die of starvation or thirst is punished by God in the fire of hell.[44] Furtheremore, he directed human beings to provide for needy animals in general, telling of a person whose sins God pardoned for the act of giving water to a dog in desperate thirst. Then the people asked, O messenger of God, is there a reward in doing good to these animals?

---

[40] (No author name), *Selected Sayings of the Holy Prophet of Islam,* (Punjab: Nazarat Isha'nt Qadian, n.d.), 1.

[41] Mohd. Kaleemur Rahman, "Environmental Awareness in Islam", in *Islam and the Environment,* ed., A.R. Agwan, (New Delhi: Institute of Objective Studies, 1997), 147.

[42] Mohd. Kaleemur Rahman, "Environmental Awareness in Islam," 147-148.

[43] Cited in Abubakar Ahmad Bakadar, "Islamic Principles for the Conservation of the Natural Envirornment," in *Islam and the Environment,* ed., A.R. Agwan, (New Delhi: Institute of Objective Studies, 1997), 82

[44] Abubakar Ahmad Bakadar, "Islamic Principles for the Conservation of the Natural Environment", 82.

He said, there is reward in doing good to every living thing. Thus,, hunting and fishing for food is permitted in Islam; however, the prophet cursed anyone who uses a living creature as target, taking a life for mere sport.[45] Prophet Muhammad said, "if a Muslim plants any plant and human being, beast birds eat of it, he shall be rewarded as if he had given that much in charity."[46] Allah's messenger has a great concern for the environment as he knows that it is from God which has been created for us, therefore it needs to be cared specially.

4) Eco-Concerns in *Shariah*

The Arabic term *"Shariah"* means the way or path to the watering hole. The word refers to God's law in its divine and revealed sense. Following the original meaning of the Arabic wore, it is said to be the source from which all properly Islamic behaviours derive.[47] One of the unique characteristics of Islamic law is that it aims explicitly at the universal common good of all created beings. This reflects a conviction that the best interests of all species, generation, peoples, regions and individual are ultimately in harmony and not in conflict, in the scheme of God, the Almighty, all Knowing.[48]

An important aspect of Islamic law is that all animals have certain legal rights, enforceable by the courts and by the office of the *hisbah*. It means to reckon or sum up, the term refers to the institution in Islamic state to regulate markets and maintain public orders. This was formulated seven centuries ago on the basis of the prophetic traditions. They are, "If an animal is sick or aged no benefits would come from them; animal should not be burdened beyond what they can bear; never break their bones until they become cold and their lives have passed away; never slaughter their young ones within their sight; males and females should put together during their mating season, etc. Islam looks upon these creatures as subjected in the service of human fulfilling vital roles in the development of this world.[49]

Islamic Criminal Law does not permit to do harm, injury, wrong or crime against any living creature. This is regardless of the nature of such a creature, whether human,, animal or otherwise. Islamic law states clearly that if there is

---

[45] Abubakar Ahmad Bakadar, "Islamic Principles for the Conservation of the Natural Environment", 82.

[46] Al-lmam Zain-ud-din, Ahmed bin Abdul-Lateef and Az-Subaidi, comps., *The Translation of the Meaning of summarised Sahih Al-Bukhari Arabic – English,* Trans. Muhammadd Mushin Khan (Soudi Arabia, Maktba Dar-us-Salam, 1994), 956.

[47] Cf. Gordon D. Newby, *The Concise Encyclopedia of Islam,*(England: One World Publication, 2002), 82-83.

[48] Abubakaar Ahmad Bakadar, "Islamic Principles for the Conservation of the Natural Environment", 101.

[49] Abubakar Ahmad Bakadar, "Islamic Principles for the Conservation of the Natural Environment", 83-84.

an injustice or crime against another creature, one not only has to try to repair the damage by compensation to the victim of one's violation or the right which had been taken away from him/her, but also he/she has to beg for the forgiveness of Allah. On the basis of these rules, activities against animals and the natural environment are crimes against one's immediate victim, and also a crime against God, since the criminal conduct in question constitutes a violation of Divine instructions. Muslim jurists maintain, in connection to environment, that conservation of environment is one of the rights of Allah to which human is entrusted responsibility. Misusing the natural environment is not only an injustice committed to self and his/her generation, but also an injustice committed against future generations, which is crime as per Muslim law, and punishable.[50]

5) Islam's Major Eco-concerns

Let me sum up Islam's major ecological concerns that are very clear which based on Qur'an and other Islamic sources.[51]All things that God has created in this universe in due proportion and measure both quantitatively and qualitatively (Surah 54:49; 13:8: 15:19; 24:41; 20:53). God did not create anything in this universe in vain, without wisdom, value and purpose (Surah 44:38-39; 6:95). All created beings are created to serve God by performing their ordained roles as best to benefit each other. This leads to a cosmic symbiosis (*takaful*). The universal common good is a principle that pervades the universe and an important implication of God's unity.[52]

Humans are part of this universe, the elements of which are complementary to one another in an integrated whole. Indeed, humans are distinct part of the universe and have a special position among its other parts. The relation between humans and universe, as defined and clarifies by Quran and the Sunna:[53]

> A relationship of meditation on, and consideration and contemplation of, the universe and what it contains.
>
> A relationship of sustainable utilization, development and employment for human's benefit and for the fulfilment of his/her interests.
>
> A relationship of care and nurture, for human's good works are not limited to the benefit of the human species, but rather extend to the benefit of all created beings.

God's wisdom has ordained to grant human beings stewardship (*khilafah*) on the earth. Therefore, in addition to being part of the earth and part of the

---

[50] Nurdeng Deuraseh, "Maintaining a Healthy Environment: An Islamic Ethical Approach", in *European Journal of Scocial Sciences*, 8/4 (2009), 529.

[51] Bakadar, *Islamic Principles...*, 72.

[52] Bakadar, *Islamic Principles...*, 72.

[53] Bakadar, *Islamic Principles...*, 73.

universe, humans are also executors of God's instructions and commands. And as such humans are only managers of this earth and not proprietors; beneficiaries and not disposers or ordainers.[54] Prophet declares: "The world is beautiful and verdant and verily God, be he exalted, has made you his stewards in it and he sees how you acquit yourselves."[55]

All of the resources upon which life depends have been created by God and entrusted humans. He has ordained sustenance for all people and for all living things (Surah 41:10). Thus the utilization of these resources is, in Islam, the right and privilege of all people and all species. Similarly, he should not regard such use as restricted to one generation above all other generations. It is rather a joint usufruct in which each generation uses and makes the best use of nature, according to its need, without disrupting or adversely affecting the interests of future generations. Therefore, human should not abuse, misuse or distort the natural resources as each generation is entitled to benefit from them but does not entitle to "own" them in an absolute sense.[56]

The right to utilize and harness natural resources, which God has granted human, necessarily involves an obligation on human's part to conserve them both quantitatively and qualitatively. It follows that human has no right to cause the degradation of the environment and distort its intrinsic suitability for human life and settlement.[57] While the attitude of Islam to the environment, the sources of life, and the resources of nature are based in part on prohibition of abuse, it is also based on construction and sustainable development. This integration of the development and conservation of natural resources is clear in the idea of bringing life to the land and causing it flourish through agriculture, cultivation and construction. Quran says, "It is he who has produced you from the earth and settled you therein (Surah 11:61)." The Prophet declared, "if any Muslim plants a tree or sows a field, and a human, bird or animal eats from it, it shall be reckoned as charity from him;"[58] and "if the day of resurrection come upon any one of you while he has a seedling in hand, let him plant it."[59] This positive attitude involves taking measures to improve all aspects of life: health, nutrition and the

---

[54] Bakadar, *Islamic Principles...*, 73.

Humans are granted stewardship to manage the earth in accordance with the purposes intended by its creator; to utilize it for his/her own benefit and the benefit of other created beings, and for the fulfilment off his/her interests and of theirs. He/she is entrusted with its maintenance and care, and must use it as a trustee, within the limits dictated by his trust.

[55] Hadith of Abu Said al-Khudri.

[56] Bakadar, *Islamic Principles...*, 74.

[57] Bakadar, *Islamic Principles...*, 74.

[58] Hadith of al Bukhari.

[59] Hadith of al Musnad.

psychological and spiritual dimensions for man's benefit and the maintenance of his welfare, as well as for the betterment of life for all future generations.[60]

A Call for Change

Let me sum up briefly the forgoing discussion. We must note the fact that failing to follow the Quranic injunctions or any other religion, we have, of course, upset the ecological balance. And it is up to us to set it right again. This will require great effort, and courageous personal change. We need to do our best to restore and preserve the balance in nature; to take up our responsibility as viceroys of God and hence as custodians, stewards, and trustees in whose trust God has placed the resources we enjoy. We need to maintain the ecosystems that harbour the dazzling array of life forms God has created, including animals, birds, insects, and plants. But the required personal changes are sometimes simple and manageable. We can easily reduce, reuse, and recycle waste. We can to a large extent conserve our use of water and other natural resources. We can in some small way reverse the process of deforestation by planting one tree at a time. It is time to pay better attention to the principles set forth in God's message, including this one: "Man shall have nothing but what he strives for" (Quran 53:39).

We have caused corruption on land and sea, and it is up to us to mend our ways. Our present crisis calls on religious leaders to find faith-based messages that will inspire the faithful towards a heightened environmental awareness. We have seen that there is ample content in the sacred traditions of Islam to meet this need. What remains to be seen is the extent to which we will rally to this call for personal change.

---

[60] Bakadar, *Islamic Principles...*, 75.

Chapter 10

Prominent Ecological Movements in India

The "ecological (eco) movements" are also sometimes treated as environmental movements, also including conservation and green politics, are diverse scientific, social, and political movements for addressing environmental issues. Environmentalists advocate the sustainable management of resources and stewardship of the environment through changes in public policy and individual behaviour. In its recognition of humanity as a participant in (not enemy of) ecosystems, the movement is centered on ecology, health, and human rights.

The environmental/ecological movement is an international movement, represented by a range of organizations, from the large to grassroots and varies from country to country. Due to its large membership, varying and strong beliefs, and occasionally speculative nature, the environmental movement is not always united in its goals. The movement also encompasses some other movements with a more specific focus, such as the climate movement. At its broadest, the movement includes private citizens, professionals, religious devotees, politicians, scientists, non-profit organizations and individual advocates. The major concern of this chapter is to discuss some popular ecological movements only related to Indian context.

The environment in which we are living plays a vital role in our survival. The environment includes all the natural resources such as air water, land, forests, minerals and so on. It is our responsibility to protect the natural resources. However, due to several reasons, there is a lot of misuse of these natural resources, in the form of land degradation, water pollution, air pollution, and deforestation. All these factors lead to deterioration of our environment. There have been many efforts made in order to reclaim the environment by people through voluntary organizations, which are concerned about the environment. There are instances where people have revoked and adopted non-violent action movements for protecting their environment.

Environmental and ecological movements are among the important examples of the collective actions of several social groups. Protection and recognition of constitutional and democratic rights, which are not defined by law but form an important part of the day to day living of the subaltern masses like the control over their resources, the right of indigenous people to preserve their culture, protection of environment and maintenance of ecological balance are significant concerns of these movements, as they affect the human life to a great extent. These movements also reflect an enlarged vision of economics and politics. Economic justice sought by these movements does not mean mere distribution of resources but encompass a larger vision like enhancement in the quality of life through recognition of people's right over their natural resources, their right to live with dignity, and their participation in the decision–making.

The concerns of human environment received spectacular attention of scholars following the conclusion of the United Nations Conference on Human Environment, Stockholm in 1972. By the 1980s the "**green movement**" became a worldwide phenomenon encompassing various countries of the world including India. It is signified by several movements of people for the protection of their environmental and ecological rights in India, 'eco-greens' or 'green movement' in Germany and North America. Environmental or ecological movements gained worldwide attention only in the second half of the twentieth century. These movements focus not only on basic survival issues but also on larger ecological concerns. In fact, there has been no single unified and homogenous environmental discourse in India. There has been what Guha calls 'varieties of environmentalism'. In this context the present chapter attempts to understand history of environmental movements in India. Some of the prominent environmental/ecological movements will be discussed in brief.

1) Eco-Movements in India: Issues and Concerns

The environmental or ecological movement is a broad generic term which is generally used to describe and understand different types of local struggles and conflicts concerning with livelihood issues and ecological security within the larger context of the development debate. These movements in fact assess critically and questioned the notion of development and preservation ecology pursued by the Indian state and its officials since colonial time. The genesis of the environmental movement in India can be traced to the Chipko movement (1973) in Garhwal region in the new state of Uttaranchal. In fact, between 1970s and 1980s there were several struggles in India around issues of rights to forest and water which raised larger ecological concerns like rights of communities in forest resources, sustainability of large scale environmental projects like dams, issues of displacement and rehabilitation.

The Indian environmental movement is critical of the colonial model of development pursued by the post–colonial state. The post–independent state failed to build up a development agenda based on the needs of the people and continued to advocate the modern capitalist agenda which led to the destruction of environment, creating poverty and marginalisation of rural communities. Formation of national parks, sanctuaries, protected areas in India, in fact represents the conventional environmentalism which the Indian state advocated with the aim of preserving wildlife and biodiversity by pushing people out of these areas. In response to this conventional environmentalism which considered the Indian state to be the custodian of natural resources, the environmental movement in India advocated the ideology of 'environmentalism of the poor'. It not only criticized modern developmentalism, but also strongly advocated the revival of traditional 'self–sufficient village economy'. It brought communities to the centre stage of Indian environmental discourse.

The ecologists/environmentalists believed that local communities were best suited to conserve natural resources as their survival depended in the sustainable use of such resources. They argued that in order to make the sustainable use of the resource the customary rights or traditional rights should be given back to the people, which were taken away by the State, and traditional institutions should also be recognised. In a nutshell, the environmental movement in India concentrates on the issue of equity in relation to access and use of natural resources. Unlike in the West, a significant characteristic of environmental movements in India is that they have mainly involved the women, the poor and disadvantaged masses who have been directly affected by or are victims of environmental degradation. Thus, these movements are primarily political expressions of the struggle of local communities and people who are victims of environmental degradation or abuse of resources.

Gadgil and Guha identify four broad strands within the environmental movements in India based on vision, ideology and strategy. The first types are those which emphasise on the moral necessity to restrain overuse and ensure justice to the poor and marginalised. Mainly Gandhians belong to this strand. The second strand stresses on the need to dismantle the unjust social order through struggle. Marxists mostly follow this strand. The Third and fourth strands advocate reconstruction, i.e., employing technologies appropriate to the given context and time. They reflect the concerns of the scientists or the spontaneous efforts of the communities at the village level who aim at protecting local community forests or the right to pursue environment-friendly agricultural practices. Before we discuss some examples of environmental and ecological movements in India it will be relevant to reproduce the following table from Ghanshyam Shah's book *Social Movements: A Review of Literature*. This table will help us to have an overview of the issues, categories and examples of environmental movements, which have taken place in India.[1]

Table

Categories	Issues	Some Examples
Forest and land based	- Right of access to forest resources - Non commercial use of natural resources - Prevention of land degradation - Social justice and human rights	Chipko, Appico and tribal movements all over the country, for example, Jharkand/ Bastar belt
Marine resources and fisheries, aquaculture	- Ban on trawling, preventing, commercialization of shrimp and pawn culture - Protection of marine resources - Implementation of coastal zone regulations	National Fishermen Forum working for traditional fisher folk on Kerala, Chika Bachavo Andolan, Orissa
Industrial Pollution	- Stricter pollution control measures, compensation - Prevention of reckless expansion of industries without considering design, vocational factors and livelihood issues of local population	Zahiro Gas Morcha in Bhoopal; Ganga Mukti Andolan in Bihar, Movement against Harihar Polyfibrc factory in Karnataka; Movement against pollution of Sonc River by Gwalior Rayon factory led by Vidushak Karkhana Group of Shahdol district, MP; Movements against poisoning of Cheliya river in Kerala by Kerala Shastra Sahitya Parishadd (KSSP)

[1] Ghanshyam Shah, *Social Movements: A Review of Literature,* (2004), 257-258; Janki Andharia and Chandan Sengupta. 1998. 'The Environmental Movement: Global Issues and the Indian Reality', in *The Indian Journal of Social Work,* (59 (1), 1998), 429-431.

Development projects: a) Dams and irrigation projects	- Protection of tropical forests - Ecological balance - Destructive development - Rehabilitation and resettlement of the displaced	Silent Valley movement by KSSP, Narmada Bachao Andolan; Movements against Tchri by Tchri Bandh Virodhi Samiti; the Koshi Gandhak Bodhghat and Bedthi; Bhopalpatnam and Ichampalli in the west ; the Tunghbhadra, Malaprabha and Ghatprabha Schemes in the south; Koyna Project affected Communities
b) Power Projects	- Ecological balance, Rehabilitation and resettlement, high costs	Jan Andolan in Dabhol against Enron; Koc-Karo Jan Sanghatana in Bihar; Anti-mine project in Doon valley.
c) Mining	- Depletion of natural resources.	Anti-Bauxite mine movement (Balco Project) in Orissa and also in AP
d) Industrial plants/ Railway projects/Airport projects	Land degradation Ecological imbalance Realignment Rehabilitation and resettlement of displaced Ecological	Protests and demands of Kakana Raillway Realignment Action Committee Citizen's group against Dupont Nylon 6.6 Goa. Amravati Bachao Abhyan against a large chemical complex
e) Military bases	- Ecological balance - Rehabilitation - Resettlement and safety	Anti-missiles test range in Baliapal and at Nctrahat, Bihar.
Wild-life sanctuaries National parks	- Displacement, rehabilitation and resettlement, loss of livelihood	Ekjoot in Bhimashankar region of Maharashtra, Shramik Kukti Andolan in Sanjay Gandhi Nationnal Park, Bombay

Tourism	- Displacement, cultural changes, social ills.	Himachal Bachao Saadd, Goa
Advocacy groups/ individual campaigns, citizen's Action Groups	- Policy inputs, stricter measures for protected area - Clear policy on national park and wild-life sanctuaries, lobbying, research, training and documentation on wild-life, conservation, education, community-based environmental management. Publications on environmental issues	Society for Clean Cities, Bombay Natural History Society (BNHS), Centre for Science and Environment (CSE), Delhi, Research, training and documentation organization such as Bombay Environmental Action Group, Save Bombay Committee, Save Pune Citizen's Committee, etc.
Appropriate technology/ organic farming	- International debates - Sustainable development, Eco-Friendly models of development - Low cost environmental friendly housing and technology	Ralegaon Siddhi (Anna Hazare's village) SOPECOMM. Laurie Baker's housing experiments Peoples Science Institute, Dehradun

2) Prominent Ecological Movements in India

This section discusses some of the forest-based movements, Anti-dam movements and movements caused due to the environmental pollution. The forest-based movements discussed here include Chipko and Appico movements; the anti-Dam movement includes NBA; the anti pollution–movement includes those which took place in Delhi.

A) *Chipko* Movement

The term '*chipko*' means (*chipak jayenge*) to hug or embrace (trees). As it is noted earlier, the origin of modern environmentalism and environmental movements in India can be ascribed to the Chipko movement in the central Himalayan region in the early 1970s. Chipko movement, launched to protect the Himalayan forests from destruction, which has its' roots in the pre-independence days. Many struggles were organised to protest against the colonial forest policy during the early decades of 20th century. Peoples' main demand in these protests was that the benefits of the forest, especially the right to fodder, should go to local people. These struggles have continued in the post-independent era as the forest policies of independent India are no different from that of colonial ones.

The origin of 'Chipko' movement took place during 1973. In the early 1973 the forest department refused to allot ash trees to the *Dashauli Gram Swarajya Sangha* (DGSS), a local cooperative organisation based in Chamoli districts, for making agricultural implements. On the other hand, the forest department allotted ash trees to a private company, i.e., Symonds Company. This incident provoked the DGSS to fight against this injustice through lying down in front of timber trucks and burning resin and timber depots as was done in Quit India movement. When these methods were found unsatisfactory, Chandi Prasad Bhat - one of the leaders, suggested of embracing the trees and thus 'Chipko' was born. This form of protest was instrumental in driving away the private company from felling the ash trees. With its success the movement spread to other neighbouring areas and subsequently the movement came to be popularly known as Chipko movement both nationally and internationally.

From its beginning the Chipko movement concentrated on ecological issues such as depletion of forest cover and soil erosion. Three important aspects were responsible for the success of Chipko movement. First, the close links between the livelihoods of the local people and the nature of the movement. The local people consider Chipko as a fight for basic subsistence which have been denied to them by the institutions and policies of the State. In addition, specificity of the area where Chipko movement took place; involvement of women in the contribution to households' subsistence and the overwhelming support to anti-alcohol campaign have led to the overwhelming support of women which is unique to the Chipko movement. The second aspect is with regard to the nature of agitation. Unlike other environmental movements Chipko has strictly adhered to the Gandhian tradition of freedom struggle, i.e., non–violence. Third, the simplicity and sincerity of the leaders like Sunderlal Bahuguna and their access to national leaders like Mrs. Indira Gandhi, other politicians and officials also helped to the success of the movement to a large extent. The demands of the Chipko movement were as follows:

i) complete stoppage of cutting trees for commercial purposes;
ii) the traditional rights should be recognised on the basis of minimum needs of the people;
iii) making the arid forest green by increasing people's participation in tree cultivation;
iv) formation of village committees to manage forests;
v) development of the forest related home-based industries and making available the raw materials, money and technique for it; and
vi) giving priority to a forestation in the light of local conditions, requirements and varieties.

What is distinctive about Chipko movement is that it was the forerunner as well as direct inspiration for a series of popular movements in defence of community rights to natural resources. Sometimes, these struggles revolved around forests, in other instances, around control and use of pasture, mineral or fish resources.

B) *Appiko* Movement

Inspired by the *Chipko* movement the villagers of Western Ghats, in the Uttar Kannada region of Karnataka started *Appiko Chalewali* movement during September – November, 1983. Here, the destruction of forest was caused due to commercial felling of trees for timber extraction. Natural forests of the region were felled by the contractors which resulted in soil erosion and drying up of perennial water resources. In the Saklani village in Sirsi, the forest dwellers were prevented from collecting forest products such as twigs, dried branches, non timber forest products for the purposes of fuel wood, fodder, honey, gum and so on. They were denied of their customary rights to these products.

In September 1983, women and youth of the region decided to launch a movement similar to *Chipko*, in South India. Women and youth from Saklani and surrounding villages walked five miles to a nearby forest and hugged trees there. They forced the fellers and the contractors of the state forest department to stop cutting trees. The people demanded a ban on felling of green trees. The agitation continued for 38 days and this forced the state government to finally concede to their demands and withdrew the order for felling of trees. For some time government stopped felling of trees which was resumed again after some time that started the movement again. The movement was backed by the local people. Even the daily wage labourers hired by the contractors to fell trees stopped doing their work.

In October, the movement entered into its second phase and this took place in Bengaon forest. Here, the forest was of mix tropical semi–evergreen type and mostly on hilly terrain. The inhabitants of the region who were primarily tribal or the indigenous people depended on the forest for their survival and livelihood. Disappearance of bamboo due to commercial felling deprived them of the basic source to make items like baskets, mats, etc. The main source of their income was the sale of these items. When felling of trees did not stop people started the movement. The movement was spontaneous in nature. The local indigenous people hugged tree to stop them from cutting and finally the government had to give in to their demands. Similar movements also started in other areas like Husri. It also inspired the local people to launch the movement. In fact, *Appiko* movement became a symbol of people's power for their rights of natural resources vis-a-vis the state. In November, the movement spread to Nidgod village in Siddapur taluka preventing the state from commercial felling of trees in this deciduous forest of the region.

The *Appiko* movement was successful in its three fold objectives, i.e., 1) protection of the existing forest cover, 2) regeneration of trees in denuded lands and 3) utilising forest wealth with proper consideration to conservation of natural resources. The movement also created awareness among the villagers throughout the Western Ghats about the ecological danger posed by the commercial and industrial interests to their forest which was the main source of sustenance. Like the *Chipko,* the *Appiko* movement adopted the Gandhian way of protest and mobilisation for sustainable society in which there is a balance between human and nature.

C) *Narmada Bachao Andolan* (NBA)

Narmada Bachao Andolan is a social movement consisting of tribal, farmers, environmentalists and human rights activists against a number of large dams being built across the Narmada River, which flows in India through the states of Gujarat, Madhya Pradesh and Maharashtra. Narmada river project is the most important case study in terms of maturation of environmental movement and dynamics related to politics of development. No other development project in India has brought into focus the intensity of magnitude of eco-development problems to such a level of informed debate, political mobilisation and grass root activism as this project. The controversy which surrounded this project has challenged the government at all levels and at the same time was successful in creating and forging linkages with civil society organisation and NGOs, both at the national and international level. In fact, it has contributed to the political discourse of alternative development in India.

Sardar Sarovar Project which is an interstate multi-purpose project with a terminal major dam in Gujarat is being built on river Narmada which is the fifth largest river in India–1312 km long. The Narmada Valley Project, with its two mega projects- Sardar Sarovar Project and Narmada Sagar Project in Madhya Pradesh, is the largest single river valley project with the objective of making the world's largest human–made lake. The consequences of the project are, however, quite glaring and alarming. The reservoir will submerge 37,000 hectares of land of which 11,000 hectares are classified as forest. It will displace about one lakh persons of 248 villages- 19 of Gujarat, 36 of Maharashtra and 193 of Madhya Pradesh. The opponents of the dam see it as "the World's worst man-made ecological disaster."[2]

The state government initiated the project as Gujarat was one of the worst water–starved regions in India and there was drastic shortage of water for domestic, commercial, agricultural and industrial needs. Further, the state had witnessed one of the worst droughts between 1985 and 1988 which further reinforced this

---

[2] M. Karpagam, *Green Management Theory and Applications,* (New Delhi: Ane Books Pvt. Ltd., 2010), 58.

project. However, according to the critics, it is seen as "the world's worst human–made ecological disaster" and it is considered unviable. It may be mentioned here that originally Narmada project was considered to be an irrigation project of a 161 feet high dam. Later it was found that water could be technologically harnessed making it a multipurpose dam if its level is raised to 455 feet.

Consequently, the state governments started looking for finances not only from the centre but also from the World Bank. Plans for damming the river at Gora in Gujarat surfaced as early as 1946. In fact, Prime Minister Jawaharlal Nehru laid the foundation for a 49.8-meter-high dam in 1961. After studying the new maps the dam planners decided that a much larger dam would be more profitable. The only problem was hammering out an agreement with neighbouring states–Madhya Pradesh and Maharashtra. In 1969, after years of negotiations attempting to agree on a feasible water-sharing formula, the Indian government established the Narmada Water Disputes Tribunal. Ten years later, it announced its award – the Narmada Water Disputes Tribunal Award. The award envisaged that land should be made available to the ousters at least year before submergence.

1978, the Narmada Water Disputes Tribunal approved the Narmada Valley Development Project, which included 30 large dams, 135 medium dams, and 3,600 small dams.[3] The government claimed that the SSP alone would irrigate almost 1.8 million hectares of land in Gujarat and an additional 73,000 hectares in the dry neighbouring state of Rajasthan, in addition to providing potable water to over 8,000 Gujarati villages and 135 urban centres. The benefits, however, would come at a high cost, including the displacement of tens of thousands of individuals and considerable environmental damage. Despite these foreseeable consequences, and in the absence of consultation with indigenous communities that would experience the environmental impact and involuntary displacement.[4] Before the Ministry of the Environment even cleared the Narmada Valley Development Projects in 1987, the World Bank sanctioned a loan for $450 million for the largest dam,[5] the Sardar Sarovar, in 1985. In actuality, construction on the Sardar Sarovar dam site had continued sporadically since 1961, but began in earnest in 1988.

---

[3] Kevin Wehr, *America's fight over Water, The Environmental and Political Effects of large-Scale Water Systems*, (New York: routledge, 2004), 194-195.

[4] https://essentialthinkers.wordpress.com/2013/10/13/the-story-of-narmada-bachao-andolan-human-rights/, 22-07-2016.

[5] Refer for information - https://essentialthinkers.wordpress.com/2013/10/13/the-story-of-narmada-bachao-andolan-human-rights/, 28-08-2016; https://en.wikipedia.org/wiki/Narmada_Bachao_Andolan, 01-08-2016:

https://essentialthinkers.wordpress.com/2013/10/13/the-story-of-narmada-bachao-andolan-human-rights/, 28-08-2016. N K Uberoi, *Environmental Management*, (New Delhi: Excel Books, 2007), 78.

Questions arose concerning the promises about resettlement and rehabilitation programme set up by the government. As a consequence, each state had a people's organisation which addressed these concerns. Soon, these groups came together to form the Narmada Bachao Andolan (NBA), or, the Save the Narmada Movement under the leadership Medha Patekar, a social activists. NBA became a powerful mass movement, started in 1985, against the construction of a huge dam on the Narmada River. It may be mentioned here that the NBA began as a fight for information about the Narmada Valley Development Projects but developed as a fight for just rehabilitation for the lakhs of people to be ousted by the Sardar Sarovar Dam and other large dams along the Narmada River. Eventually, when it became clear that the magnitude of the project precluded accurate assessment of damages and losses, and that rehabilitation was impossible, the movement challenged the very basis of the project and questioned its claim to development.

Unlike other social justice organizations in India at the time, the NBA directly opposed dam construction altogether and proposed various development alternatives, including decentralized methods of water harvesting. They demanded World Bank accountability for the displacement of millions and initially sought to verify the claims regarding benefits of the dams. Much of the early campaign was focused on transparency from the government and World Bank. NBA employed peaceful marches, protests, and large-scale hunger fasts. They also campaigned against paying taxes and denied government officials entry into villages.

In 1989, Lori Udall of the Environmental Defence Fund worked with a U.S. Congressional Committee to hold an oversight hearing on *Sardar Sarovar*, where Patkar could testify against the dam. In addition to working with the Environmental Defence Fund, the NBA would later partner with numerous other human rights, environmental, and solidarity organizations overseas, including the Narmada International Action Committee, Friends of the Earth, and Japan's Overseas Economic Cooperation Fund.[6]

NBA resistance operated at local, national, and international scales, redefining the terms of development, democracy, and accountability. In September 1989, Baba Amte, another prominent social activist and moral leader, led a 60,000 people in an anti-dam NBA rally in Harsud, a town of 20,000 people in Madhya Pradesh that faced submersion. The dam site and its surrounding areas were under the Indian Official Secrets Act, which prohibited the gathering of groups of more than five people. The whole area was turned into a police camp.

In response, local opponents, environmental activists, and academic, scientific and cultural professionals founded a cluster of NGOs. These NGOs allied in 1989 to form the Narmada Bachao Andolan (NBA), or the 'Save Narmada

---

[6] http://www.ecoindia.com/education/narmada-bachao-andolan.html, 12-7-2016.

Movement', led by Medha Patkar.[7] Since 1985, Patkar had been organizing protest marches against the dam, local people participated in large numbers at *Harsud* in September 1989 was attended by over 50,000 people, mostly local tribal.

Despite the police barricades, one year later in 1990, thousands of villagers marched to the town of Badwani, threatening to drown in the dams rising waters rather than be relocated. The slogan, '*koi nahin hatega: bandh nahin banega*!' (No one will move; the dam will not be built!) became much popular. These rallies and marches helped secure the allies of the Indian middle class and liberal intellectuals, as well the attention of other countries. The *Chakkajam* agitation in March 1990 saw participation of more than 10,000 local people.

In May of 1990, NBA organized a 2,000-person, five-day sit-in at Prime Minister V. P. Singh's residence in New Delhi, which convinced the Prime Minister to 'reconsider' the project. In December of the same year, five to six thousand men and women began the *Narmada Jan Vikas Sangharsh Yatra* (Narmada People's Progress Struggle March), marching over 100 kilometres. Marchers accompanied a seven-member team, including Medha Patkar, who all decided to give up their lives for the river. They were stopped on the Gujarat border. The government deployed Gujarati police and bussed thousands of government-supported pro-dam demonstrators from urban centers to counter-protest. The confrontation would last nearly two weeks. Marchers, who each had their hands voluntarily tied together to demonstrate their non-violence, were beaten, arrested, and dragged into trucks in which they were driven miles away and dumped in the wilderness.

Finally on January 7, 1991, the seven-member team began an indefinite hunger strike. Two days earlier Baba Amte had himself committed to a sit-in unto death. As tension rose, Indian and international press, TV, and documentary crews increased their coverage. Environmental activists increased pressure on Washington. Then 10,000 tribals participated in the Long March in January 1991. Representatives of local people have also been part of every indefinite hunger strike that has been one of the most effective strategies used by the initiative. Local people have also borne the brunt of the state repression in numerous incidents throughout the valley.[8]

---

[7] **Medha Patkar,** (born December 1, 1954, Bombay [now Mumbai], Maharashtra state, India) Indian social activist known chiefly for her work with people displaced by the Narmada Valley Development Project (NVDP), a large-scale plan to dam the Narmada Riverand its tributaries in the Indian states of Madhya Pradesh, Gujarat, and Maharashtra. An advocate of human rights, Patkar founded her campaigns on two basic tenets in the Indian constitution: the rights to life and to livelihood. Born to socially active parents, Patkar grew up in an environment imbued with a sense of social justice and freedom. She graduated with a bachelor's degree in science from Ruia College in Mumbai and earned a master's degree in social work from the Tata Institute of Social Sciences in the early 1980s. https://www.britannica.com/biography/Medha-Patkar, 28-09-2016.

[8] John Byrne, "The Long march of Live hood," *Environmental Justice*, vol-8 (London: transaction Publishers, 2009), 81.

Shaken by the unfavourable news coverage, the World Bank announced it would institute an Independent Review of the Sardar Sarovar projects. The review was the first of its kind and included sweeping mandates and oversight procedures. It may have been the first time in the history of the World Bank that a people's movement influenced their policy decisions.

On January 28, the fasters ended their hunger strike after 22 days without food. Medha Patkar, one of those fasting, was near death. The short-term victory was bittersweet: many were distrustful of the World Bank, but they returned home with the other protesters. After some claimed the end of the hunger strike to be a victory for the Indian government, NBA protesters claimed they would stay in villages until drowning from the Sardar Sarovar reservoir. In response, the government banned Patkar and other activists from the villages during the monsoon, and prohibited the villagers from holding anti-dam protests. The NBA defied the bans, and hundreds of their supporters were arrested during the monsoon months. Known as 'monsoon *satyagrahas*,' hundreds of individuals refused to move as rising waters entered fields and homes. In most of the monsoon *satyagrahas*, police physically dragged people out of flooding areas in an attempt to rob the protest of its symbolic power. Arrests, beatings, and detentions rose in Madhya Pradesh, where many declared readiness for monsoon *satyagraha* between 1992 and 1993.

International human rights NGOs began documenting abuses against NBA activists. A June 1992 report by Human Rights Watch noted increases in arbitrary arrests, illegal detentions, beatings, rape and other forms of physical abuses. Some reports document Indian police shooting and killing individuals during forced relocation. Other NGOs worked to form the Narmada International Human Rights Panel, which garnered support of 42 environmental and human rights NGOs representing 16 countries. The Bank's Independent Review, known as the Morse Commission, issued its report in June 1992. The report exposed the Bank's violation of its own policies and recommended drastic reform of the relocation programs and environmental assessment. It warned that opposition to the dam was so strong in the affected villages that the authorities would have to use "unacceptable means" to get the dam built. However, the Bank reassured the Indian government it would continue support, but only if the government met benchmarks for reform.

In response to the Morse Commission's report, environmental activists wrote an open letter to World Bank President Lewis Preston, which they published as a full-page advertisement in the London Financial Times. It warned that if the Bank refused to withdraw funding for Sardar Sarovar then NGOs would launch a campaign to cut government funding of the Bank. The letter was endorsed by 250 NGOs and coalitions from 37 countries. Similar actions were taken in the Washington Post and the New York Times. A February 1993 "Peoples'

Referendum" in the Narmada Valley, carried out by the NBA, organized over 22,500 families in opposition to forced relocation.[9]

With mounting pressure from NBA, other citizen activists, and international NGOs and Economic Funds, the Indian government soon cancelled the remaining loans knowing that it could not meet the Bank's guidelines, thus ending support from the World Bank for the Sardar Sarovar dam. The controversy led to the creation of the World Bank Inspection Panel in 1993. It was a milestone for the human rights movement and the first mechanism established to enable local groups to challenge World Bank projects.

While the withdrawal of the World Bank was a milestone accomplishment for NBA and social movements across the globe, it was unfortunately not the end of the Narmada dam struggle. Even without the World Bank's support, the Indian government pledged to continue the dam project with its own funds. In response, the Gujarati government decided to raise $200 million and go ahead with the project. The Bank's withdrawal in 1993 affected dam construction much less than anticipated. Further, the withdrawal reduced the Indian government's accountability to the outside world.

The campaign against the dam refocused their effort on the Supreme Court of India. One criticism of NBA's strategy is that it avoided the Supreme Court until the withdrawal of the World Bank left them no choice. Construction continues to this day (March 2010). The Sardar Sarovar dam has already displaced well over 320,000 people, with over a million affected by related canal systems and other projects. NBA continues direct action and legal processes with international involvement to stop further dam construction on the Narmada.[10] Many issues of the project are yet unresolved. However, what is more important is that the Movement has been successful to a considerable extent. The achievements of the movements include:1) exit of the World Bank from *Sardar Sarovar* in 1993; 2) halt of *Sardar Sarovar* construction 1994-99; 3) withdrawal of foreign investors from Maheshwar dam 1999-2001.

The NBA is unique in the sense that it underlined the importance of people's right to information which the authorities finally had to concede under media and popular pressure. It was successful not only in mobilising hundreds of thousands people from different walks of life to put pressure on the State government for its anti-people policies, affecting and displacing lakhs of tribals from their homes and livelihoods. It also received immense international support. Resorting to non–violent mode of protest and following Gandhian vision of constructive work, NBA, as its popularly known is distinctive landmark in the

[9]https://essentialthinkers.wordpress.com/2013/10/13/the-story-of-narmada-bachao-andolan-human-rights/, 22-07-2016.

[10] http://nvdatabase.swarthmore.edu/content/narmada-bachao-andolan-nba-forces-end-world-bank-funding-sardar-sarovar-dam-india-1985-1993

history of environmentalism in India. However, in the face of recalcitrant attitude of the governments, the NBA continues with the involvement of effected people and civil society organisations.

D) Urban-based Environmental Movements

In the recent past environmental pollution caused due to the industrialisation has become the focus of collective action by the civil society organisations, NGOs, concerned individuals, especially lawyers, scientists, environmentalists and social activists. They sought the intervention of the judiciary and drew the attention of the state for showing concern to the pollution caused by the process of industrialization, urbanisation and modernisation. However, the main focus of the collective action against pollution has been in the urban areas. Certain tragedies like gas leakage in Bhopal based Union Carbide MNC, Chernobyl in former Soviet Union where thousands of people were killed created worries among the people on the negative effect of the industrialisation. Though the 1990s have seen increased concern about the environmental pollution, awareness about the disastrous impact of the environmental pollution started growing in the 1960s.

All the major cities of India are facing acute air, water and other kinds on environmental pollution. Continuous immigration of the people from rural areas into the cities, their habitat in the congested areas which exist along with the polluting small scale industries; increasing number of vehicles; and unplanned expansion of cities, open drainage, etc., have created levels of environmental hazards. This pollution made people susceptible to multiple diseases. The protection of environment did not form significant part of the policies of the state. The Nehruvian model gave more emphasis to the industrialisation without showing much concern for the pollution it was going create. However, in 1976 a Constitutional Amendment called upon the state "to protect and improve the environment and to safeguard the forest and wildlife of the country" and made the fundamental duty of every citizen "to protect and improve the natural environment including forests, lakes, rivers and wildlife, and to have compassion for living creatures".

In the following decades the state passed legislations to prevent air pollution and environmental protection like **The Air Act of 1981** and **Environmental Protection Act of 1986**. The judiciary has become the arbiter of people's rights which include their protection from the environmental protection also since the emergence of the device of the **Public Interest Litigation (PIL)**. In the face of indifference of the executive and legislature about the people's problems, the PIL has become an effective weapon through which people seek the intervention of the state on these issues. The intervention of the judiciary forced the state to introduce some measures for prevention of environmental pollution. **Justice Krishna Iyer, Justice Kuldeep Singh** and advocate **MC Mehta** have made remarkable contribution in protection of the environment.

Delhi is one of the most polluted cities in the world. Three issues related to the environmental pollution have been focus of activities of some concerned of the civil society components in the recent past. These are air pollution caused due to the vehicular and industrial pollution and water pollution in river Yamuna. The number of private and public vehicles has increased many folds in the recent past. This has polluted the environment and made people, especially children and old vulnerable to multiple diseases. Reacting to the court order which was result of a PIL, the government made it compulsory to introduce the CNG vehicles and make the pollution check mandatory for all private vehicles. The introduction of the CNG vehicles has resulted in the reduction of the environmental pollution in the city. Similarly, the Delhi government has been forced to shift the polluting industries out of the city and launch the Yamuna River cleaning operation. The closing down of the polluting factories and industries proved the labour unrest in the city. It resulted in the police firing, which killed one labourer. In fact, this is related to the unplanned development policy. The migration to the cities from the villages is inevitable. Unless some measures are adopted to absorb the migrating population, and increasing usage of the vehicles is stopped, it seems the environmental pollution will remain.

Government programs at central and state levels taken in favour of environment protection, such as ***Swacha Bharat*** initiated by Indian central government to make India clean from pollution and ***Harita Haram*** initiated by Telangana State government as a project to plant 5 crores of plants within two years to protect eco-balance are note worthy from ecological point of view.

To sum up, environmental and ecological movements became prominent in India since the 1970s, like other such movements. The concerns of these movements are not confined to any particular groups. They are all encompassing – the entire village and urban communities, women, tribals, peasants, middle classes and nature. Even the issues raised by them concern all sections of society in varying degrees. These issues are: protection of people's right to access of natural resources, prevention of land degradation, preventing commercialisation of nature resources and environmental pollution, maintenance of ecological balance, rehabilitation of displaced people and so on. These issues are also related to people's dignity, environmental rights and their decision-making rights on the issues concerning them. The state in collaboration with the donor agencies disturbed the ecological balance in the society following independence. In the process this adversely affected the people. The latter launched environmental and ecological movement with their leadership, NGOs and other civil society organisations. These movements have raised the levels of people's consciousness, and achieved some success. They form a significant aspect of democracy in India.

Chapter 11

Contributions of Ecologically Enlightened

It is, indeed, noteworthy to know about and much helpful of study the lives and contributions of ecologists/environmentalists those who enlightened the people bringing awareness towards care for environment where they are living. Many persons, who were/are ecologically enlightened, dedicated their lives to the cause of protecting environment from degradation of modern trends. "Ecology" has become an important discipline of university curriculums paying the way to study environment from multi-disciplinary dimensions.

Environ in French means to encircle, and everything that surrounds an organism is understood to be its environment. Environmental science is basically a branch of biology and it examines the effect of human beings on the environment, as well as the relationships between the environment and the organisms living within it. It is a multidisciplinary science, and the environmental scientist integrates and makes use of many other branches of science including biology, soil science, physics, chemistry, ecology, geology, geography, philosophy and theology as well as quite a few other branches of social sciences too. The environmental scientist is concerned with all the impacts of human activities on earth and its biodiversity. Environmental scientists were not much known publicly before the 1960s but their work came into prominence after some great publications. This chapter is an attempt to review briefly the important ecologists of the world and prominent/popular environmentalists in India.

1) World Famous Environmental Scientists

There are many to mention, but we will see few prominent ecologists and environmentalists who enlightened world community through their researches and other contributions on ecological problems.

A) Rachel Carson

Rachel Carson was born to Maria Frazier and Robert Warden Carson on May 27, 1907 in Springdale, Pennsylvania, U.S. and died on April 14, 1964 at the age of fifty-six years, in Silver Spring, Maryland, U.S. She is best known for her book *Silent Spring,*[1] published in 1962. She is also known for her bestselling book *The Edge of the Sea*. Although, she was opposed by the synthetic pesticides producers, her book caused two major decisions of historical importance, being the ban on DDT and formation of U.S. Environmental Protection Agency. Jimmy Carter awarded her posthumously the Presidential Medal of Freedom.

Silent Spring began with a "fable for tomorrow" – a true story using a composite of examples drawn from many real communities where the use of DDT had caused damage to wildlife, birds, bees, agricultural animals, domestic pets, and even humans. Carson used it as an introduction to a very scientifically complicated and already controversial subject. This "fable" made an indelible impression on readers and was used by critics to charge that Carson was a fiction writer and not a scientist.

Serialized in three parts in *The New Yorker*, where President John F. Kennedy read it in the summer of 1962, *Silent Spring* was published in August and became an instant best-seller and the most talked about book in decades. Utilizing her many sources in federal science and in private research, Carson spent over six years documenting her analysis that humans were misusing powerful, persistent, chemical pesticides before knowing the full extent of their potential harm to the whole biota.

Carson's passionate concern in *Silent Spring* is with the future of the planet and all life on Earth. She calls for humans to act responsibly, carefully, and as stewards of the living earth. Additionally *Silent Spring* suggested a needed change in how democracies and liberal societies operated so that individuals and groups could question what their governments allowed others to put into the environment. Far from calling for sweeping changes in government policy, Carson believed the federal government was part of the problem. She admonished her readers and audiences to ask "Who Speaks, And Why?" and therein to set the seeds of social revolution. She identified human hubris and financial self-interest as the crux of the problem and asked if we could master ourselves and our appetites to live as though we humans are an equal part of the earth's systems and not the master of them.

Carson expected criticism, but she did not expect to be personally vilified by the chemical industry and its allies in and out of government. She spent her last years courageously defending the truth of her conclusions until her untimely death in 1964. *Silent Spring* inspired the modern environmental movement,

---

[1] Rachel Carson, *Silent Spring,* (Houghton Mifflin Company; September 27, 1962; Anniversary edition October 22, 2002).

which began in earnest a decade later. It is recognized as the environmental text that "changed the world." She aimed at igniting a democratic activist movement that would not only question the direction of science and technology but would also demand answers and accountability. Rachel Carson was a prophetic voice and her "witness for nature" is even more relevant and needed if our planet is to survive into a 22nd century.[2]

B) Dame Jane Morris Goodall

Dame Jane Morris Goodall DBE was born to Herbert Morris-Goodall and Margaret Myfanwe Joseph on April 3, 1934 in London. She is a multidisciplinary environmental scientist and is better known as a primatologist, ethnologist, and anthropologist. She is a UN Messenger of Peace. She is the world number one specialist on chimpanzees and is best known for her forty-five years study of the wild chimpanzees in Gombe Stream National Park of Tanzania. She is the founder of the world famous Jane Goodall Institute. She developed the lasting interest in chimpanzees since her early childhood, when she was presented a stuffed toy chimpanzee. About that toy, which she still retains with her, she remarked, 'My mother's friends were horrified by this toy, thinking it would frighten me and give me nightmares.' Goodall is the eighth exceptional person to study and receive a Ph.D. at the Cambridge University, without first having a bachelor's degree. Based on her five years research at the Gombe reserve, she wrote her thesis, titled Behaviour of the "Free-Ranging Chimpanzee".

C) Dr. James Hansen

Dr. James Hansen was born to James Ivan Hansen and Gladys Ray Hansen on March 29th 1941 in Denison, Iowa, U.S. He received his bachelor's degree in Physics and Mathematics, M.Sc., in Astronomy and Ph.D., in Physics from the University of Iowa. From 1962 to 1966 he participated in a NASA graduate traineeship. He is best known for his work on "Climatology" and for his testimony to Congressional Committee on climatic change in 1988. This contributed towards enhancing awareness about "global warming". Based on the meteorological data analysis from 1880 to 1985, he established that in the past century the mmean temperature of the globe has increased by 0.5^{0}C to 0.7^{0}C and that according to the 2006 update, the temperatures are 0.8^{0}C warmer than the past century. His first study of NASA global temperature analysis was publisher in 1981. In 2009 he published his book *Storms of My Grandchildren.*[3]

---

[2] http://www.rachelcarson.org/SilentSpring.aspx, accessed on March 31st 2018.

[3] James Hansen, *Storms of My Grandchildren: The Truth About the Coming Climate Catastrophe and our last Chance to Save Humanity,* (Bloomsbury, USA, New York, 2009).

James Hansen, the world's leading climatologist, shows that exactly contrary to the impression the public has received, the science of climate change has become even clearer and sharper since the hardcover was released. In *Storms of My Grandchildren*, Hansen speaks out for the first time with the full truth about global warming: The planet is hurtling even more rapidly than previously acknowledged to a climatic point of no return. In explaining the science of climate change, Hansen paints a devastating but all-too-realistic picture of what will happen in our children's and grandchildren's lifetimes if we follow the course we're on. But he is also an optimist, showing that there is still time to take the urgent, strong action that is needed- just barely.[4]

D) Philip Weller

Philip Weller is a Canadian environmental scientist. Since 2003, he has been the executive secretary of the International Commission for the Protection of the Danube River. He was born in 1956 and he received his Masters degree in Urban and Regional Planning from the University of Waterloo, Canada. He served as director of Great Lakes United and as Program director of WWF International and of the Danube Carpathian Programme in Austria. He has also worked as consultant in Canada. He was appointed as a member of the Baia Mare Task Force in 2003. He has authored many books on environmental science including *Freshwater Seas,*[5] which is a history of the Great Lakes of North America.

E) John Hartley Lawton

John Hartley Lawton was born on September 24th 1943. Since his early childhood, he was interested in birds and was a member of the Young Ornithologists Club. He received his Ph.D. from the University of Durham in 1969. He is a British Ecologist and chairs the Yorkshire Wildlife Trust. He has volunteered for the RSPBs Operation Osprey at Loch Garten. He served as demonstrator in the zoology department at the University of Oxford. His main interest has been in impact of global environment change on the population of birds and insects. He played a pivotal role in the establishment of The Royal Society for the Protection of Birds.

F) Marjory Stoneman Douglas

Marjory Stoneman Douglas was born to Frank Bryant Stoneman andd Lillian Trefethen on April 7th 1890 in Minneapolis, Minnesota, US and died on May 14th 1998 at the age of 108 years in Coconut Grove, Miami, Florida. She was an environmental scientist, journalist and feminist. She is best known for her active

---

[4] https://www.amazon.com/Storms-My-Grandchildren-Catastrophe-Humanity/dp/1608195023, 31-03-2018.

[5] Philip Weller, *Freshwater Seas,* (Between the Lines, Canada, May1, 1991); https://www.amazon.com/Fresh-Water-Seas-Saving-Great/dp/0921284187, March 31st, 2018.

resistance against drainage of the Everglades to reclaim land for development. She is known for her book *The Everglades: River of Grass*[6] published in 1947. It created awareness about the importance of seeing the Everglades as a valuable river, instead of taking it for a waste swamp. Her book is considered as influential as Carson's *Silent Spring.* There are many prominent environmental scientists in different countries that were enlightened in ecological sustainability and spend their lives to bring awareneness among people about environmental issues and care.[7]

2) Indian Famous Ecologists/Environmentalists

A) Raman Sukumar

Raman Sukumar is well known, as an Indian ecologist, for his work on the ecology of the Asian Elephant and wildlife-human conflict. He also works on climate change[8] and tropical forest ecology. He was born in India in 1955. In 1986 he also helped design the Nilgiri Biosphere Reserve, the first of its kind in India. In 1997, he set up the Asian Nature Conservation Foundation,[9] a public charitable trust that incorporates the Asian Elephant Research and Conservation Centre, an organization that has carried out several field projects in India and other Asian countries on elephants and their habitats.[10] He was awarded the International Cosmos Prize, Japan, in 2006, the first Indian to get this award[11] He was also commended by the Prime Minister of India for contributions to the Intergovernmental Panel on Climate Change (IPCC) that shared the Noble Peace Prize in 2007.

He got his BS from the University of Madras in 1977 and did a Masters in Botany from the same university. He obtained a Ph.D., from the Indian Institute of Science in 1985. He was a Fulbright Fellow at Princeton University in 1991 and was the Chair at the Centre for Ecological Sciences at the Indian Institute of Science for over eight years (2004–2012). He continues to pursue conservation based scientific research as a Professor at this Centre and is often called upon to represent Indian wildlife scientists in a number of international, national and regional governmental committees.

---

[6] Marjory Stonemean, Douglas, *The Everglades: River of Grass,* (Pineapple Press. Inc., Sarasota, Florida, 1947).

[7] Refer for more information: Famous Environmental Scientists – A Knowledge Archive, http://informory.com/famous/famous-environmental-scientists/#ixzz4HP31MI00.

[8] *The Asian Elephant: Ecology and Management,* (Cambridge University Press, 1989).

[9] www.asiannature.org.

[10] *Elephant Days and Nights: Ten Years with the Indian Elephant,* (Oxford University Press, 1994).

[11] *The Living Elephants: Evolutionary Ecology, Behaviour and Conservation,* (Oxford University Press, 2003); *The Story of Asia's Elephants,* (Marg Publishers, 2011).

The following Awards and Fellowships he has received so far:

i) Presidential Award of the Chicago Zoological Society, USA, in 1991
ii) Order of the Golden Ark (The Netherlands), in 1997
iii) Fellow of the Indian Academy of Sciences, in 2000
iv) Whitley Gold Award for International Nature Conservation UK, in 2003
v) T.N. Khoshoo Memorial Award for Conservation Science, Ashoka Trust for Research in Ecology and Environment, India, in 2004
vi) Fellow of the Indian National Science Academy, in 2005
vii) International Cosmos Prize, Japan, in 2006
viii) Fellow, Geological Society of India, in 2006
ix) Fellow, The World Academy of Sciences, Italy, in 2013

B) Mylamma

Mylamma is anti-coke crusader of Kerala and she is well known for her life and initiatives as one of the fire-branded leaders of the anti-coke agitation of Plachimada in Kerala. The major problem local people faced from this coke company were illustrated in the following lamentations:

> They came to our village with glittering offers; that our people would get many job opportunities in the plant; the overall development of our village would be taken care of; the economic growth of the area would be strengthened, etc. We waited and waited… nothing miraculous happened. On the contrary, six months went by, slowly we started facing the reverse effects. Except a few, nobody from the locality was given jobs. The water level in the wells of the surrounding colonies showed a sharp depletion. The quality of the water -its odour, taste, hardness- got worsened. It became non-potable. We stopped using it. We were forced to fetch water from a distance of three to five kilometres. Several uncommon diseases started showing their neck out. The farmers around the plant stopped cultivation due to severe shortage of water. This was another thunderbolt on us that took away our daily little earnings. We were forced to migrate to faraway lands, seeking for some work or other to make our living. Suddenly we felt terribly helpless, facing the fact that we were being robbed. Our precious water resource had been stolen… lakhs of liters every day… Where would I get some fresh and pure drinking water any more? How many kilometres should we have to walk to fetch a drop of water? Who will compensate the heavy loss incurred upon us by this giant plant?

These lamentations synchronized with anger and despair were from a 55 year old lady, Mylamma, a resident of Vijayanagar colony in Plachimada village in the southern Indian state of Kerala, situated adjacent to the mega bottling plant of Hindustan Coca-Cola Beverages Pvt. Ltd. Company.

She has been one of the leaders in the villages, along with other tribal leaders who kept the struggled against the multi-national alive despite the attempts by the global company to use every trick in the book to break the people's resistance. She kept at the bay some of the outside political influences out to exploit the people's struggle. At the same time, she was the product of the people's democratic process.

She belonged to an Adivasi family. When she began to organize the poor women of the village she was about fifty years old. She was presumably illiterate but she upheld the rights of the villagers for their water and its sources. Mylamma became a source of inspiration for all those who stand for nation and oppose imperialist penetration. In truth Mylamma was fighting hegemonization. While she was fighting she contracted Psoriasis all over her body which she believed to be the result of drinking poisonous water adulterated with cola chemicals. Scabies began to haunt her. And Mylamma is no more today and she died at the age of fifty seven which is no old age according to Kerala standards. Strenuous efforts and hard work aggravated her disease and she had to succumb to death.

But the cause for which she fought and won and lost still remains unresolved. People of Plachimada and for that matter the people of the whole world should continue this struggle until victory is achieved. Water is a free source of life to all and the best beverage which nature gives us. The legacy of Mylamma continues to encourage people everywhere to fight for their due rights over natural sources.

C) Suzanna Arundhati Roy

Suzanna Arundhati Roy is an Indian author who is best known for her novel *The God of Small Things*, (1997), which won the Man Booker Prize for Fiction in 1997. This novel became the biggest-selling book by a non-expatriate Indian author. She is also a political activist involved in human rights and environmental causes.[12] She was born on November 24th 1961[13] in Shillong, Meghalaya, India, to Rajib Roy, a Bengali Hindu tea plantation manager from Calcutta and Mary Roy, a Malayali Syrian Christian women's rights activist from Kerala. When she was two years old, her parents divorced and she returned with her mother and brother to Kerala.[14] For a time, the family lived with Roy's maternal grandfather in Ooty, Tamil Nadu. When she was fivers old, the family moved back to Kerala, where her mother started a school.

Roy attended school at Corpus Christi, Kottayam, followed by the Lawrence School, Lovedale, in Nilgiris, Tamil Nadu. She then studied architecture at the

---

[12] Dhanusha Gokulan, "'Fairy princess' to 'instinctive critic'", *Khaleej Times,* (11 November, 2012). Retrieved 2014-11-02. http//www.khaleejtimes.com

[13] "Arundhati Roy", *Encyclopædia Britannica,* Retrieved 12 May, 2013. http//www.britanica.com/Arundhati Roy

[14] Siddhartha Deb, "Arundhati Roy, the Not-So-Reluctant Renegade Archived 21 April, 2016 at the Wayback Machine.", *New York Times,* 5 March 2014. Accessed March 5th, 2014. http//www.nytimes.com/2014/03/09/magazine.

School of Planning and Architecture, Delhi, where she met architect Gerard da Cunha. The two lived together in Delhi, and then Goa, before they broke up. Roy returned to Delhi, where she obtained a position with the National Institute of Urban Affairs. In 1984 she met independent filmmaker Pradip Krishen, who offered her a role as a goatherd in his award-winning movie *Massey Sahib*. The two were later married. They collaborated on a television series on India's independence movement and on two films, *Annie* and *Electric Moon*. Disenchanted with the film world, Roy worked various jobs, including running aerobics classes. Roy and Krishen eventually split up. She became financially secure by the success of her novel *The God of Small Things*, published in 1997. Roy is a cousin of prominent media personality Prannoy Roy, the head of the leading Indian TV media group NDTV.[15] She lives in Delhi.

Early in her career, Roy worked for television and movies. She wrote the screenplays for *In Which Annie Gives It Those Ones* (1989), a movie based on her experiences as a student of architecture, in which she also appeared as a performer, and *Electric Moon* (1992),[16] both directed by her then husband Pradip Krishen. Roy won the National Film Award for Best Screenplay in 1988 for *In Which Annie Gives It Those Ones*.[17] She attracted attention in 1994, when she criticised Shekhar Kapur's film *Bandit Queen*, based on the life of Phoolan Devi.[18] In her film review entitled, "The Great Indian Rape Trick", she questioned the right to "restage the rape of a living woman without her permission", and charged Kapur with exploiting Devi and misrepresenting both her life and its meaning.[19]

Arundhati Roy's Literary Contributions

Arundhati's major and first literary contribution, perhaps, is her novel *The God of Small Things.* She began writing her first novel, *The God of Small Things*, in 1992, completing it in 1996.[20] The book is semi-autobiographical and a major

---

[15] Nayare Ali,. "There's something about Mary", *Times of India,* (14 July, 2002), Retrieved 12 May 2013.

[16] "Arundhati Roy, Author-Activist", Archived November 24th 2010 at the Wayback Machine., *India Today*. Retrieved June 16th 2013.

[17] "36th National Film Awards (PDF)", *Directorate of Film Festivals*, Retrieved 25 February 2015.

[18] "Arundhati Roy, Author-Activist", Archived November 24th 2010 at the Wayback Machine., *India Today*. Retrieved June 16th 2013.

[19] The Great Indian Rape-Trick Archived 14 April 2016 at the Wayback Machine. @ SAWNET -The South Asian Women's NET work. Retrieved November 25th 2011; "Arundhati Roy: A 'small hero'", *BBC News,* March 6th 2002; Ramesh, Randeep, "Live to tell", *The Guardian, London,* (17 February, 2007), Archived from the original on 6 May 2009. Retrieved 6 April, 2009.

[20] *Roy, Amitabh, The God of Small Things: A Novel of Social Commitment,* (Atlantic. 2005), 37–38.(ISBN 978-81-269-0409-9.); htpps://books. google.com.

part captures her childhood experiences in Aymanam. The publication of *The God of Small Things* catapulted Roy to international fame. It received the 1997 Booker Prize for Fiction and was listed as one of the *New York Times* "Notable Books of the Year for 1997."[21] It reached fourth position on the *New York Times* "Bestsellers list for Independent Fiction".[22] From the beginning, the book was also a commercial success: Roy received half a million pounds as an advance. It was published in May, and the book had been sold to eighteen countries by the end of June.[23]

The God of Small Things received stellar reviews in major American newspapers such as *The New York Times* (a "dazzling first novel,")[24] "extraordinary", "at once so morally strenuous and so imaginatively supple"[25] and the *Los Angeles Times* ("a novel of poignancy and considerable sweep")[26] and in Canadian publications such as the *Toronto Star* ("a lush, magical novel").[27] By the end of the year, it had become one of the five best books of 1997 by *Time Magazine*.[28] Critical response in the United Kingdom was less positive, and that the novel was awarded the Booker Prize caused controversy; Carmen Callil, a 1996 Booker Prize judge, called the novel "execrable", and *The Guardian* called the contest "profoundly depressing."[29] In India, the book was criticised especially for its unrestrained description of sexuality by E. K. Nayanar,[30] the then Chief Minister of Roy's home state Kerala, where she had to answer charges of obscenity.[31]

Since the success of her first novel, Roy has written a television serial, *The Banyan Tree*,[32] and the documentary *DAM/AGE: A Film with Arundhati Roy*

---

21 "Notable Books of the Year 1997", *New York Times,* December 7th 1997. Archived from the original on 9 December 2008; Retrieved 21 March, 2007.

22 "Best Sellers Plus", *New York Times,* 25 January 1998; Retrieved March 21st 2007.

23 Roy, Amitabh, *The God of Small Things.*

24 *Kakutani, Michiko, "Melodrama as Structure for Subtlety", The New York Times,* (June 3rd 1997).

25 Truax, Alice, "A Silver Thimble in Her Fist". *The New York Times,* (May 25th 1997).

26 Eder, Richard, "As the world turns: rev. of The God of Small Things", *Los Angeles Times,* (1 June 1997), p. 2, retrieved January 18th 2010.

27 Carey, Barbara, "A lush, magical novel of India", *Toronto Star,* (7 June 7th 1997), p. M.21.

28 "Books: The best of 1997", *Time Magazine,* (December 29th 1997), retrieved January 18th 2010.

29 "Books: The best of 1997", *Time Magazine,* (December 29th 1997).

30 Kutty, N. Madhavan, "Comrade of Small Jokes", *The Indian Express,* (November 9th 1997), retrieved January 18th 2010.

31 Bumiller, Elisabeth, "A Novelist Beginning with a Bang", *New York Times,* (July 29th 1997), retrieved January 18th 2010.

32 Vir Sanghvi, "I think from a very early age, I was determined to negotiate with the world on my own", Archived March 3rd 2016 at the Wayback Machine., *The Rediff Special,* Retrieved April 18th 2012.

(2002). In early 2007, Roy stated that she was working on a second novel.[33] She contributed to *We Are One: A Celebration of Tribal Peoples*, a book released in 2009[34] that explores the culture of peoples around the world, portraying their diversity and the threats to their existence. The royalties from the sale of this book go to the indigenous rights organisation Survival International. She has written numerous essays on contemporary politics and culture. They have been collected by Penguin India in a five-volume set.

Since publishing *The God of Small Things* in 1997, Roy has spent most of her time on political activism and nonfiction (like collections of essays about social causes). She is a spokesperson of the anti-globalization/alter-globalization movement and a vehement critic of neo-imperialism and U.S. foreign policy. She opposes India's policies towards nuclear weapons as well as industrialization and economic growth (which she describes as "encrypted with genocide potential" in *Listening to Grasshoppers: Field Notes on Democracy*).[35]

Activist on Sardar Sarovar Project

Roy has campaigned along with activist Medha Patkar against the Narmada Dam Project, saying that the dam will displace half a million people, with little or no compensation, and will not provide the projected irrigation, drinking water, and other benefits. Roy donated her Booker Prize money as well as royalties from her books on the project to the *Narmada Bachao Andolan.* Roy also appears in Franny Armstrong's *Drowned Out*, a 2002 documentary about the project.[36] Roy's opposition to the Narmada Dam Project was criticised as "maligning Gujarat" by Congress and BJP leaders in Gujarat.

In 2002, Roy responded to a contempt notice issued against her by the Indian Supreme Court with an affidavit saying the court's decision to initiate the contempt proceedings based on an unsubstantiated and flawed petition, while refusing to inquire into allegations of corruption in military contracting deals pleading an overload of cases, indicated a "disquieting inclination" by the court to silence criticism and dissent using the power of contempt.[37] The court found Roy's statement, which she refused to disavow or apologise for, constituted criminal contempt and sentenced her to a "symbolic" one day's imprisonment and fined Roy with Rs. 2500. Roy served the jail sentence for a single day and

---

[33] Randeep Ramesh , "An activist returns to the novel", *The Sydney Morning Herald,* (March 10th 2007), Retrieved March 13th 2007.

[34] *We Are One: A Celebration of Tribal Peoples,* Survival International, October 16th 2009, Retrieved November 25th 2009.

[35] http://en.wikipedia.org/wiki/Arundati_Roy.

[36] *"Case registered against Arundhati, Geelani", The Hindu,* 29-11-2010. ISSN 0971-751X. Retrieved November 22nd 2015.

[37] *Arundhati Roy,* "The Greater Common Good". *Frontline,* ***16(11)*** (22 May – 4 June, 1999).

opted to pay the fine rather than serve an additional three months' imprisonment for default.

Environmental historian Ramachandra Guha has been critical of Roy's Narmada dam activism. While acknowledging her "courage and commitment" to the cause, Guha writes that her advocacy is hyperbolic and self-indulgent,[38] "Ms. Roy's tendency to exaggerate and simplify, her Manichaean view of the world, and her shrill hectoring tone, have given a bad name to environmental analysis."[39] He faulted Roy's criticism of Supreme Court judges who were hearing a petition brought by the *Narmada Bachao Andolan* as careless and irresponsible. Roy counters that her writing is intentional in its passionate, hysterical tone: "I *am* hysterical. I'm screaming from the bloody rooftops. And he and his smug little club are going 'Shhhh... you'll wake the neighbours!' I want to wake the neighbours, that's my whole point. I want everybody to open their eyes."[40] Gail Omvedt and Roy have had fierce yet constructive discussions, in open letters, on Roy's strategy for the Narmada Dam movement. The activists disagree on whether to demand stopping the dam building altogether (Roy) or searching for intermediate alternatives (Omvedt).

The Muthanga Incident

In 2003, the Adivasi Gothra Maha Sabha, a social movement for Adivasi land rights in Kerala, organised a major land occupation of a piece of land of a former Eucalyptus plantation in the Muthanga Wildlife Reserve, on the border of Kerala and Karnataka. After 48 days, a police force was sent into the area to evict the occupants—one participant of the movement and a policeman were killed, and the leaders of the movement were arrested. Arundhati Roy travelled to the area, visited the movement's leaders in jail, and wrote an open letter to the then Chief Minister of Kerala, A. K. Antony, saying "You have blood on your hands." She is not only the critique of environmental decline, but also deliberately criticized

---

[38] "Arundhati's contempt: Supreme Court writes her a prison sentence", *The Indian Express*, March 7th 2002; V. Venkatesan and Sukumar Muralidharan, "Of contempt and legitimate dissent", *Frontline*, (18–31 August 2001). Archived from the original on February 20th 2012.

[39] *Arundhati Roy.... Contemner*, JUDIS (Supreme Court of India bench, Justices G.B. Pattanaik & R.P. Sethi 6 March 6th 2002).

[40] Arundhati Roy, "Statement by Arundhati Roy", (7 March 2002), *Friends of River Narmada*, Retrieved March 21st 2007.

several contextual issues of her time such as terrorism,[41] naxalism,[42] corruption and Anna Hazare's anti-corruption campaign.[43]

Awards

Arundhati Roy was awarded the 1997 Booker Prize for her novel *The God of Small Things*. The award carried a prize of about US$30,000/- and a citation that noted, "The book keeps all the promises that it makes". Prior to this, she won the National Film Award for Best Screenplay in 1989, for the screenplay of *In Which Annie Gives It Those Ones*, in which she captured the anguish among the students prevailing in professional institutions. In 2015, she returned the national award in protest against religious intolerance and the growing violence by rightwing groups in India.[44]

In 2002, she won the “Lannan Foundation's Cultural Freedom Award” for her work "about civil societies that are adversely affected by the world's most powerful governments and corporations", in order "to celebrate her life and her ongoing work in the struggle for freedom, justice and cultural diversity". In 2003, she was awarded "special recognition" as a Woman of Peace at the Global Exchange Human Rights Awards in San Francisco with Bianca Jagger, Barbara Lee, and Kathy Kelly. Roy was awarded the “Sydney Peace Prize” in May 2004 for her work in social campaigns and her advocacy of non-violence. In January 2006, she was awarded the “Sahitya Akademi Award”, a national award from India's Academy of Letters, for her collection of essays on contemporary issues. In November 2011, she was awarded the Norman Mailer Prize for Distinguished Writing. Roy was featured in the 2014 list of *Time* 100, the 100 most influential people in the world.

D) Mahesh Chandra Mehta

Mahesh Chandra Mehta is a public interest attorney from India. He was awarded the Goldman Environmental Prize in 1996[45] for his continuous fights in Indian courts against pollution-causing industries. He received the Ramon Magsaysay

[41] Arundhati Roy, "And His Life Should Become Extinct", Archived March 3rd 2016 at the Wayback Machine., *Outlook*, October 30th 2006.

[42] Singh, Tavleen, "The Real Enemies", *The Indian Express,* (21 December 2008), Retrieved 18 January 2010; "Naxals are patriots: Arundhati", *Hindustan Times,* Retrieved August 18th 2014.

[43] I'd rather not be Anna: Arundhati Roy, Archived June 23rd 2015 at the Wayback Machine, *The Hindu*, August 21st 2011, Retrieved June 18th 2012.

[44] Hannah Ellis, "Arundhati Roy returns award in protest against religious intolerance in India", *Guardian,* (November 5th, 2015), Retrieved November 5th 2015.

[45] Goldman Environmental Prize: M.C. Mehta, Retrieved on November 28th 2007: https://en.wikipedia.org/wiki/Mahesh_Chandra_Mehta#cite_ref-goldman_1-0

Award for Asia towards Public Service in 1997. The Government of India awarded him the civilian honour of the *Padma Shri* in 2016.[46]

A lawyer by profession and a committed environmentalist by choice, he has made the fight to protect India's environment as his unending mission. He has pioneered legal activism for environmental protection and is proof that one man can make a difference. Born on October 12th 1946, Mehta hails from a small village in district Rajouri in the State of Jammu & Kashmir (India). It was here that his love for nature instilled in him a sense of commitment towards protecting the environment. He got his education up to primary level in his village Dhangri. Later, to get higher education he had to join school at Rajouri. For few years he travelled from his village to school and back by crossing two rivers and about 15 km. of distance every day. After his schooling at Rajouri he moved to Jammu and completed his post graduation in political science and law degree from Jammu University and started his practice in Jammu & Kashmir High Court. During his stay in Jammu, he took an active part in social and political issues. He raised his voice against corruption and motivated students and youth to fight against discrimination taking place with the Jammu region. He remained president of The Youth Action Committee and pioneered the social and political causes.

His career as a Supreme Court lawyer began in 1983, when he migrated to Delhi. In 1984, he began focusing on environmental litigation. In the words of Ms Smita Gate "Often described as the One Man Enviro-legal Brigade, Mr Mehta is probably the only Supreme Court lawyer to have taken up legal cudgels with the polluting Indian Industries and come out victorious. A dedicated, fearless and extremely honest man, he pursues his goals with single-minded devotion. He has been conferred with several prestigious awards. Some of these are the Governor's Gold Medal, the Goldman Environmental Prize, considered on alternative Noble Prize in USA and Europe, the UN's Global 500 Award for 1993 and above all the Magsaysay Award for 1997. He is the man that helps to include the environmental science in all technical branch and he want that every educated person must know about our environment and they have to protect.

E) Medha Patkar

Medha Patkar was born in Mumbai, Maharashtra, to Indumati and Vasant Khanolkar, a freedom fighter and labour union leader, on 1 December 1954.[47] Patkar earned an MA in Social Work from Tata Institute of Social Sciences (TISS). She worked with voluntary organisations in Mumbai's slums for 5 years and tribal districts of North-East districts of Gujarat for 3 years. She worked as a member

---

[46] "Padma Awards 2016", *Press Information Bureau, Government of India- 2016,* Retrieved February 2nd 2016.

[47] "A mother speaks: I worry for her but I know Medha is right", *The Times of India,* April 19th 2006.

of faculty at TISS but left her position to take up the field work. She was a PhD scholar at TISS, studying Economic development and its impact on traditional societies. After working up to M.Phil level she left her unfinished PhD when she became immersed in her work with the tribal and Peasant communities in the Narmada valley spread over three states.

Medha Patkar is an Indian social activist working on various crucial ecological, political and economical issues raised by Tribals, Dalits, Farmers, labourers and Women facing injustice in India.[48] She is an alumnus of TISS, a premier institute of India.[49] Patkar is the founder member of the 32 years old people's movement called Narmada Bachao Andolan (NBA) in three states: Madhya Pradesh, Maharashtra and Gujarat. Narmada Bachao Andolan (NBA) has been engaged in a struggle for justice for the people affected by the dam projects related to the Sardar Sarovar Dam projects, especially those whose homes will be submerged, but have not yet been rehabilitated. She is also one of the founders of the National Alliance of People's Movements (NAPM), an alliance of hundreds of progressive people's organisations.[50]

In addition to the above, Patkar was a commissioner on the World Commission on Dams, which did a thorough research on the environmental, social, political and economic aspects and impacts of the development of large dams globally and their alternatives.[51] She was the national co-ordinator and then convenor of National Alliance of People's Movements for many years and now continues to be an advisor to NAPM. Under the banner of NAPM she has participated in and supported various mass struggles across India against inequity, non-sustainability, displacement and injustice in the name of development. Her work challenges Casteism, Communalism and all kinds of discrimination. She has been a part of numerous teams and panels that work on initiating and formulating various national policies and enactments including those related to land acquisition, unorganized sector workers, hawkers, slum-dwellers and forest-dweller Adivasis. NAPM filed a number of public interest litigations including those against Adarsh society, Lavasa Megacity, Hiranandani (Powai) and as well as other builders. Narmada Bachao Andolan and Ghar Bachao Ghar Banao Andolan are allies of NAPM founded by Medha Patkar with others.

---

[48] Patkar, Medha, "'The unprotected class of workers is the real India", (18 September 2013), Rediff, Retrieved July 25th 2017.

[49] "TISS official website - About TISS", www.tiss.edu.TISS, Retrieved July 25th 2017.

[50] "National Alliance of People's Movement Website".

[51] "Final report of World commission on dams" (PDF), United Nations Environment Programme. http://www.unep.org/dams/WCD/report

Activism and Agitations

She has been involved in several activities and agitations protecting environment in India.

1) Narmada Bachao Andolan (NBA):

NBA is a social movement which began in 1985 consisting of adivasis, farmers, fish workers, labourers and others in the Narmada valley along with the intellectuals including environmentalists, human rights activists, scientists, academicians, artists who stand for just and sustainable development. Sardar Sarovar Dam (SSD) in Gujarat is one of the biggest dams on Narmada where the non-violent people's struggle has questioned social and environmental costs, undemocratic planning and unjust distribution of benefits. The struggle is still on in the Sardar Sarovar affeced areas and also other large and medium dams on Narmada and its tributaries. It has led to thousands of project affected families receiving land based rehabilitation and continues to fight against submergence and displacement without rehabilitation of more than 40,000 families residing in these submergence areas of Sardar Sarovar till date. Many of its claims and critique on economic, social and environmental aspects of Sardar Sarovar and Narmada valley development project stand vindicated today. Patkar has also questioned the wisdom of the currently popular developmental strategy of linking rivers in India as a means to address issues of water shortage.[52]

NBA has been running JEEVANSHALAS- schools of life, since 1992 with about 5,000 students having passed out and many graduated. Tens of them are under training in athletics and some have won many awards. NBA also successfully established and managed two micro hydral projects which got submerged due to SS dam. It has been working in many sectors over last 30 years including health, employment guarantee, Right to Food and PDS, rehabilitation and environment protection.

2) Ghar Bachao Ghar Banao Andolan (GBGBA):

It is a struggle for housing rights in Mumbai, started in 2005 and continues to fight for rights of slum-dwellers and those cheated by the builders in various rehabilitation and re-development projects. It all began when the government of Maharashtra demolished 75,000 houses of the poor in 2005, against its own promises before election. strong people's movement was founded by Medha Patkar and others when she gave the slogan in a large public meeting at Azaad Maidaan Mumbai. It was through mass action that the communities were re-built on the same sites and continue to assert and attain their right to shelter, water, electricity, sanitation and livelihood. As members of working class GBGBA

[52] Patkar, Medha, River Linking: A Millenium Folly? (First ed.). National Alliance of People's Movements, (1 August 2004).

respects the slum-dwellers for contribution to the life of the city and involves them in equitable and inclusive planning for urban development.

3) National Alliance of People's Movements (NAPM):

The National Alliance of People's Movements is an alliance of people's movements in India, with the stated aim of working on a range of issues related to socio-economic justice, political justice and equity.[53] Medha Patkar founded the National Alliance of People's Movements with the objective of "facilitating unity and providing strength to peoples' movements in India, fighting against oppression, further questioning the current development model so as to work towards a just alternative". She is the national convener of the NAPM.[54]

4) Tata Nano Plant Singur:

Tata Motors started constructing a factory to manufacture their $2,500 car, the Tata Nano at Singur.[55] She protested against the setting up of the plant at Singur, West Bengal. Patkar's convoy was assaulted, allegedly by CPI(M) activists, at Kapaseberia in East Midnapore district while on her way to strife-torn Nandigram. At the height of the agitation, Ratan Tata had made remarks questioning the source of funds of the agitators.In October 2008 Tata announced that the factory would not be completed and that the production of the Nano will be set up in Sanand, Gujarat.

5) Resistance to forcible land grab in Nandigram, West Bengal (2007):

She participated in and initiated various supportive actions including a fast during Diwali in Kolkata, Mass-mobilisation, and complaints at various national forums and building support of intellectuals and various citizens across the country. The battle was ultimately won in favour of the local people who had to lay their lives in large numbers during State Violence.

6) Lavasa Project:

Lavasa is a project by Hindustan Construction Corporation, in Maharashtra. It is a yet-to be completed city. Lavasa Project is criticised by P. Sainath for unjust use of water in a worst hit farmer suicide state.[56] Medha Patkar with villagers of Lavasa protested for the environmental damage in Nagpur.[57] She also filed a PIL in Supreme Court against the Lavasa project.

---

[53] *"Website National Alliance for People's Movement". NAPM.*

[54] http://napm-india.org/

[55] *The Hindu Business Line*, November 26th 2006 , Archived June 5th 2009 at the Wayback Machine.

[56] "How the other half dries", *The Hindu.* http://www.thehindu.com/opinion/columns/Sainath/how-the-other-half-dries/article4456130.

[57] *"Lavasa battles to get environmental clearance", CNN IBN.*

7) Golibar Demolition:

A demolition took place on 2 and 3 April 2013 in the Golibar area, Mumbai, Maharashtra evicting 43 houses and displacing more than 200 people. The whole project is to displace thousands of families and 50–100 years old communities that are demanding in-situ and participatory housing rights. Medha Patkar with more than 500 slum dwellers set on indefinite fast to protest against any further demolition until the inquiry into the matter is completed.[58] Patkar has alleged corruption and "atrocities" by builders in the city's slum rehabilitation scheme, and called for the halting of six projects by the Slum Rehabilitation Authority, until a proper inquiry is conducted. The inquiry was conducted giving partial solutions hence communities continue with their struggle.

8) Save Sugar-Cooperatives Mission:

To save Sugar-Cooperative sector in Maharashtra from falling into the hands of politicians including tens of ministers in the Maharashtra cabinet till 2014, Medha Patkar organised protests. She explained that "the politicians are interested in the prime plots of land, old equipment and machinery," of sugar co-operatives and accused the state government of selling assets of industry at throw away rates. A case against Girna Sugar factory at Malegaon, Nasik, Maharashtra and members of Chhagan Bhujbal Family pending before the Supreme court of India and the unused land of the factory is re-occupied and cultivated by the local farmers who were the donors of the cooperative that was privatized by the former minister purchasing it at throw away price.[59]

9) Kovvada Nuclear Project:

Patkar expressed a strong opposition to the land acquisition in Kovvada of Ranasthalam mandal in Srikakulam district, Andhra Pradesh saying that the nuclear plant would be a disaster for ecology as well as people of region.[60]

10) Awards and Honours:

She received many awarded
1991: Right Livelihood Award[61]
1992: Goldman Environment Award[62]

---

[58] "Medha Patkar enters Day 8 of indefinite fast", *Hindustan Times.* http://www.hindustantimes.com/india-news/mumbai/medha-patkar/indefinitefast

[59] "Medha Patkar, Anna Hazare on sugar co-operative save mission", *CNN IBN.*

[60] "Medha Patkar cries halt to Kovvada nuclear project", *The Hindu.*

[61] "Laureates 1991-Medha Patkar & Baba Amte / Narmada Bachao Andolan". Archived from the original on 13 November 2007.

[62] *Malhotra, Aditi.* "A Guide to Aam Aadmi Party's National Candidates", *Wall Street Journal,* Retrieved 30 March, 2014.

1995: Green Ribbon Award for Best International Political Campaigner by BBC, England
1999: Human Rights Defender's Award from Amnesty International, Germany
1999: M.A. Thomas National Human Rights Award from Vigil India Movement
1999: Person of The Year BBC
1999: Deena Nath Mangeshkar Award[63]
1999: Kundal Lal Award for Peace
1999: Mahatma Phule Award[64]
2001: Basavashree Award[65]
2013: Bhima Bai Ambedkar Award
2014: Mother Teresa Award for Social Justice.[66]

There are many, in similar way, to mention those who dedicated their lives to the cause of ecological sustenance and healthy environment though their names arc not much popularized by print media or electronic media, but their efforts brought great awareness among the local communities. For example, we will see human created forest if we go to Puliyankulam area in Kerala. Abdul Karim belongs to Kasaragod village in Kerala State. He studied up to 10th standard. He created forest in 32 acres which is 25 km away to his village. This place was rocky 25 years ago and it was government land. Due to lack of any tree underground water rapidly decreased. People went to long distance for collecting water. Karim started to plant trees on that rocky land first in 5 acres and then every year he increased plantation. Plants became trees and underground water levels have been increased. Scientists also surprised and they are doing researches how plantation became successful on rocky land.[67] In a similar way, Ramaiah, native of Daripalli village of Khammam (dist) in Telangana State believed "*vruksho rakshithi rakshitaha*", means that saving trees is safety for us. People called him as *chetla ramaiah*. He is a small farmer, but believe trees give shelter so he loved trees much. His habit is to plant trees wherever he finds empty land. So far he planted more than one crore plants. Once somebody gave Rs.5000/- to his son's

[63] "Quicktakes Indian Express", *The Indian Express,* Retrieved February 25th 2014

[64] "Medha Patkar – The People's Protestor", *Tehelka Magazine.*

[65] "Basavashree Award for Medha Patkar", *The Hindu,* April 29th 2001. Retrieved January 31st 2018.

[66] *"Mother Teresa Memorial International Award for Social Justice held on Sunday",* dna. Diligent Media Corporation Ltd, November 11th, 2014, Retrieved December 14th 2014.

[67] "Athadu Adavini Srustinchadu' (He created forest) in "Funday" of *sakshi*, Sunday, August 14th 2016, p 14.

wedding, but he used that amount to plantation .[68] There are many unpopularised persons like this who were enlightened ecologically and worked for ecological and environmental awareness among the people where they are living. I feel that it needs a special study on the contributions of ecologically enlightened to record their contributions, which perhaps, becomes a source of inspiration for future generations to protect environment.

[68] "*Akshrala vruksha koteeswarudu*" (He planted one crore plants), in "Funday" of *sakshi*, Sunday, August 14th 2016, p 20.

Chapter 12

Inter-religious Cooperation for a Healthy Environment

Eco-crisis and environmental degradation are the problems of whole world, irrespective of racial, religious and gender limitations, indeed it is universal problem of all people, therefore inter-religious or inter-faith cooperation is essential to safeguard healthy environment on the planet earth for the survival of human and other living beings. The environmental problem/eco-crisis is challenging and profoundly alerting every aspect of religious life, everyday conduct of religious people, and rituals. Religious environmentalism as a global movement is described and some interesting problems which the movement faces are discussed. The main concern lies in restoring the prevalence of severed, non-cooperative and isolationist ideologies and cultural tendencies in a context of globalization where our unparalleled interdependency with other human cultures and the life world require unity, cooperation and mutual flourishing. Interreligious Eco-theologians identify multiple sites for healing the divides that threaten our social, spiritual and ecological future. Therefore, this chapter deals with interfaith contributions and understanding of Eco-theology to promote healthy environment.

1) Interfaith Partnership

The Interfaith Partnership for the environment (IPE) was founded in the late 1986 as a United Nation Environmental Program (UNEP) project to inform North American congregation about the serious environmental problems facing living beings on Earth. It has since evolved into a global network of faith traditions and organizations working to bring together the forces of religion and ecology. Since its inception, the IPE has organized numerous seminars and conferences, as well as produced several books and related materials. Among events held at UN Headquarters was a Symposium on our Environmental Future: Ethical and

Spiritual Perspectives and the culminating Conference for the Harvard Project on Religion and Ecology.[1]

2) The Geneva Interfaith Forum

The Geneva Interfaith Forum (2011) on Climate Change, Environment and Human Rights is an informal group of faith-based NGOs that gathered to reaffirm the responsibility of each faith and spiritual tradition to care for the environment and play a role in addressing climate change and its impact on the human rights of the world's population.[2] Thus, it is imperative that the international community and all sectors of civil society urgently mobilize to tackle the hurdles that obstruct adequate and equitable international action on climate change. It becomes vital to act to bring about the changes needed to generate rapid solutions to the consequences of climate change; the cost of delaying further responsible decision making will disrupt the social, economic, political and cultural life of peoples and nation states.[3]

The 10th Assembly of the WCC at Bussan (2013) under the general theme, "God of life, let us do justice and peace" also speaks of a Theo-centric understanding of eco-justice in the world today. As life is the gift of God, there is a divine authorization to preserve and promote life at its best in the whole World. In such an attempt, there comes a hymn of praise in the order of creation as the psalmist perceived and interpreted it in psalm 150:6 "Let all that breathe praise the Lord". In search of a Green Spirituality, the humans encounter the divine as Moses experienced it in the burning bush or Adam in the Garden of Eden. All the religions of the World speak of the integrity of creation "as a cosmic vision in nature". A sustainable future for all is a vision to be realized through the combined efforts of all the religious people and others with secular ideologies. The WCC's scheduled consultation on Religion and Sustainable Development will certainly be a milestone in its pilgrimage toward justice and peace.[4]

---

[1] Interfaith Partnership for the Environment UNEP www.unep.org/newyork/InterfaithPartnershipfortheEnvironment/tabid/.../Default.aspx (Accessed on 07/092016 at 05:48 pm).

[2] Call for action by Geneva Interfaith Forum on Climate Change, Environment and Human Rights 20 September 2011 https://www.oikoumene.org/en/resources/documents/wcc-programmes/justice-diakonia-andresponsibilityforcreation/climate-change-water/call-for-action-by-geneva-interfaith-forum (Accessed on 07/08/2016 at 06:31 pm).

[3] Call for action by Geneva Interfaith Forum on Climate Change, Environment and Human Rights 20 September 2011 https://www.oikoumene.org/en/resources/documents/wcc-programmes/justice-diakonia-andresponsibilityforcreation/climate-change-water/call-for-action-by-geneva-interfaith-forum (Accessed on 07/08/2016 at 06:31 pm).

[4] M.J. Joseph, "The Integrity of Creation", *Theology for our Times: Indian School of Ecumenical Christian Centre, Vol. Number 18, March* (Bangalore: Ecumenical Christian Centre, 2016), 26-27.

3) Interreligious Concern for Eco-Crisis

The eco-crisis has a number of threatening and frightening dimensions, such as Global climate change, species extinction, wilderness loss, and the huge amount of toxic chemicals have been pumped into the air, water, and earth leading to pollution of air, water and soil. Future prospects of genetic engineering and nano-technology loom devastatingly larger than present and past consequences of other "miracle" developments such as nuclear engineering/weapons.[5] Let us see some important eco-concerns of religious communities for joining together and fight against the destructive forces of God's creation.

As a family of the Abrahamic tradition, Jews, Christians, and Muslims think of the world not simply as a collection of inert material lying around for human use, but as the gift of a loving God. The world is "creation" – an act of generosity. Even more, the traditions often teach that the world is ours only temporarily – it still belongs to God. Is this any way to treat the gift of the Master of the Universe?[6] There are specifically religious practices which are called into doubt. Can Jews sanctify wine if they know it contains poisonous pesticide residues? Can the communion wafer really be the "body of Christ" if it was grown with destructive chemical fertilizers and the people who worked the farms on which it was grown suffers from disproportionate amounts of cancer from using those fertilizers?[7]

All religions – share one basic belief: that they have some kind of privilege knowledge of what God wants and how a person should act. What happens to this theological and moral self-confidence when, for example, a fourth grader in religious school ask "Why have you let this happen?" How much respect can religious teachers demand of a younger generation of future members of the faithful when the older generation seems, rather obviously, to have failed so dismally?[8] Religions must ask themselves the embarrassing question of how they could have been so dumb about all this for so long. It was, after all, not the leading religious authorities or theologians who noticed that modern industrial practices had some real problems. It was free-lance mystics and nature lovers, the occasional believer with no institutional influence, anti-communist western Marxists, and the occasional more or less pagan phenomenologist, who raised questions about what humanity, was doing to nature and what that might signify in terms of humanity's treatment of itself. For their part, religions concentrated on whether

---

[5] Roger S. Gottlieb, religion and the environment http://users.wpi.edu/~gottlieb/files/32CHAP29GOTTLIEB_PP[1]_with_corrections.pdf (Accessedon 05/09/2016 at 10:15 pm).

[6] John B. Cobb, "Protestant Theology and Deep Ecology," in Roger S. Gottlieb, ed., *This Sacred Earth, Second Edition* (New York: Rutledge, 2004), 99-100.

[7] Cobb, "Protestant Theology and Deep Ecology," ..., 99-100.

[8] Roger S. Gottlieb, religion and the environment http://users.wpi.edu/~gottlieb/files/32CHAP29GOTTLIEB_PP[1]_with_corrections.pdf (Accessed on 05/09/2016 at 10:15 pm).

or not the fruits of industrialization were being distributed with a small amount of social justice, that's all.[9]

Religions become used to ecological problems and environmental issues they become increasingly open to ecumenical and interfaith efforts of all kinds. A good number of religious environmental organizations and actions have enlisted a variety of religious participants. Interfaith Power and Light, for example, a national U.S. group focusing on local responses to climate issues, includes Protestants, Catholics, Jews, Buddhists, and Muslims among its members. Well publicized statements by important religious figures on global warming have often been signed by leaders of widely different faiths. Religious Witness for the Earth included Jewish, Unitarian, and Episcopalian clergy in its leadership. Even in Israel-Palestine, perhaps the place one would least expect to find interreligious cooperation; Jewish and Muslim leaders have combined forces on common ecological concern, most notably the sadly deteriorated state of the Jordan River.[10]

4) Environmental Movements

There are some important environmental movements, for example to mention, working with interfaith cooperation to safeguard environment. In northern California the "Redwood Rabbis"[11] engaged in a public struggle to protect one of the areas last remaining stands of Redwood trees. Redwood Rabbis protect northern California trees, 1995-1999. Goals: Primary: to protect an old growth forest in Humboldt County (Northern California) called Headwaters Forest. Secondary: the protection of all redwood forests in Northern California. Their mission statement is: "The Redwood Rabbis seek to carry out the Judaic imperative, laid out in the Book of Genesis, to guard the earth. Invoking the Jewish tradition in defence of ancient forests and other threatened ecosystems, the Redwood Rabbis are part of a larger effort to create an environmental constituency within the Jewish community and to build bridges between diverse religious and secular communities to advocate more effectively for ecological land management and environmental protection." They challenged the logging company's head, a leader in his own Jewish community, with going against Jewish values. In violating legal orders the group engaged in direct action by planting new Redwood seedlings in the grove.[12]

---

[9] Roger S. Gottlieb, religion and the environment http://users.wpi.edu/~gottlieb/files/32CHAP29GOTTLIEB_PP[1]_with_corrections.pdf (Accessed on 05/09/2016 at 10:15 pm).

[10] Roger S. Gottlieb, *The Oxford Handbook of Religion and Ecology* (New York: Oxford University Press, 2006), 65-67.

[11] See, Redwood Rabbis protect northern California trees, 1995-1999 ...nvdatabase.swarthmore.edu/content/redwood-rabbis-protect-northern-california-trees-1995-1999 (Accessed on 23/06/2018).

[12] Murphy Charles, *At Home on Earth: Foundations for a Catholic Ethic of the Environment* (NY: Crossroad, 1989), 56.

In Tanzania fishermen were dissuaded from their ecologically disastrous policy of dynamite fishing by a local sheik who ruled that the practice was un-Islamic. The fishermen had ignored government decrees and scientific cautions, but were convinced by a religious structure.[13] In the U.S. the Methodist Church engaged in a focused campaign to demand that Staples stores stop selling paper the production of which led to Dioxin pollution.[14] In India the Sikh religion has committed itself to a three hundred year policy of responsible ecological practices. Since the Sikhs fulfill one of their religious commitment by giving free food to the poor – providing tens of millions of meals a day – this means changing their patterns of energy use, packaging, clean up, etc.[15]

Religious Witness for the Earth, an interfaith activist environmental group centered in New England, engaged in civil disobedience protesting against the Bush administration's energy policy, demonstrated at the U.N., and held a 125 mile "Climate Walk" publicizing the dangers of and possible responses to global warming.[16] In Taiwan the Shu Tzi[17] organization, founded by charismatic nun decades ago and concentrating on charity and relief work in Taiwan and abroad, has included ecological issues in its activities. One year it helped recycle millions of pounds of paper and metal.[18]

In the U.S. a loose network of nuns, the "Sisters of Earth," practice and teach organic agriculture, model low impact living, take part in local ecological efforts, save seeds, and monitor and criticize the ecologically destructive practices of local and national governments and transnational institutions such as the World Bank and the World Trade Organization.[19] In a fascinating instance of the intersection of religion, environmentalism, and political life, there is the case of Nambaryn Enkhbayar, the Prime Minister of Mongolia, who has led a Buddhist oriented attempt to combine economic development with real sustainability, particular in regard to preserving forests, biodiversity, and Mongolia's unique seven foot long river fish (the Taimen). Embahkar said "Buddhism considers the creation of a good balance or, let us put it in a broader sense – of a healthy environment where

---

[13] Charles, *At Home on Earth: Foundations for a Catholic Ethic of the Environment* ..., 57.

[14] Charles, *At Home on Earth: Foundations for a Catholic Ethic of the Environment* ..., 58.

[15] Max Oelschaeger, *Caring for Creation: An Ecumenical Approach to the Environmental Crisis* (New Haven and London, Yale University Press, 1994), 98.

[16] Oelschaeger, *Caring for Creation: An Ecumenical Approach to the Environmental Crisis* ..., 99-100.

[17] Shu-Tzi is the world's largest business network, helping professionals like Peng Shu-Tzi discover inside. See, Peng Shu-Tzi | LinkedInwww.linkedin.com/in/peng-shu-tzi-61171879 (Accessed on 28/09/2016 at 12:40 am).

[18] Intercultural Ecotheology: Integral Visions of Healing www.acu.edu.au/__data/assets/pdf_file/0014/.../Rider_Practical_Theol_GH.pdf*(Accessed on 05/09/2016 at 10:45 pm).*

[19] Oelschaeger, *Caring for Creation: An Ecumenical Approach to the Environmental Crisis*..., 101-102.

everyone and everything can enjoy freedom to realize or improve its potential – is the condition for the qualitative development.[20]

5) Inter-faith Networks to Promote Healthy Environment

In 2015, Green Faith, a US-based Inter-faith environmental network, commissioned Climate Outreach to identify language around climate change that could speak across all the world's five main faiths (Christianity, Buddhism, Judaism, Hinduism, and Islam).[21] "The natural world is a precious gift. Caring for the natural world is an act of worship. We have a sacred responsibility to care for the earth and be its stewards." Although, the underlying concept of a responsibility to care for and protect the world is strong across all faiths, the most commonly used frame of "Creation Care" does not work well outside the Abrahamic faiths. The terms "natural world" and "the earth" were found to be sufficiently neutral to work across all faiths, but were weaker as a consequence. However, the language of the world being a gift that we have a responsibility to respect did work well across all faiths, and was mentioned spontaneously in all of the focus groups.[22]

"Climate change is a moral challenge. Climate change is harming the poor and vulnerable. We should be generous and care for them. It is our responsibility to preserve the legacy of our parents and provide for the future for our children." All faiths contain sacred values condemning violence and harm to others (and, for Hindus and Buddhists, this extends to all living things), being charitable, and protecting the vulnerable. Future generations are important to all groups. As noted earlier, psychological distancing often leads people to frame climate change as a future problem. For this reason, the narrative places it within the intergenerational timeline of respect for both those who came before us and those as yet unborn.[23]

"Climate change is disrupting the natural balance. There is a divine balance to the world. Climate change is disrupting that balance. Climate change is a message that something is wrong. By taking action on climate change we can restore that natural order and balance." All faiths, especially in their more

---

[20] Intercultural Ecotheology: Integral Visions of Healing www.acu.edu.au/__data/assets/pdf_file/0014/.../Rider_Practical_Theol_GH.pdf (Accessed on 05/09/2016 at 10:45 pm).

[21] G. Marshall, A. Corner, O. Roberts, and J. Clarke, (2016). Faith & Climate Change ---A guide to talking with the five major faiths. Oxford: Climate Outreach. http://climateoutreach.org/resources/climate---change---faith/ (Accessed on 07/09/2016 at 09:15 pm)

[22] Climate Justice is a Matter of Faith, US Catholic, Vol. 81, No. 4, April 2016 pp 22–26 www.uscatholic.org/articles/201603/climate---justice---matter---faith---30604#sthash.ovEqjY3N.dpuf (Accessed on 08/09/2016 at 03:20 am).

[23] A. Corner, (2013). A new conversation with the centre---right about climate change: Values, frames and narratives. Oxford: Climate Outreach and Information Network (Accessed on 08/09/2016 at 03:17 am).

traditional or conservative expressions, are concerned with order, authority and stability, which are presented in constant opposition to disorder and instability. This narrative works especially well with the Hindu and Buddhist understanding of a universal order. Islam also has a strong concept of balance, embodied in the Arabic word *mīzān,* which denotes equilibrium, balance, and the scales on which all deeds are weighted. The framing of balance appears throughout the 2015 Islamic Declaration on Global Climate Change, for example: "The Earth functions in natural seasonal rhythms and cycles. Climate change is a result of the human disruption of this balance."[24]

"Taking action brings us closer to God. Climate change is taking us all away from the divine system, will or plan. Through action on climate change we can become closer to God, deeper in our faith and better people individually and collectively. And by being closer to God we will be better able to take action on climate change."[25] For Hinduism and Buddhism, language around the interconnectedness of humanity and the natural world, and the divine or cosmic order of universe, was most effective. Although not fully tested, participants and faith experts felt that climate change could be presented as a form of violence, and action against it framed within the theology of *Dharma* as an abhorrence of Violence and causing harm to others (*ahimsa*).[26]

For Jews, language around justice and intergenerational equity was especially meaningful. Compared with other faiths, Judaism has a particularly strong understanding of the morality of inaction and missed opportunities, and requires atonement for the specific "sin of omission" when "a man fails to fulfil the duty serving upon Him."[27] All of these approaches could be particularly relevant to this complex issue that is so often marginalized through a social silence.

6) Interfaith Rain-Forest Initiative

"We must use our faith/religion to protect environment on the Earth." Setting aside their religious differences, Christian, Muslim, Jewish, Hindu, Buddhist and

---

[24] http://islamicclimatedeclaration.org/islamic---declaration---on---global---climate---change/ (Accessed on 07/09/2016 at 10:20 pm).

[25] G. Marshall, 2014. Hearth and Hiraeth: Constructing Climate Change Narratives around National Identity, Climate Outreach (Accessed on 08/09/2016 at 03:12 am).

[26] For example, Rebecca Solnit's article "Call climate change what it is: violence" www.theguardian.com/commentisfree/2014/apr/07/climate---change---violence---occupy---earth (Accessed on 08/09/2016 at 03:43 am).

[27] George Marshall, Communicating with Religious Communities on Climate Change: Research Overview and Emergent Narratives http://irdialogue.org/wp-content/uploads/2016/08/Communicating-with-Religious-Communities-8.14-FINAL.pd f(Accessed on 07/09/2016 at 09:15 pm).

Daoist leaders have launched a global effort to end deforestation.[28] Launching the Interfaith Rainforest Initiative at a conference in Oslo on June 19-21, religious and indigenous leaders from 21 countries spoke with forest advocates, climate scientists and human rights experts to develop goals and actions, along with milestones to mark their progress. They expect to follow up with an action plan and a global interfaith rainforest summit in 2018.

"The story of creation in the book of Genesis tells us of trees that are beautiful to behold and a source of sustenance. Rainforests are pivotal for life on earth, provisioning people's needs, promoting biodiversity and protecting the climate", said World Council of Churches general-secretary Rev. Dr Olav Fykse Tveit. "Today when the rainforests are threatened by deforestation driven by a short-sighted, profit-oriented economy, we must use the knowledge of what is good and our faith-driven action to protect and care for the rainforests and therefore the Earth and all life."

The leaders said the initiative will bring needed moral attention and spiritual commitment to bear on global efforts to end deforestation and protect the tropical rainforests – forests that are fundamental to human life, the planet's health and reducing the emissions fuelling climate change. This marks the first time religious leaders from a broad spectrum of faiths are working hand-in-hand with indigenous peoples, the world's leading rainforest guardians, to call upon and activate billions of people of faith worldwide to stand up for rainforests. The gathering was attended by His Majesty King Harald V of Norway.

Tropical rainforests in South America, sub-Saharan Africa and Asia are falling rapidly due to a range of forces, including palm oil plantations, cattle, soy and crop production, and rapacious and often illegal mining and logging operations. The losses amount to an area the size of Austria each year. With their capacity to store billions of tons of carbon, the preservation of tropical rainforests is widely viewed as fundamental to halting climate change. Many climate experts note that forests are the only proven approach for capturing and storing large amounts of carbon. Thus, staving off their destruction could keep carbon emissions at bay, buying time for the world to transition to a low carbon energy future, and also playing an indispensable role in reaching global carbon neutrality in the second half of this century.

Tropical rainforests also provide food, water and income to 1.6 billion people. They contain most of the planet's land-borne biodiversity and help regulate rainfall and temperature globally, regionally and locally. The group was convened

---

[28] Benjamin Glatt, "Religious leaders launch interfaith rainforest initiative" in **Meeting Rivers** <meeting-rivers@googlegroups.com>, June 27th 2017, 10:50am. Source: http://www.jpost.com/Christian-News/Religious-leaders-launch-interfaith-rainforest-initiative-497517. Meeting Rivers is a global platform of religious, spiritual and secular actors who bring fresh understandings, experiences and solutions to the inter-related challenges of personal change, social transformation and ecological engagement.

by Norway's International Climate and Forest Initiative, Rainforest Foundation Norway and the United Nations Development Program, in cooperation with the Forum on Religion and Ecology at Yale University, Green Faith, the Parliament of the World's Religions, Religions for Peace, REIL Network and the WCC.

"Our goal – working in concert with the spiritual and indigenous leaders gathered here – is to define a shared action plan to create a popular movement for expanded political will and on-the-ground action to protect rainforests," said Bishop Emeritus Gunnar Stålsett, honorary president of Religions for Peace. "The scope of this initiative is global. But we are also putting special focus on religious and indigenous leaders, networks and institutions in countries with the most significant tropical rainforests."

The initiative is linked to a surge of recent grassroots action in which environmental, climate and indigenous rights issues are being embraced as spiritual imperatives that strike a chord with multiple faiths and traditions. Other leaders of Evangelical Christian and Muslim organizations, and the Archbishop of Canterbury, have stressed the shared human responsibility to protect the planet. Lending crucial leadership and indispensable momentum to these efforts was the official letter issued in 2015 by Pope Francis that called on all people of the world to quickly bring, "the whole human family together to protect our common home." The pope also noted the unbreakable link between indigenous peoples and the environment. "For them land is not a commodity, but rather a gift from God and from their ancestors who rest there, a sacred space with which they need to interact if they are to maintain their identity and values."

7) Need of Interreligious Eco-theology

Interreligious Eco-theology is a young field that draws on long histories. While is take up the long held mantle of spiritual and cultural development passed through the heritage of the world's religious traditions, it is young and still inexperienced in terms of practical application. There are many faith communities who practice interfaith dialogue with their neighbours and Eco-theology in their communities. But the movement is still fledgling (an immature or inexperienced person). It now needs the leaders, activists, dedicated members and committed scholars of these faith communities to critically engage with these theoretical assumptions and contribute to the development of intercultural/interreligious "Eco-theology". The field itself needs to be diversified in the interests of genuine dialogue.[29]

As a largely white middle-class movement of the west, Intercultural Eco-theology needs to seek contributions and critiques from a variety of socio-religio-cultural perspectives, national contexts, class groups and faiths.

[29] G. Marshall, A. Corner, O. Roberts, and J. Clarke, (2016). Faith & Climate Change ---A guide to talking with the five major faiths. Oxford: Climate Outreach. http://climateoutreach.org/resources/climate---change---faith/ (Accessed on 07/09/2016 at 09:15 pm)

Challenging questions need to be asked and explored. To what extant do will faith communities allow themselves to adapt to new circumstances without feeling that they are threatening their unique integrity and heritage? Can faith communities reinterpret their theologies in a way that can incorporate these themes and contemporary callings? How can faith communities imagine the divine and their specific relationship to the divine in this multi-faith context? How do we maintain collectively a fair and fruitful arena for discussion and exchange and prevent any particular ideology or belief system from colonizing that space? These questions and many more present the practical dilemmas that can only be navigated through practice.[30]

Therefore, intercultural Eco-theology needs to become more of a widespread practical theology, one that is practiced in churches, mosques, synagogues and temples in a variety of cultural contexts. This practical knowledge and experience can open up further potentials and directions of thought and practice that cannot be preconceived. When dealing with new approaches to old traditions we need to be open to play, open to the expression of ideas and practices that lay beyond the page, and are inclusive of the knowledge's transferred in ritual and experiences. We need to be open to experimentation in safe environments and we need to be brave enough to introduce our long held traditions to new possibilities.

At this historic juncture, collecting these experiences of transformation and using this knowledge in developing and strengthening ourselves and each other is a courageous task. In a world where faith communities are already challenged and undermined in so many ways new transformations and interactions seem threatening and the pull of separatist fundamentalism may appear a safer haven. But perhaps it is in these uncertain circumstances, that faith communities can remember and exercise the only truly common aspect of their identity of faith.

[30] Oelschaeger, *Caring for Creation: An Ecumenical Approach to the Environmental Crisis...*, 102.

Conclusion

Our contemporary generation is witnessing the drastic changes in the universe, particularly on the earth, threatening the existence, survival and continuity of several biotic and abiotic creatures of the world due to eco-crisis and environmental degradation. We are hearing everywhere in the world the intensity of the increasing problem of ecological imbalance causing environmental vulnerability pushing the living creatures into insecurity on this globe the earth. This ecological/ environmental problem is not limited to one area, one nation, or few countries; it is not the only problem of Christians, or Muslims, or Hindus, or Buddhists; but is the problem of whole world and all people irrespective of nation and region; faith and religion; and gender and caste, hence, it is responsibility of all human beings to search for resources and solutions to solve the problem and improve healthy environment. This research is based on eco-concerns in India and on the study of major religious traditions from the perspective of ecology and environment searching the ways and means to re-construct eco-spirituality in order to bring environmental awareness of Indian masses.

With a population of over 1.3 billion, India is soon set to dislodge China as the most populous country of the world. While India has one of the fastest growing populations in the world today, it's far behind most others when it comes to preserving the environment and the ecology. Today, our country is riddled with a number of environmental concerns which have only aggravated in the last few decades. It is high time we tackled these issues head on as turning a blind eye is no solution. Even as India races ahead to join the league of top economies internationally, it must stick to a growth path that is environmentally friendly and ecologically sustainable. Neglecting the environment can create havoc and the damage done may become irreparable. So, we must wake up to face the challenges boldly and actively. Let me sum up some of the major environmental concerns contemporary India is struggling with today.

Air pollution is one of the worst scourges to have affected India. According to a report from the International Energy Agency (IEA), by 2040 there are likely to be about 9 lakh premature deaths in the country due to the drastic rise in air pollution in the country. Average life expectancies are likely to go down by about 15 months because of air pollution. India is also home to 11 out of 20 of the most polluted (in terms of air pollution) cities in the entire world. According to the rankings of the 2016 Environmental Performance Index, India ranks 141 out of 180 countries in terms of air pollution.

Rapidly depleting levels of groundwater is one of the biggest threat to food security and livelihood in the country. Accessing the groundwater has become increasingly difficult over the decades. According to news reports, excessive exploitation of limited groundwater resources for irrigation of cash crops such as sugarcane has caused a 6 percentage point decline in the availability of water within 10 metres from ground level. Low rainfall and drought are also reasons for groundwater depletion. The north western and south eastern parts of the country are the worst hit. These are also the regions responsible for most of the country's agricultural production and food crisis is a natural consequence.

Global warming and climate change are other crucial ecological problems of our country as well as whole world. In May 2016, Phalodi in Rajasthan recorded a temperature of 51 degrees Celsius – the highest ever in the country; Adilbad in Telangana and some parts of Andhra also reached $50°_C$. The increasingly tormenting heat waves in the past few years are but an indication that global warming and climate change are real challenges that the country is facing today. With the Himalayan glaciers melting at an alarming rate, floods and other such natural disasters are occurring with increasing frequency. The number of forest fires, floods, earthquakes and such other calamities over the past five years has been unprecedented.

Uncontrolled use of plastics is another major threat for the healthy environment of our country. According to data from the Plastindia Foundation, India's demand for polymers is expected to go up from 11 million tonnes in 2012-13 to about 16.5 million tonnes in 2016-17. India's per capita plastic consumption went up from about 4 kg in 2006 to some 8 kg in 2010. By 2020, this is likely to shoot up to about 27 kg. To understand the damage that this can cause to the environment, it is important to understand that plastics are one of the least biodegradable materials. An average plastic beverage bottle could take up to 500 years to decompose naturally.

Garbage Disposal and Sanitation systems are also intensifying a great problem in India. According to a 2014 report by The Economist, about 130 million households (and 600 million population) in the country lack toilets. Over 72 percent of India's rural population defecate in the open. Ancient practices such as manual scavenging are still in vogue in the country. Lack of safe garbage disposal systems in the country make India one of the most unhygienic countries in the world. The rural regions of the country are worse off than urban tracts in this regard. This is one of the areas where the country's government and people need to work hard and improve the prevailing conditions and improve healthy environment.

Deforestation, industrialization and urbanisation are some other major factors increasing ecological problems and environmental degradation. For example, millions hectors of forests have been disappearing through "deforestation" either converting to "agricultural, industrial, urban projects" or leaving as "deserts". Forests became rich sources of production of woody biomass for commercial purpose, as raw material for industries, particularly for timber merchants. The interests of the timber merchants and their customers clash with the interest of the *Adivasis*/Tribes who live in the forests and with the forests, and depend on the sources that are available in forests, economically as well as spiritually. Deforestation affects to a larger extent the life of *Adivasis* – Tribes and wild life of many forest living creatures. Industrialization and urbanization added further the fuel to deforestation leading to increasing air pollution, water scarcity, bio-diversity, climate change and natural calamities.

An important alarming eco-concern is, perhaps, loss of biodiversity. According to the International Union for Conservation of Nature's Red Data Book, some 47 species of plants and animals in India are listed as critically endangered. Loss of ecology and natural habitats have left many indigenous species, including important ones such as the Siberian crane, Himalayan wolf and Kashmir stag in grave danger of going extinct, even frogs and sparrows are also in danger of extinction. Rapid urbanization, poaching and indiscriminate hunting for leather fur and food, etc., has rendered these animals, birds and other living creatures critically endangered and the flora or herbal treasure of India in near-extinction conditions. Many of the plants commonly harvested for their medicinal properties are vanishing along with the legacy of Ayurvedic treatment.

Although, India has a rich and long history of environmental laws dating back to the 1970s, it still ranks very low on air and water pollution levels compared to the rest of the world resulting in higher rates of infant mortality and lower life expectancy rates. Poor sanitation conditions and sewage problems compound the problem affecting the health of ordinary citizens in India. The reasons for this disconnect between enlightened environmental laws and high levels of pollution could be traced to lax enforcement of existing environmental laws, discrepancies in the environmental guidelines for businesses to follow between the central government and at the state levels, and the existence of a large number of untrained employees who neither have the resources nor the technical skills to adhere to the existing environmental laws.

Using extensive research, this suggests a series of steps to help the country achieve safe air and water pollution levels resulting in improved health conditions for its citizens. The cornerstone of the prescription for improvements in the environment is a collaborative arrangement that brings together the various government agencies, the citizens, large domestic companies, and NGOs to participate in a collaborative arrangement to educate, streamline effective policies, develop the necessary institutional infrastructure, and provide adequate funding for improving the environment.

There are two main reasons India's environmental challenges are assuming gigantic proportions. Firstly, the exploding population and the needs of billions make environmental sustainability a very difficult issue. The other big challenge is lack of environmental awareness and conservation. Despite the efforts of government and environmental agencies, there is a lack of substantial efforts from the masses. Unless this changes, there is little hope for improvement. We can only look forward to the youth and the younger generations of the nation to remain conscientious and act in the best interests of future generations.

Environmental awareness, indeed, is essential in our country. India, as a pluralistic country, where people profess various faiths, confesses diverse creeds and follows different religious traditions, perhaps, lacks in the knowledge on ecological concerns from their religious traditions and faiths. This work is, indeed, a scientific study to search various religious traditions of India for resources to reflect on important eco-concerns and to reconstruct eco-spirituality of Indian major religious traditions. Eco-crisis is a common and universal problem; therefore it needs the cooperation and coordination of all people irrespective of their religious and faith backgrounds, to work together for the safeguard of health environment.

Some Suggestions to Church and it's Ministry in India:

Finally let me suggest, as an ordained Christian minister, some action plans to be adapted into the life of Indian Church, Christian ministry, especially to Pastoral Ministry in India.[1] Local congregations and all pastors must be aware of the present ecological crisis and environmental disorder, therefore, the pastors and churches are ought to organise ecological awareness campaigns, seminars and other related programs in congregations. Pastors and leaders of congregations should resolve to be as thoroughly informed as possible about the diverse aspects of the ecological crisis. We cannot share Christ's ministry of resting the life of God's creation unless we are fully aware of factors in the process that are destroying

[1] For more clarification on role of pastoral ministry and ecological concerns in India refer Eric J. Lot, "The Ecological Crisis and the Pastoral Ministry" and particularly his scholarly articles on ecological concerns and Indian Religions, for example, "The Image for Mission: The Epiphanic Body"; "Changing Eco-Faith Perspectives in India" in *Bangalore Theological Forum*, UTC, Bangalore, Oct-Dec 1986; "The Indian Contribution to a Global Eco-Theology"; "Indian Culture and Earth Care Facing our Ecological Crisis", first published by Indian Institute of World Culture, Bangalore, as Transaction No. 68, 1986; and "Religion and the Future of Creation", a lecture delivered at Wesley College, Bristol, in May 1998. This author fortunately accessed to these writings on eco-concerns from Eric J. Lott unpublished personal micro soft word (MS) documents.

it and that alienate the human race from other parts of that creaturely world. And how can we become better informed? One way of educating all Pastors and leaders would be to provide them literature in their vernacular languages about ecological concerns.

The central focus of Christian ministry should be to create ecological or holistic awareness among Christians and non-Christians too. Basic to true eco-development is the strengthening of a local sense of community and if people participating in all local resources, developing such a local people's participant consciousness is perhaps the most important way to enable local resistance to the destructive tendencies in much, though not all, modern technology. It is necessary to build up and mobilise local cells on environmental concerns, especially, Sunday schools, youth groups, women groups, elders retreats, of those prepared to pioneer the way on ecological concerns.

Church property resources, especially landed resources, should be developed in tune with the eco- friendly developmental aims. There are still large missionary compound lands lying, either unused or perhaps misused, for example, missionary grounds belong to Andhra Evangelical Lutheran Church, in the heart of Guntur, Bhimavarm and Rajamundry towns of Andhra Pradesh are witnessing the same fact. If a pastoral ministry is involved with educational training institutions of any kind, from Primary to College level, great efforts should be made to develop an environmentally conscious style of education. Pastoral ministry needs to focus on tree plantation and species preservation programs. Pastors need to join with the organizations, governmental or non-governmental, that are working on environmental concerns. Pastoral ministry also focus to bring awareness among rural people to adopt eco-friendly agriculture rather than organic and commercial based agricultural products. Churches also bring awareness among people in rural areas particularly in avoiding age old practices of cooking/heating habits such as burning wood or cow dung. Instead they will be provided to use smokeless gas stoves and so on. Finally pastors come forward with openness to organize/ participate in inter-faith and inter-religious programs to mobilize/utilize inter-faith cooperation in order to promote healthy environment at least locally, if not possible globally.

Bibliography
(Referred and Related)

Abd-al-Hamid, "Exploring the Islamic Environmental Ethics," in *Islam and the Environment*, A.R. Agwan (ed.), New Delhi, Institute of Objective Studies, 1997.

Abdulla Yusuf'Ali, *The Meaning of the Holy Qur'an: Text, Translation and Commentary,* New Delhi, Al Hasanat Books Pvt.Ltd, 1973.

Abraham, K.C., *Eco–Justice- A New Agenda for Church Mission*, Bombay, BUILD Publication, n.d.

Abraham, K.C., *Eco–Justice- A New Agenda for Church Mission,* Bombay: BUILD Publication, n.d.

Abubakar Ahmad Bakadar, "Islamic Principles for the Conservation of the Natural Envirornment," in *Islam and the Environment,* A.R. Agwan (ed.), New Delhi, Institute of Objective Studies, 1997.

Agwan, A.R., "Introduction," in *Islam and the Environment,* A.R. Agwan (ed.), New Delhi, Institute of Objective Studies, 1997.

Agwan, A.R., "Towards an Ecological Consciousness", in *Islam and the Environment,* A.R. Agwan (ed.), New Delhi, Institute of Objective Studies, 1997.

Al Mawil Samarai, "The Human Appointment and Creation"," in *Islam and the Environment,* A.R. Agwan (ed.), New Delhi: Institute of Objective Studies, 1997.

Al-lmam Zain-ud-din, Ahmed bin Abdul-Lateef and Az-Subaidi, (Comps.), *The Translation of the Meaning of summarised Sahih Al-Bukhari Arabic – English,* Muhammadd Mushin Khan (Trans.), Soudi Arabia, Maktba Dar-us-Salam, 1994.

Anil Agarwal, "Facing a Silent Spring, Pesticides and Ecological Devastation and Cancer: The Story of an Environmental Victim" in *Down to Earth,* November 30, 1996.

Anil Agarwal, "My Story Today, Your Story Tomorrow: An Environmentalist Searches for the Genesis of His Own Cancer," *Down To Earth,* 5, no. 13, 30 November, 1996.

Arjun Makhijani et al., "Ozone Depletion: Cause and Effects" in *Economic and Political Weekly*, March 10th 1990.

Arne Naess, *Ecology, Community, and Lifestyle: Outline of an Ecosophy,* David Rothenberg (trans.), Cambridge and New York, Cambridge University Press, 1989.

Arputhamurthy, J.E.M. "Ecology, Economics and Ecumenics," in *TBT Journal,* Ken Gnanakan and Paul Mohan Raj (eds.), Bangalore, The Theological Book Trust, 2000.

Aruna Gnanadason, "Woman, Patriarchy and Creation: Insights from Eco-Feminist Theology, in *Green Theology*, Wati Longchar (ed.), Kolkata, Shrach, 2014.

Aruna Gnanadason, "Women, Economy and Ecology," in *Green Theology*, Wati Longchar (ed.), Kolkatta, PTCA, 2012.

Augustine Perumalil, *Religious Cosmologies,* Delhi, ISPCK, 2007.

Bas Wielenga, *Towards an Eco-Just Society*, Bangalore, Centre for Social Action, 1999.

Bernard J. Frieden, *The Environmental Protection Hustle,* Cambridge, Mass, MIT Press, 1979.

Bernard L. Cohen, "The Costs of Nuclear Power", in *The State of Humanity,* Julian L. Simon (ed.), New York: Blackwell, 1995.

Bhaskar, Bhagchandra Jain, "Ecology and Spirituality in the Jain Tradition", *Jainism and Ecology: Nonviolence in the Web of Life*, Christopher Key Chapple (ed.), vol. XXII, Delhi, Motilal Banarsidass Publishers, 2006.

Boff, Leonardo, *Ecology and Liberation*, John Cumming (Trans.), New York, Orbis Book, 1995.

Bose, A.C., *The Call of the Vedas,* Bhartiya Vidya Bhavan, Mumbai, 1999.

Brewer, R., *The Science of Ecology,* 1988.

Brown, David A., *A Guide to Religion*. New Delhi, ISPCK, 1973.

Byrne John, "The Long march of live hood" in *Environmental Justice*, vol-8, London, Transaction Publishers, 2009.

Calvin Beisner E., "Sixpence None the Richer: Economics–A Millennium of Human Progress," *World*, 14 July 31, 1999.

Calvin Beisner E., *Prospects for Growth: A Biblical View of Population, Resources, and the Future,* Wheaton, Ill., Crossway Books, 1990.

Calvin Beisner E., *Prosperity and Poverty: The Compassionate Use of Resources in a World of Scarcity,* Wheaton, Ill., Crossway Books, 1988.

Calvin Beisner, E., "Anomalies, the Good News, and the Debate over Population and Development: A Review of Susan Power Bratton's Six Billion and More," *Stewardship Journal* – 3, Summer, 1993.

Calvin Beisner, E., "*Imago Dei* and the Population Debate," in *Where Garden Meets Wilderness: Evangelical Entry into the Environmental Debate,* Grand Rapids, Mich., Eerdmans Publishing/Acton Institute, 1997.

Calvin Beisner, E., "Stewardship in a Free Market," in *The Christian Vision: Morality and the Marketplace,* Michael Bauman et al. (eds.), Hillsdale, Mich., Hillsdale College Press, 1994.

Calvin Beisner, E., *Prospects for Growth: A Biblical View of Population, Resources, and the Future,* Wheaton, Ill., Crossway Books, 1990.

Calvin Beisner, E., *Where Garden Meets Wilderness: Evangelical Entry into the Environmental Debate,* Grand Rapids, Mich., Eerdmans Publishing/Acton Institute, 1997.

Calvin Beisner, E., *Where Garden Meets Wilderness: Evangelical Entry into the Environmental Debate,* Grand Rapids, Mich., Eerdmans Publishing/Acton Institute, 1997.

Chakrabarti, *The Oxford Companion to Indian Archaeology: The Archaeological Foundations of Ancient India Stone Age to 13th Century,* New Delhi; New York, Oxford University Press, 2006.

Charles T. Rubin, *The Green Crusade: Rethinking the Roots of Environmentalism,* New York, Free Press, 1994.

Charles, Murphy, *At Home on Earth: Foundations for a Catholic Ethic of the Environment,* New York, Crossroad, 1989.

Cobb, John B., "Protestant Theology and Deep Ecology," in *This Sacred Earth, Second Edition,* Roger S. Gottlieb (ed.), New York, Rutledge, 2004.

Colinvaux P. A., *Introduction to Ecology,* 1973.

Darnell, R. M., *Ecology and Man,* 1973.

David G. Hallman, *Ecotheology: Voices from South and North,* New York: Orbis Books.

Deegan Chris, "The Narmada in Myth and History" in *Toward Sustainable Development Struggling over India's Narmada River,* William F. Fisher(ed.), Landon, M. E. Sharpe. 1995.

Derek M. Elsom, "Atmospheric Pollution Trends in the United Kingdom", in *The State of Humanity,* Julian L. Simon (ed.), New York, Blackwell, 1995.

Desrochers et. al., *Social Movements,* Bangalore, Centre for Social Action, 1991.

Drengson A. & B. Devall (eds.), *The Ecology of Wisdom Writings by Arne Naess,* Berkeley, Counterpoint, 2008.

Drengson, A. and Y. Inoue (eds.), *The Deep Ecology Movement: An Introductory Anthology*, Berkeley, North Atlantic Publishers, 1995.

Elizabeth Brubaker, *Property Rights in the Defense of Nature,* London and Toronto, Earthscan/Environment Probe, 1995.

Emmel, T. C., *An Introduction to Ecology and Population Biology,* 1973.

Francis A. Schaeffer, "How Should We Then Live?" in *The Complete Works of Francis A. Schaeffer: A Christian Worldview,* Westchester, Ill., Crossway Books, 1982.

George Zachariah, *Gospel Groaning World: Climate Injustice and Public Witness*, Thiruvalla, CSS & NCCI, 2012.

Ghanshyam Shah, *Social Movements: A Review of Literature,* 2004.

Gnanadason, Aruna, "Women, Economy and Ecology" in *Green Theology*, Wati Longchar (ed.), Kolkatta: PTCA, 2012.

Goeller, H. E., "Trends in Nonrenewable Resources", in *The State of Humanity,* Julian L. Simon (ed.), New York: Blackwell, 1995.

Gordon D. Newby, *The Concise Encyclopedia of Islam,* England, One World Publication, 2002.

Gordon D. Newby, *The Concise Encyclopedia of Islam,* England, One World Publication, 2002.

Gottlieb, Roger S., *The Oxford Handbook of Religion and Ecology*, New York, Oxford University Press, 2006.

Griffith, R.T.H., *The Hymns of the Atharvaveda*, D.K. Publishers, Delhi, 1995.

Guattari, Félix, "Remaking Social Practices", in Genosko, Gary, *The Guattari Reader,* Oxford, Blackwell, 1996.

Habib, Irfan, *A Peoples History of India 2: The Indus Valley Civilization.* New Delhi, Tulika Books, 2002.

Huang Po Ho, *Embracing The Household of God – A Paradigm Shift From Anthropocentric Tradition to Creation Responsibility in Doing Theology,* Kolkata: SCEPTRE, 2014.

Hugh W. Ellsaesser, "Trends in Air Pollution in the United States," in *The State of Humanity,* Julian L. Simon (ed.), New York, Blackwell, 1995.

Jacinta Prakashappa, "Re-reading the Creation Story," in *Envisioning a New Heaven and a New Earth*, Lalrinawmi Ralte (ed.), Nagpur: NCCI/ISPCK, 1998.

Jain, Arun Kumar, *Faith and Philosophy of Jainism*, Delhi, Kalpaz Publications, 2009.

James Hansen, *Storms of My Grandchildren: The Truth About the Coming Climate Catastrophe and our last Chance to Save Humanity,* Bloomsbury, USA, New York, 2009.

James, Woba, *Major Issues in the History of Christianity in India: A Post Colonial Reading*, Mokokchung, TDCC Publications, 2013.

Janki Andharia and Chandan Sengupta, 'The Environmental Movement: Global Issues and the India Reality', in *The Indian Journal of Social Work,* 59 (1), 1998.

Jessica Hellman et al., *Ecofables/Ecoscience,* Stanford, Calif, Stanford University/ Center for Conservation Biology, 1998.

John A. Baden and Douglas S. Noonan, (ed.), *Managing the Commons,* 2nd ed. Bloomington, Indiana University Press, 1998.

John G. Myers, Stephen Moore, and Julian L. Simon, "Trends in Availability of Non-Fuel Minerals" in *The State of Humanity,* Julian L. Simon (ed.), New York: Blackwell, 1995.

John Harris, Stanley Godlovitch, and Roslind Godlovitch, *Animals, Men, and Morals,* New York: Taplinger Publishing, 1972.

John Tuxill and Chris Bright, "Losing Strands in the Web of Life," in *The State of the World 1998,* Lester R. Brown, Christopher Flavin, and Hilary French (eds.), New York, W. W. Norton, 1998.

Jose Abraham, "An Ecological Reading of the Qur'anic Understanding of Creation," in *Bangalore Theological Forum,* 33/1, June, 2001.

Joseph, M.J., "The Integrity of Creation," in *Theology for Our Times,* Vol. Number 18, March, Bangalore, Indian School of Ecumenical Christian Centre & Ecumenical Christian Centre, 2016.

Judy Pearsall and Bill Trumble (eds.), *The Oxford English Reference Dictionary,* New York, Oxford University Press, 1995.

Julian L. Simon (ed.), *The State of Humanity,* New York, Blackwell, 1995.

Julian L. Simon and Aaron Wildavsky, "On Species Loss, the Absence of Data, and Risks to Humanity," in *The Resourceful Earth,* Julian L. Simon and Herman Kahn (eds.), Oxford and New York, Blackwell, 1984.

Julian L. Simon, *The Ultimate Resource 2,* revised edition. Princeton, Princeton University Press, 1996.

Julian L. Simon, *Population Matters: People, Resources, Environment, and Immigration,* New Brunswick, N.J., Transaction, 1990.

Julian L. Simon, *The Economics of Population Growth,* Princeton: Princeton University Press, 1977.

Kansara, N.M., *Agriculture and Animal Husbandry in the Vedas*, Delhi, Nag Publishers, 1995.

Kapil Dev Dwivedi, *Vedic Sahitya Avam Sanskriti*, Varanasi, 2000.

Karpagam M., Green *Management: Theory and Applications,* New Delhi, Ane Books Pvt. Ltd., 2010.

Keitzar, Renthy, *In Search of a Relevant Gospel Message*, Guwahati, CLC, 1995.

Kochappilly, Paulachan, "Ecological Crisis and Christian Response" in *Theology for Our Times*, Reji Samuel (ed.), Bangalore, Ecumenical Christian Centre, 2015.

Kosambi, D. D, *The Culture and Civilisation of Ancient India in Historical Outline,* New Delhi, Vikas Publishing House Pvt. Ltd, 1996.

Kumar, Mritunjay, "Religious Ecology in Buddhism", *Ecological Perspective in Buddhism*, K. C. Pandey (ed.). New Delhi, Readworthy Publications Pvt. Ltd., 2008.

Kwok Pui-Lan, "Ecology and the Recycling of Christianity," in *Ecotheology- Voices from South and North,* David G. Hallman (ed.), New York: Orbis Books.

Lasetso, Razouselie, "Tribal Theology and the Bible: A Contextual Reading of the Bible", in *Tribal Theology -A search for Quality Theological Education and Relevant Ministry*, Yangkahao Vashum (ed.), Jorhat, Tribal Study Series, 2009.

Lasetso, Razouselie. "Exploring Ecological Values from Tribal Resources", in *Tribal Ecology*, Razouselie Lasetso, Marlene Ch.Marak and Yangkahao Vashum (eds.), Jorhat, ETC Programme Coordination, 2012.

Lemtur, Zulunungsang, "Climate Change and Climate Refugees" in *Green Theology*, Wati Longchar (ed.), Kolkata, SCEPTRE, 2014.

Leonardo Boff, *Ecology and Liberation*, John Cumming (Trans.), New York, Orbis Books, 1995.

Lockyer, N.J., *The dawn of Astronomy,* Massachusetts, Institute of Technology.

Long, Jeffery D., *An Introduction to Jainism*, London/New York, I.B.TAURIS, 2010.

Longchar, Wati, "Ecumenical Responses to Ecological Crisis: A Critique from the Indigenous Peoples' Perspective", in *The Journal of Theologies and Cultures in Asia*, Vol. 11, A.Wati Longchar (ed.), Kolkata, PTCA, 2012.

Longchar, A. Wati, "Myth: A Source for Conceptualizing Tribal Theology", in *An Exploration of Tribal Theology*, A. Wati Longchar (ed.), Mokokchung, TzÜdikong Baptist Church, 1997.

Longchar, A. Wati, *The Traditional Tribal Worldview and Modernity*, Jorhat, N. Limatula Lkr, 1995.

Longchar, A. Wati, *The Tribal Religious Traditions in North East India – An Introduction*, Jorhat, A. Wati Longchar, 2000.

Longchar, Wati, "Ecumenical Responses to Ecological Crisis: A Critique from the Indigenous Peoples' Perspective," in *Green Theology - Asian Ecumenical Response to Eco-Justice*, Wati Longchar (ed.), Kolkata: JTCA, 2012.

Longchar, Wati, "Green Theology: Resources from Primeval Traditions", in *The Journal of Theologies and Cultures in Asia,* Vol. 11, A. Wati Lonchar (ed.), Kolkata: PTCA, 2012.

Longchar, Wati, "Green Theology: Resources from Primeval Traditions", in *Green Theology*, Wati Longchar (ed.), Kolkata, SCEPTRE, 2014.

Longchar, Wati, *Returning to Mother Earth: Theology, Christian Witness and Theological Education: An Indigenous Perspective,* Taiwan, Program for Theology and Culture in Asia, 2012.

Lourdunathan, S., "Ecosophical Concerns in the Sikh Tradition" presented as a paper at a conference Sikhism and Global Living, organized by Guru Nanak Devji Chair, School of Religions, Philosophy and Humanistic Thought, Madurai Kamaraj University, Madurai, April 1996.

MacDonnell, A.A., *A History of Sanskrit Literature*, MLBD, 1965.

Marjory Stonemean, Douglas, *The Everglades: River of Grass,* Pineapple Press. Inc., Sarasota, Florida, 1947.

Mark H. Williamson, *Island Populations,* Oxford, Oxford University Press, 1981.

Mawil Y. Izzi Dien, "Islamic Ethics and the Enviornment," in *Islam and Ecology*, Fazlun M. Khalid and Joanne O'Brien (eds.), London, Cassell Publishers Limited, 1992.

Max Singer, *Passage to a Human World: The Dynamics of Creating Global Wealth,* Indianapolis, Hudson Institute, 1987.

McHenry Robert, *The Encyclopedia Britannica,* Chicago, Encyclopaedia Britannica, inc. 1993.

Michael B. Barkey, "A Framework for Translating Environmental Ethics into Public Policy," *Journal of Markets and Morality*, in *The Christian Vision: Morality and the Marketplace,* Michael Bauman et al. (eds.), Hillsdale, Mich., Hillsdale College Press, 1994.

Michael B. Barkey, "Translating Environmental Ethics into Public Policy," *Journal of Markets and Morality*, 2, Fall 1999.

Michael B. Barkey, Paul Cleveland, and Gregory M. A. Gronbacher, "Population, the Environment, and Human Capital".

Michael Cromartie, ed., *The Nine Lives of Population Control,* Washington, D.C., and Grand Rapids, Mich., Ethics and Public Policy Center/Eerdmans Publishing, 1995.

Mikhail Bernstam, "Comparative Trends in Resource Use and Pollution in Market and Socialist Economies," in *The State of Humanity,* Julian L. Simon (ed.), New York: Blackwell, 1995.

Minz, Nirmal, "Tribal Perspective on Ecology", in *The Tribal Worldview and Ecology*, A. Wati Longchar and Yangkahao Vashum (eds.), Jorhat, Tribal Study Centre, 1998.

Mohd. Kaleemur Rahman, "Environmental Awareness in Islam", in *Islam and the Environment,* A.R. Agwan (ed.), New Delhi, Institute of Objective Studies, 1997.

Morris A. Adelman, "Trends in the Price and Supply of Oil", in *The State of Humanity,* Julian L. Simon (ed.), New York: Blackwell, 1995.

Murthy, S.R.N., *Vedic View of the Earth*, D.K. Print World, New Delhi, 1997.

Naess, Arne, "The Shallow and the Deep Long-Range Ecology Movement: A Summary" in *Inquiry*, 1973.

Nandita Singhavi, *Vedame Paryavarana*, Sonali Publications, Jaipur, 2004.

Narula Smita, *Human Rights in the Global Economy and the Struggle Against the World Bank,* New York University Public Law and Legal Theory, Working Papers, 12-17-2008.

Narula Smita, *The Story of Narmada Bachao Andolan: Human Rights in the Global Economy and the Struggle Against the World Bank,* New York, University Public Law and Legal Theory, Working Papers, 12-17-2008.

Nathan Rosenberg and L. E. Birdzell, Jr., *How the West Grew Rich: The Economic Transformation of the Industrial World,* New York, Basic Books, 1986.

Nayare Ali, "There's something about Mary", *Times of India,* 14 July 2002.

Nicholas Eberstadt, "Population, Food, and Income: Global Trends in the Twentieth Century," in *The True State of the Planet,* Ronald Bailey (ed.), New York, Free Press, 1995.

Nicholas Eberstadt, "World Depopulation: Last One Out Turn Off the Lights," *Milken Institute Review* 2, First Quarter, 2000.

Nicholas Eberstadt, "World Depopulation: Last One Out Turn Off the Lights," in *Milken Institute Review,* 2, First Quarter 2000.

Nicholas Eberstadt, "World Population Prospects for the Twenty-First Century: The Specter of 'Depopulation'?" in *Earth Report 2000: Revisiting the True State of the Planet,* Ronald Bailey (ed.), New York McGraw-Hill, 2000.

Nurdeng Deurashe, "Maintaining a Healthy Environment: An Islamic Ethical Approach," in *European Journal of Social Sciences,* 8/4, 2009.

Odum, E. P, *Fundamentals of Ecology,* 3rd ed., 1971.

Oelschaeger, Max, *Caring for Creation: An Ecumenical Approach to the Environmental Crisis,* New Haven and London, Yale University Press, 1994.

Panchamukhi, A.R., *Socio-economic Ideas in Ancient Indian Literature,* Rashtriya Sanskrit Sansthan, Delhi, 1998.

Paul R. Ehrlich and Anne Ehrlich, *Extinction: The Causes and Consequences of the Disappearance of Species,* New York, Random House, 1981.

Paulachan Kochappilly, "Ecological Crisis and Christian Response," in *Theology for Our Times,* Reji Samuel (ed.), Bangalore, Ecumenical Christian Centre, 2015.

Peter J. Hill, "Biblical Principles Applied to a Natural Resources/Environment Policy," in *Biblical Principles and Public Policy: The Practice,* Richard Chewning (ed.), Colorado Springs, NavPress, 1991.

Peter J. Hill, "Can Markers or Government Do More for the Environment" in *Creation at Risk? Religion, Science, and Environmentalism,* Michael Cromartie (ed.), Washington, D.C.: Ethics and Public Policy Center/Eerdmans Publishing, 1995.

Peter J. Hill, "Takings and the Judeo-Christian Land Ethic: A Response," *Religion and Liberty* 9, March/April 1999.

Peter Singer, *Animal Liberation: A New Ethics for Our Treatment of Animals,* New York, Random House/New York Review of Books, 1975.

Philip Weller, *Freshwater Seas,* Between the Lines, Canada, May 1, 1991.

Po Ho, Huang, "Embracing The Household of God – A Paradigm Shift From Anthropocentric Tradition to Creation Responsibility", *in Doing Theology,* Kolkata, SCEPTRE, 2014.

Podimattam, Felix M., *The Ten Commandments in the Law of Christ – Ecological Ethics,* Vol. ix. New Delhi: Media House, 2013.

Prakashappa, Jacinta, "Re-reading the Creation Story," in *Envisioning a New Heaven and a New Earth,* Lalrinawmi Ralte (ed.), Nagpur, NCCI/ISPCK, 1998.

Pui-Lan, Kwok, “Ecology and the Recycling of Christianity” in *Ecotheology- Voices from South and North,* David G. Hallman (ed.), New York, Orbis Books.

Rachel Carson, *Silent Spring,* Houghton Mifflin Company; September 27, 1962; Anniversary edition October 22, 2002.

Rahula,Walpola Sri; *What the Buddha Taugh*t, London, Gordon Fraser Gallery Ltd., 1978.

Raj, P. J. Sanjeeva, “Ecology and Development: A Theological Perspective” in *Ecology and Development,* Daniel D. Chetti (ed.), Chennai, United Evangelical Lutheran Churches in India, Gurukul Lutheran Theological College & Research Institute, BTESSC, 1991.

Raja Ram Mohan Roy, *Vedic Physics, Scientific Origin of Hinduism,* Toronto, Golden Egg Publishing, 1999.

Ramesh, Randeep, "Live to tell", *The Guardian,* London, 17th February 2007.

Razu, Indukuri John Mohan, *Global Capitalism as Hydra- A New Look at Market, Money and MNCs,* New Delhi, ISPCK, 2006.

Riane Eisler, *The Chalice and the Blade: Our History, Our Future,* Cambridge, Mass., Harper and Row, 1987.

Robert C. Balling, *The Heated Debate: Greenhouse Predictions Versus Climate Reality,* San Francisco, Pacific Research Institute, 1992.

Robert M. May, "Conceptual Aspects of the Quantification of the Extent of Biological Diversity," in *Biodiversity: Measurement and Estimation,* D. L. Hawksworth (ed.), London, Royal Society/Chapman and Hall, 1995.

Robert Royal, *The Virgin and the Dynamo: Use and Abuse of Religion in Environmental Debates,* Grand Rapids, Mich., Eerdmans Publishing, 1999.

Robert William Fogel, "The Contribution of Improved Nutrition to the Decline in Mortality Rates in Europe and America," in *The State of Humanity,* ed. Julian L. Simon (ed.), New York, Blackwell, 1995.

Roger A. Sedjo and Marion Clawson, "Global Forests Revisited," in *The State of Humanity,* Julian L. Simon (ed.), New York: Blackwell, 1995.

Ronald Bailey (ed.), *Earth Report 2000: Revisiting the True State of the Planet,* New York, McGraw-Hill, 2000.

Ronald Bailey, "Earth Day: Then and Now," *Reason* 31, May 2000.

Rosalie Bertell, *No Immediate Danger, Prognosis for a Radioactive Earth,* London,The Women's Press, 1985.

Rowan B. Martin, "Biological Diversity: Divergent Views on Its Status and Diverging Approaches to Its Conservation," in *Earth Report 2000: Revisiting the True State of the Planet,* Ronald Bailey (ed.), New York, McGraw-Hill, 2000.

Seyyed H. Nasr, "Islam and the Environmental Crisis," in *Islam and the Environment,* A. R. Agwan (ed.), New Delhi, Institute of Objective Studies, 1997.

Seyyed Hossein Nasr, "Islam and the Environmental Crisis," in *The Islamic Quarterly,* 34/4, 1990.

Seyyed Hossein Nasr, "The Cosmos and the Natural Order", in *Islamic Spirituality: Foundations,* Seyyed Hossein Nasr (ed.), London, SCM Press Ltd., 1989.

Sharma, A, "Dr. B. R. Ambedkar on the Aryan Invasion and the Emergence of the Caste System in India", in *Journal of the American Academy of Religion, 73*(3), 2005.

Shashi Tiwari, "Origin of Environmental Science from Vedas."

Shivaji Rao, T., *Nuclear Plants – The Silent Killers,* Hyderabad, Navya Bharathi Publications, 1989.

Silva, Lynn A de., "The Buddhist Religious Tradition" in *The Religious Tradition of India,* P.S. Daniel, David C. Scott, G. R. Singh (eds.), New Delhi, ISPCK, 2011.

Smith, R. L. (ed)., *The Ecology of Man: An Ecosystem Approach,* 1971.

Snaitang, O. L, *Asia Journal of Theology, Vol. 18, Issue 2,* October 2004.

Sutton D. B.and N. P. Harman, *Ecology: Selected Concepts,* 1973.

Swami Raju, T., "Paryavarana Aadhyathmikata – Aavasyakatha: Samakaleena Samaja Badhyata (Telugu)" in *Samaikya,* Golden Jubilee issue, ed. Praveen Prabhu Sudheer, ACTC, Hyderabad, 2014.

Swami Raju, T, "Eco-Justice: Contemporary Global Concern" in *Social Justice and Eco Concern,* in *ACTC Golden Jubilee One Day State Level Women Meet,* Hyderabad, ACTC, 2014.

Swami Raju, T, *Christian Theological Responses: Contemporary Contextual Concerns,* New Delhi, Christian World Imprints, 2014.

Swami Raju, T., "Eco-sophy and Eco-spirituality", in Richardson, K.L (ed.), *Samaikya,* Hyderabad, Andhra Christian Theological College, April 2015.

Takis Fotopoulos, "The Ecological Crisis as Part of the Present Multidimensional Crisis and Inclusive Democracy", in *International Journal of Inclusive Democracy,* Vol. 3, No. 3, June 2007.

Terry L. Anderson and Donald R. Leal, *Free Market Environmentalism,* San Francisco, Pacific Research Institute, 1991.

Terry L. Anderson, (ed.), *Multiple Conflicts over Multiple Uses,* Bozeman, Mont, Political Economy Research Center, 1994.

Thanzauva, K., *Theology of Community – Tribal Theology in the Making,* Bangalore, Asian Trading Corporation, 2004.

Thingo, Zunecho, "Deriving Ecological Values from the Chakhesang Naga Tribal Perspective" in *Tribal Ecology,* Razouselie Lasetso, Marlene Ch. Marak and Yangkahao Vashum (eds.), Jorhat, ETC Programme Coordination, 2012.

Thomas Blom Hansen, *The Saffron Wave: Democracy and Hindu Nationalism in Modern India,* Princeton, N.J.: Princeton University Press, 1999.

Thomas Sieger Derr, Environmental *Ethics and Christian Humanism,* Nashville, Tenn., Abingdon Press, 1996.

Thomas, Jaison, "Cosmic Groaning for Creation Stewardship: Excavating Green Theology" in *Olive Theological Institute,* 4/ I (February 2014).

Thumra, Jonathan H., "The Primal Religious Tradition", in *Religious Traditions of India,* P.S. Daniel, David C. Scott and G.R. Singh (eds.), Delhi, ISPCK, 2011.

Timothy C. Whitmore and Jeffrey A. Sayer, (eds.), *Tropical Deforestation and Species Extinction,* London and New York, Chapman and Hall, 1992.

Timothy D. Terrell, "Property Rights and Externality: The Ethics of the Austrian School," *Journal of Markets and Morality,* 2, Fall 1999.

Uberoi N K, *Environmental Management,* New Delhi, Excel Books. 2007.

Vandana Shiva, "The Enclosure of the Commons", in *The Third World Resurgence,* No. 84, August 1997.

Vandana Shiva, "Why the Engineering Paradigm in Life-Forms is Flawed", in *Third World Resurgence,* No. 53-54, 1995.

Vandana Shiva, *Earth Democracy, Living Democracy: Rebuilding Security in an Age of Insecurity,* Whitefield-Bangalore, Ecumenical Christian Centre, n.d..

Vannucci, M., *Ecological Readings in the Veda,* New Delhi, D.K. Print World, 1994.

Vasantha Rao, Ch., *Let the Mother Bird Go,* Hyderabad, National Christian Writers Forum, 1996.

Vashum, Yangkahao, "A Tangkhul Creation Myth: Implication for Holistic View of Human Rights", in *The Tribal Worldview and Ecology,* A. Wati Longchar and Yangkahao Vashum (eds.), Jorhat, Tribal Study Centre, 1998.

Vashum, Yangkahao, "Theology of Land: A Naga Perspective", in *The Tribal Worldview and Ecology,* A. Wati Longchar and Yangkahao Vashum (eds.), Jorhat, Tribal Study Centre, 1998.

Vashum, Yangkahao, "Tribal Theology: A Search for Relevant Theology and Ministry in Tribal Context" in *Tribal Theology – A Search for Quality Theological Education and Relevant Ministry,* Yangkahao Vashum (ed.), Jorhat, Tribal Study Centre, 2009.

Vasudha Narayanan, "'One Tree Is Equal to Ten Sons': Hindu Responses to the Problems of Ecology, Population, and Consumption," *Journal of the American Academy of Religion,* 65, no. 2, 1991.

Vladimir Chernousenko, "We Shall be Killed in Silent Ways", in *Third World Resurgence,* No. 69, May 1996.

Wallis, H.W., The *Cosmology of the Rigveda*, Cosmo Publications, 1999.

Watt K. E. F., *Principles of Environmental Science,* 1973.

Wehr Kevin, *America's fight over Water:* The *Environmental and Political Effects of large-Scale Water Systems*, New York, Routledge, 2004.

Wielenga Bas, *Towards an Eco-Just Society*, Bangalore, Thomas K.C., 1999.

William J. Baumol and Wallace E. Oates, "Long-Run Trends in Environmental Quality", in *The State of Humanity,* Julian L. Simon (ed.), New York, Blackwell, 1995.

William J. Hausman, "Long-Term Trends in Energy Prices", in *The State of Humanity,* Julian L. Simon (ed.), New York: Blackwell, 1995.

Woba James, *Major Issues in the History of Christianity in India: A Post Colonial Reading,* Mokokchung, TDCC Publications, 2013.

Worster, D., *Nature's Economy,* 1977.

Yangkahao Vashum, "Tribal Theology: A Search for Relevant Theology and Ministry in Tribal Context," in *Tribal Theology – A Search for Quality Theological Education and Relevant Ministry,* Yangkahao Vashum (ed.), Jorhat, Tribal Study Centre, 2009.

Yudhishthira Mimansaka, *Vaidika Siddhanta Mimansa*, Sonipata, 1976.

Yunus Negus, "Science Within Islam: Learning How to Care for Our World," in *Islam and Ecology*, Fazlun M. Khalid and Joanne O'Brien (eds.), London, Cassell Publishers Limited, 1992.

Zunecho Thingo, "Deriving Ecological Values from the Chakhesang Naga Tribal Perspective," in *Tribal Ecology*, Razouselie Lasetso, Marlene Ch. Marak and Yangkahao Vashum (eds.), Jorhat: ETC Programme Coordination, 2012.

________ "Broadest Religious Coalition in US History opposes Life Patenting" in *Third World Resurgence,* No. 63, Nov. 1995.

________ "High-Tech Piracy" in *Third World Resurgence,* No. 71, July 1996.

________ "The Aquaculture Disaster", in *The Ecologist Asia*, September-October, 1995.

________ *Down to Earth*, December 15th 1996.

________ *World Resources, 1994-1995,* A Report by the World Resources Institute in collaboration with the United Nations Environmental Program (UNEP) and the United Nations Development Program (UNDP), Delhi, 1995.

________ "Human Rights and the Rights of Nature," *Journal of Markets and Morality.*

________ "Acid Rain", *Down to Earth*, May 15, 1999.

________ "Where are all the Pollinators going", in *Down to Earth,* (cover story), August 15, 1998.

________ *The Asian Elephant: Ecology and Management*, Cambridge University Press, 1989.

________ *The Living Elephants: Evolutionary Ecology, Behaviour and Conservation,* Oxford University Press, 2003.

________ *The State of India's Environment, 1984-1985,* The Second Citizens' Report, New Delhi, Centre for Science and Environment, 1985.

________ *The Story of Asia's Elephants,* Marg Publishers, 2011.

________ *Third World Resurgence*, No. 53-54, January – February, 1995.

________ *Elephant Days and Nights: Ten Years with the Indian Elephant,* Oxford University Press, 1994.

Webliography (Internet Sources)

"Arundhati Roy", *Encyclopædia Britannica,* Retrieved 12 May 2013. http//www.britanica.com/Arundhati Roy.

"Arundhati Roy, Author-Activist", Archived November 24th 2010 at the Wayback Machine., *India Today*. Retrieved June 16th 2013.

"Arundhati's contempt: Supreme Court writes her a prison sentence", *The Indian Express*, March 7th 2002.

"Case registered against Arundhati, Geelani", The Hindu, 29-11-2010. ISSN 0971-751X. Retrieved November 22nd 2015.

"Forest Rights Acts 2006." *Ministry of Tribal Affairs – Government of India.* http://www. tribal.nic.in/ Content/ ForestRight ActOtherLinks.aspx (16-08-2016).

"Oraon." http://www.everyculture. com/South-Asia/Oraon.html#ixzz4HP6GDZUX (15-08-2016).

"State/Union Territory-wise List of Scheduled Tribes in India" In *Ministry of Tribal Affairs – Government of India.* http://tribal.nic.in/content/list%20of%20scheduled%20tribes%20in % 20India.aspx (16-08-2016).

"The Constitution (Scheduled Tribes) Order 1950." http://lawmin.nic.in/ld/subord/ rule9 a.htm (12-08-2016).

"Totems." in *Tribal Zone.* http://www. tribalzone.net/history/totems.htm (15-08-2016).

"What is the Meaning of Environment? Concept, Definition of Environment." https://edukalife.blogspot.in/2013/01/definition-of-environment.html (31-07-2016).

Arundhati Roy, "The Greater Common Good" in *Frontline, 16(11),* 22 May – 4 June 1999.

Astrid. Schwarz, "Etymology and Original Sources of the Term 'Ecology.'" http://link.springer.com/chapter/10.1007%2F978-90-481-9744-6_9 (31-07-2016).

Call for action by Geneva Interfaith Forum on Climate Change, Environment and Human Rights 20 September 2011 https://www.oikoumene.org/en/resources/documents/wcc-programmes/justice-diakonia-andresponsibilityforcreation/climate-change-water/call-for-action-by-geneva-interfaith-forum (Accessed on 07/08/2016 at 06:31 pm).

Calvin Beisner E., et.al (eds.), "A Biblical Perspective on Environmental Stewardship", in *Public Policy: Environmental Stewardship in Judo-Christian Tradition: Jewish, Catholic and Protestant Wisdom on Environment*, https://acton.org/public-policy/environmental-stewardship/theology-e/biblical-perspective-environmental-stewardship (accessed on 17-07-17).

Climate Justice is a Matter of Faith, US Catholic, Vol. 81, No. 4, April 2016 pp 22–26 www.uscatholic.org/articles/201603/climate---justice---matter---faith---30604#sthash.ovEqjY3N.dpuf (Accessed on 08/09/2016 at 03:20 am).

Corner, A. (2013). A new conversation with the centre---right about climate change: Values, frames and narratives. Oxford: Climate Outreach and Information Network (Accessed on 08/09/2016 at 03:17 am).

Dhanusha Gokulan, "'Fairy princess' to 'instinctive critic'", *Khaleej Times,* 11 November 2012, Retrieved 02-11-2014. http//www.khaleejtimes.com

George Marshall, Communicating with Religious Communities on Climate Change: Research Overview and Emergent Narratives http://irdialogue.org/wpcontent/uploads/2016/08/Communicating-with-Religious-Communities 8.14FINAL.pdf (Accessed on 07/09/2016 at 09:15 pm).

http://bhumiproject.org/) for updates on this event.

http://buddhism.about.com/od/theeightfoldpath/a/rightlivelihood.htm "Right Livelihood: The Ethics of Earning a Living", 27/08/16.

http://en.wikipedia.org/wiki/Ecosophy.

http://encyclopedia2.thefreedictionary.com/biosphere; en.wikipedia.org/wiki/ecology.

http://environment-ecology.com/religion-and-ecology/283-what-does-hinduism-teach-us-about-ecology.html (accessed on July 6th 2017).

http://fore.yale.edu/publications/books/cswr/hinduism-introduction/ (Accessed on July 6th 2017).

http://informory.com/famous/famous-environmentalscientists/#ixzz4HP31MI00.

http://islamicclimatedeclaration.org/islamic---declaration---on---global---climate---change/ (Accessed on 07/09/2016 at 10:20 pm).

http://nvdatabase.swarthmore.edu/content/narmada-bachao-andolan-nba-forces-end-world-bank-funding-sardar-sarovar-dam-india-1985-1993, (accessed on 07-07-2016).

http://www.arcworld.org/faiths.asp?pageID=3, Faith and Ecology", 27/08/16.

http://www.arcworld.org/faiths.asp?pageID=73 (accessed on 14-07-17).

http://www.asiantribune.com/index.php?q=node/6210, "Judge Weeramantry,"

http://www.bbc.co.uk/schools/gcsebitesize/rs/environment/sikhstewardshiprev2.shtml (accessed 14-07-2017).

http://www.dianuke.org/letter-from-koodakulam-to-citizens-of-india (02/08/2016).

http://www.ecoindia.com/education/narmada-bachao-andolan.html, 12-7-2016.

http://www.ecosikh.org/wp-content/uploads/2011/09/Ecosophical-Concerns-in-the-Sikh-Tradition.pdf (accessed on 13-07-17).

http://www.goldmanprize.org/recipient/medha-patkar/, 25-09-2016.

http://www.jainworld.com/jainbooks/asceticism/ch8.as,

http://www.jainworld.com/jainbooks/Books/Jaindecl.htm, "The Jain Teaching", 27/08/16.

http://www.rachelcarson.org/SilentSpring.aspx, (accessed on March 31st 2018).

http://www.sanskrit.nic.in/svimarsha/v2/c17.pdf , (accessed on 28-06-2017)

http://www.sikhiwiki.org/index.php/Sikhism_and_the_environment (accessed on 13-07-17).

http://www.sikhiwiki.org/index.php/Sikhism_and_the_environment (accessed on 13-07-17).

http://www.universespirit.org/eco-spirituality-definition-principles-history http://www.universespirit.org/node/286/backlinks

https://en.wikipedia.org/wiki/Narmada_Bachao_Andolan, 01-08-2016.

https://essentialthinkers.wordpress.com/2013/10/13/the-story-of-narmada-bachao-andolan-human-rights/, 22-07-2016.

https://www.amazon.com/Fresh-Water-Seas-Saving-Great/dp/0921284187, March 31st, 2018.

https://www.amazon.com/Storms-My-Grandchildren-Catastrophe-Humanity/dp/1608195023, 31-03-2018.

https://www.britannica.com/biography/Medha-Patkar, 28-09-2016.

Intercultural Ecotheology: Integral Visions of Healing www.acu.edu.au/__data/assets/pdf_file/0014/.../Rider_Practical_Theol_GH.pdf (Accessed on 05/09/2016 at 10:45 pm).

Interfaith Partnership for the Environment UNEP www.unep.org/newyork/InterfaithPartnershipfortheEnvironment/tabid/.../Default.aspx (accessed on 07/092016 at 05:48 pm).

Kelli Mahoney, "Caring for the World Around You is an Important Part of Your Faith" in *Bible Verses About Protecting the World,* https://www.thoughtco.com/bible-verses-about-protecting-the-environment-712753 (accessed on 17-07-17).

Lourdunathan, S., "Ecosophical Concerns in the Sikh Tradition" http://www.ecosikh.org/wp-content/uploads/2011/09/Ecosophical-Concerns-in-the-Sikh-Tradition.pdf (accessed on 13-07-17).

Marshall, G., (2014), Hearth and Hiraeth: Constructing Climate Change Narratives around National Identity, Climate Outreach (Accessed on 08/09/2016 at 03:12 am).

Marshall, G; A. Corner, O. Roberts, and J. Clarke, (2016). Faith & Climate Change ---A guide to talking with the five major faiths. Oxford: Climate Outreach. http://climateoutreach.org/resources/climate---change---faith/ (Accessed on 07/09/2016 at 09:15 pm).

Pankaj Jain, "10 Hindu Environmental Teachings", http://www.huffingtonpost.com/pankaj-jain-phd/10-hindu-environmental-te_b_846245.html (accessed on 04th July, 2017).

Peng Shu-Tzi | LinkedInwww.linkedin.com/in/peng-shu-tzi-61171879 (Accessed on 28/09/2016 at 12:40 am).

Rebecca Solnit's article "Call climate change what it is: violence" www.theguardian.com/commentisfree/2014/apr/07/climate---change---violence---occupy---earth (Accessed on 08/09/2016 at 03:43 am).

Redwood Rabbis protect northern California trees, 1995-1999...nvdatabase.swarthmore.edu/content/redwood-rabbis-protect-northern-california-trees-1995-1999 (Accessed on 28/09/2016 at 12: 14 am).

Roger S. Gottlieb, religion and the environment http://users.wpi.edu/~gottlieb/files/32CHAP29GOTTLIEB_PP[1]_with_corrections.pdf (Accessed on 05/09/2016 at 10:15 pm).

Rosen, Med Alex. "Effects of the Fukushima nuclear meltdowns on environment and health" (March 9th, 2012). http://www.ippnw.de/commonFiles/pdfs/Atomenergie/FukushimaBackgroundPaper.pdf (02/08/2016).

The Great Indian Rape-Trick Archived 14 April 2016 at the Wayback Machine. @ SAWNET -The South Asian Women's NET work. Retrieved November 25th 2011.

V. Venkatesan and Sukumar Muralidharan, "Of contempt and legitimate dissent", *Frontline,* 18–31, August 2001.

www.asiannature.org

www.sakshi.com

Newspapers

________ "Arundhati Roy: A 'small hero'", *BBC News,* March 6th 2002.

"*Akshrala vruksha koteeswarudu*" (He planted one crore plants), in "Funday" of *Sakshi,* (Daily News Paper in Telugu), Sunday, August 14th 2016.

"Athadu Adavini Srustinchadu' (He created forest) in "Funday" of *Sakshi,* (Daily News Paper in Telugu), Sunday, August 14th 2016.

________ "Kids Special – Mother Earth" in *Sakshi,* Daily News Paper in Telugu, February 14, 2009.

________ "Kids Special – Mother Earth" in *Sakshi,* Daily News Paper in Telugu, February 15, 2009.

________ "Prkruthiki Punarankitam" in *Sakshi – Fun-day,* Sunday Magazine, March, 17th 2013.

________ *Funday, Sakshi Sunday Magazine,* Sunday, April 14, 2013.

Patangi Rambabu, "Mana Nagaralu "Bhopal"ku Nakallu!" in *Sakshi,* Daily News Paper in Telugu, Thursday, Jagathi Publications Limited, Hyderabad, April 04, 2013.

Prasad, ABK., "'Agni' ki Ajyam America!", in *Sakshi,* Daily News Paper in Telugu, Hyderabad, Thursday, April 11, 2011.

Sajjala Ramakrishana Reddy (Editorial Director), *Sakshi,* Daily News Paper in Telugu, Jagathi Publications Limited, Hyderabad, March 29, 2013.

________ *Sakshi,* (Daily News Paper in Telugu, February 3, 2010.

________ *Sakshi,* Daily News Paper in Telugu, Tabloid, Saturday, Jagathi Publications Limited, Hyderabad, April 13, 2013.

Singh, Tavleen, "The Real Enemies", *The Indian Express,* 21st December 2008.

________ *The Hindu,* Daily News Paper in English, Hyderabad, Sunday, April 14, 2013.

________ *The Indian Express,* December 9th, 1997.